Landmark
Essays

Landmark Essays

on
Writing Process

Edited by Sondra Perl

Hermagoras Press
1994

Landmark Essays Volume Seven

About the Editor

Sondra Perl is Associate Professor of English at Herbert H. Lehman College of the City University of New York and a Research Associate at Lehman's Institute for Literacy Studies. Co-founder and director for ten years of the New York City Writing Project, she has observed both teachers and writers at work. She is the author of numerous articles and a co-authored book, *Through Teachers' Eyes*. Among her honors are included an NCTE Promising Researcher Award, a Guggenheim Fellowship, and most recently, Lehman College's Award for Excellence in Teaching.

Table of Contents

Introduction

Essays

Introduction

Writing Process: A Shining Moment
by Sondra Perl

What happens when we write? What occurs as we compose? Can the processes by which individuals give shape and meaning to written texts be observed, documented and understood? To what theories about composing could such understanding lead? And based on what premises do we even ask such questions?

For a brief time in the life of the academy, these and other related questions became the focus of attention. It was a moment when researchers, writers and scholars looked beyond an examination of written texts to inquire into the nature of composing itself. The growing interest in these questions paralleled the growth of a new, young field: in the early 1970s, both studies of composing and composition studies emerged as exciting avenues for research and inquiry (North, 1986a).

Prior to this time, authors such as Peter Elbow, Ken Macrorie, James Moffett and Donald Murray had written about writing and its teaching in ways that helped scholars, teachers and students think about composing issues. But beginning in 1971, a steady line of new work began to appear: work that looked at individual writers and examined precisely what they did as they were engaged in the act of writing. As a result, the landmark essays written in the early days of composing research are easy to identify. But fields and inquiries do not remain static. And as the new field of composition studies began to change and redefine itself, so did interest in composing research and theory. By the mid-eighties, there were fewer studies of individual writers at work. By the early nineties, even fewer, and many of those who began the early work had moved on to study other related interests.

So too, as the field of composition studies became more sophisticated in its understanding of research, the designs and assumptions underlying the early work were called into question (Emig, 1982; Durst, 1990). Researchers were challenged to design studies that were sensitive to the varying contexts in which writers write and to the ways their own roles shaped their investigations. The more comprehensive studies called for by these critiques are only now beginning to appear, exemplified in the recent work of Anne Dyson (1994) and of Glynda Hull, Mike Rose, and their colleagues (1991).

Searching through the major journals of the field, it may appear then, at first glance, that landmark essays on writing processes have diminished. But if we read closely and look, occasionally, outside the academy, we find that interest in writing processes is still alive; it comes to us, however, in a new guise. There are writers who show us more of themselves at work than ever before, revealing their processes in the midst of their own writing. There are others who take the lessons we have learned from the early studies and use them to teach writing, even to those no longer in school. And once we broaden our understanding of what constitutes a "process approach," we can recognize, in retrospect, the authors who were mindful of the power of writing processes long before there was a field of composition or a single empirical study of composing processes.

In this introduction, I aim to tell the story of how inquiry into writing processes became the focus of attention for a substantial number of composition researchers and scholars, what happened to this inquiry, and where it has led. But like all stories, this one, too, is composed by an individual writer with a personal philosophy and view of the world. As a result, the version printed here is neither innocent nor the only one available: it is the story I tell and reflects as much about my reasons for selecting particular essays as it reflects particular movements in the field. To read it as if it were the only history, or the only truth, would be to ignore an important lesson of the post-modern era, namely, that there is always more than one version to any story and more than one form to contain it, that the voices we write in are multiple and the tales we tell never fully told. Consequently, I will begin by providing an historical sketch of the way research on composing helped to shape a field but conclude with comments on the situated nature of all composing, and in this case, especially, my own.

The Moment Begins

Nineteen seventy-one marks the movement in the field of composition from an almost exclusive focus on written products to an examination of composing processes. In that year Janet Emig published *The Composing Processes of Twelfth Graders*, hailed at the time as "an audacious venture into relatively unexplored territory" (Buxton, p. v). Emig's was the first study to ask a process-oriented question, "How do twelfth-graders write?" and the first to devise a method to study writing processes as they unfolded. By asking her students to "compose aloud," to say whatever crossed their minds while they were writing, Emig was able to document, at least in part, what happened as a small sample of twelfth graders composed.

Looking closely at the writing behaviors of eight students, Emig demonstrated that insights about composing could be gathered by using a case-study approach. One result of her work was a careful analysis of the dimensions of the composing process among twelfth graders, and the taxonomy she devised has become familiar to many teachers across the country. Less familiar but equally important, and the starting point for this volume, is her review of the literature on creativity and composing. Here Emig showed precisely why the teaching of composition had proceeded in so haphazard and contradictory a manner: on the one hand, interviews with professional writers had provided only idiosyncratic, at times puzzling, and often unreliable descriptions of creative processes while, on the other, the dicta in textbooks had offered formulaic approaches diametrically opposed to those given by professionals. After guiding us through this mass of conflicting evidence, Emig argued convincingly that one way to resolve the conflict was to observe, carefully and systematically, what student writers did as they wrote.

In 1975, Donald Graves published the second major study on composing processes. Using a case-study approach, Graves sat next to second-graders and observed them working on their writing at school and at home, and he spoke at considerable length with their parents and teachers. Graves was among the first to show that young children could write and that their writing processes, like those of adults, did not necessarily follow the linear logic of textbooks: the common instruction to plan, write and edit in a lockstep fashion. In fact, Graves found, even among young children, there was evidence of discrete patterns and developmental shifts.

Building on the work of Emig and Graves, I designed a study to examine the composing processes of basic writers, underprepared college students at the City University of New York. Given the look of their finished products, often studded with crossed-out words, misspellings, misstarts and errors, it seemed prudent to ask whether such writers even had composing processes: consistent behaviors that recurred as they wrote.

To gather my data, I observed five writers at work, and following Emig, I, too, asked them to compose aloud, tape-recording whatever they said. Since my interest was in documenting the sequence and flow of my students' composing, I devised a coding scheme to order and systematize what I was observing which then enabled me to detect patterns of composing within and among the students. Through careful coding, I discovered that students who produced flawed written products did, nonetheless, have consistent composing processes.

The designs of these early studies on composing were partly modeled on the tenets of experimental research. Even within a case-study approach, researchers looked to control as many variables as possible. Cautioned by Braddock, Lloyd-Jones and Schoer in *Research in Written Composition* (1963), that early work in composition was suspect precisely because it did not control for such variables as "the topic," "the setting," and "the length of time allotted" to writing, we designed studies that asked writers to engage in similar activities on similar occasions in similar settings, so that what we came to discover could not be dismissed as being merely idiosyncratic or as occurring only by chance.

During the ensuing years, then, researchers of writing processes conducted studies of one or more writers, often in what could be described as laboratory conditions. The writers were of different ages and abilities ranging from young children (Calkins, 1980; Lamme & Childers, 1983) to adults (Selzer, 1983), from native speakers of English (Bridwell, 1980) to speakers of Spanish (Raimes, 1985; Zamel, 1983) or Chinese (Lay, 1982), from basic writers (Hull, 1987; Pianko, 1979) to professionals (Schwartz, 1983). Audiotapes, videotapes and protocols were collected. Analyses were designed to discover pauses and patterns (Matsuhashi, 1981), to create cognitive process models (Flower and Hayes, 1981) and to produce theories (Greene, 1990; Hairston, 1986).

In tone, too, the early studies reflected the thinking of their time. Researchers were to be distant, faceless and voiceless. We were to observe and take notes but not to participate. Assuming that the premises which worked for experimental researchers in a laboratory would work equally well for us and produce findings equally useful and generalizable, we kept our distance. And we reported our findings as if we had had very little to do with producing them. In other words, as writers of these early essays, we worked at being as objective, informed, and distant as the methods we used.

The next three articles in this volume also reflect this early stance. They are controlled studies and attempt to isolate and examine features of composing in rigorous and systematic ways. Linda Flower and John R. Hayes, who have since published numerous articles on writing processes, based their work on theories derived from the information-processing branch of cognitive psychology. Using problem-solving as a frame for their studies, their aim was to uncover the thinking processes writers used in the act of solving rhetorical problems. They, too, asked writers to compose aloud; then they created transcripts which could be analyzed according to the network of goals and the hierarchy of relationships that seemed to keep the process moving. In this article from their early work, they describe their approach and then provide examples of the types of problems writers set for themselves and how these writers then devise means to solve them.

In 1980, Nancy Sommers published an article that reconceived all writing as revision. Describing the ways the process of revision worked for the college students and adult writers she observed, Sommers emphasized how narrow most students' conceptions of revision were and how truncated their processes. Her work added to the growing body of research which argued that a linear model of composing with three distinct stages was misleading. Sommers called for a theory of writing that was both holistic and recursive, "in which a sense of the whole writing both precede[d] and gr[e]w out of an examination of the parts."

In the same year, Mike Rose conducted a systematic study of a debilitating writing problem: writer's block. In the article included here, he reports the findings of a study in which he interviewed ten students, of whom half wrote with relative ease and half experienced a form of "nearly immobilizing writer's block." Looking for and discovering both patterns and differences among these students, Rose provided a foundation for conducting even more rigorous investigations using a problem-solving framework.

Close observation of writers at work led to theoretical questions too: What theories of meaning, we asked, would be adequate to convey the complexity and richness of composing? My investigations led me to consider that we write not just with our minds but also with a wider kind of knowing that is often visceral and embodied. In "Understanding Composing," I suggested ways in which this knowing works and how writing enables us to bring what is at first only implicit in our knowing, a "felt sense," into explicit form.

Ann Berthoff also pursued questions of meaning, arguing that writing must never be divorced from the shaping power of the imagination. Highly critical of research based on the positivist notion that reliable knowledge must be logically ordered and lend itself to mathematical modeling, Berthoff reminded us that writing is an act of making meaning. Materialist, behavioralist and technicist theories, she maintained, could never elucidate the power of mind. To do so, she suggested in "The Intelligent Eye and the Thinking Hand," we must inquire into composing in the tradition of such thinkers as I. A. Richards, Susanne Langer, William James, and C. S. Peirce, whose philosophical works address questions of meaning and the relationship between signs and symbols, and between representation and interpretation. Only by addressing such questions, she argued, would we arrive at a sound understanding of composing.

So vigorous was this early work and so widespread its initial impact that Maxine Hairston termed its effect on the field a "paradigm shift." In her essay, "The Winds of Change," Hairston identified the ways findings from composing research had begun to contradict what she called the "current-traditional" paradigm. The winds, as she saw them, brought a breath of fresh air as they summoned forth, particularly for practitioners, a new awareness: of writing as "recursive" instead of "linear;" of the importance of attending to composing processes as well as written products.

From the early to mid-eighties, then, composing processes were under investigation. Among the noteworthy studies published in 1983 is Carol Berkenkotter's study of Donald Murray, a well-known writer and teacher of writing. Berkenkotter observed Murray as he wrote at home and in her office, examining how he worked in both naturalistic and controlled settings, with topics he had chosen as well as those she had assigned. We come to see through her study that composing processes are, indeed, affected by the contexts in which writers locate and find themselves. Berkenkotter voiced a concern that would increasingly come to shape research on composing: the caution that writing arises out of specific contexts and that approaches which attempt to control variables may have so stripped away these contexts that what remains is only the merest trace of what might have occurred in more natural settings.

In the mid-eighties, articles appeared in which the early work on composing was analyzed and evaluated. In 1985, James Reither praised past work and then raised important and forward-looking questions: How do the social contexts that shape our lives influence what we say and write? And what is the role of "social knowing" in the processes of composing? In 1986, these questions were developed further when Lester Faigley outlined three prominent views of composing, or in Berthoff's terms three philosophies, and asked: How is social knowledge constructed in history? While Reither pointed us toward the social dimensions of composing, Faigley challenged us to examine how even our understanding of what is social is affected by historical perspectives and political contexts.

Suddenly, the once seemingly simple act of studying writing processes engendered a range of theoretical, methodological, political, pedagogical and practical questions. Among them: Who is the writer in the act of writing? To whom does she write? What is the basis of her knowledge? What is her relationship to the world? Can she be known separate from the contexts in which she lives? And who determines the contexts and her relation to them? Consequently, research on composing was no longer seen as a neutral activity conducted by an observer who stood aside watching and documenting a complex phenomenon, but as a philosophical and political act itself in which researchers were challenged to be aware of the stances they were taking and how they situated themselves in their studies.

These critiques from the mid-eighties had an impact on the way writing was subsequently studied and described. Those who wrote about writing processes began to describe the settings which gave meaning and order to their lives. Min-zhan Lu, for example, in her article "From Silence to Words," chronicled her own struggles with composing, showing explicitly how her speaking and writing, in both Chinese and English, were always a function of the differing political and social contexts in which she was living. Lu's article reminds us that language is neither neutral nor a strictly individual possession—that the social settings out of which we write also shape the meaning we express.

Increasingly, too, as the premises of studies based on experimental designs and conducted in laboratory settings were subjected to critique, researchers began to make finer distinctions and ask different kinds of questions. Elizabeth Flynn in "Composing as a Woman" argued that our construct of "the writer" had been fashioned with little regard to gender. Are our research methods or research samples "androcentric"? she asked. Are male writers "the standard" against which female writers are judged? Flynn called on us to bring the insights gained in feminist studies, particularly those dealing with difference and dominance, more fully into our thinking, scholarship and research on composing.

In work appearing, then, between the end of the eighties and the early nineties, several themes can be distinguished. Writing is no longer viewed merely as an individual act but as a social one as well (Berlin, 1988; LeFevre, 1987); contexts in which writers write are taken into account and studied (Berkenkotter *et. al*, 1988; Herrington, 1985; McCarthy, 1987); researchers no longer remain anonymous but speak through their research, making their own biases and perspectives explicit (Perl & Wilson, 1986; Sommers, 1993); writing, now viewed as a cultural act, is increasingly studied through ethnography, a method suited to the study of cultures (Doheny-Farina, 1986; Dyson, 1988); the scene of writing is more often understood now not as a room in which a writer is isolated and alone but as a room in which many voices reside: those that both shape the writer and to which he or she responds in return (Brodkey, 1987). Finally, the forms in which we tell of our discoveries, in which we report the findings of our research, expand. Stories, portraits, tales, and narrative accounts begin to supplant the more traditional reports of research as we move closer to an understanding that what we are trying to describe may not be the truths of laboratory science but the truths of living and shaping and creating—the truths of being human.

Many of these views are expressed by William Irmscher, as he reflects on 40 years devoted to the study and teaching of composition. In his article, "Finding a Comfortable Identity," Irmscher values the lessons learned from empirical research but is nonetheless critical of our borrowing models of inquiry from the sciences, models which inevitably reduce the complexities of composing. Reminding us that writing is above all a symbolic act and an essentially human activity, Irmscher encourages us to use case studies and ethnographies, methods better suited to the aims of humanistic inquiry, and to embrace methods of reporting that, like literature, "present the fullness of experience."

Studies of composing have led us then not to fuller and more detailed models or to larger and longer taxonomies as we once suspected they might. Rather we are arriving at an understanding of the complex relationship between writers and the contexts that shape their lives. In this relationship, writers are both constituents of their particular cultures and capable of playing constituting roles themselves—in other words, both creatures of varying cultures and creators of variously unique expressions and extensions of them.

In the early nineties, teachers and writers begin to rethink the ways in which writing processes have been understood and described. Lex Runciman reflects, for example, on the shaping power of metaphor. To liken the act of writing to a problem, he claims, will result in students making it one. Critical of the problem-posing language of some composing studies, Runciman reminds us that we write for many reasons, including those connected with pleasure and satisfaction. Examining his own process of writing, he shows us what many researchers ignore or overlook in their studies: the rewards of writing.

Donald Murray, too, has long known and written about the pleasures of writing. In his 1991 essay, "All Writing is Autobiography," Murray explores the cultures which have given him an identity and the pleasure he derives from reshaping his understanding of those cultures through writing. Murray reminds us that no matter what we are writing, no matter the form or the content, the structure or the point, we write out of who we are, representing ourselves in print. His article is a treatment to the ways writers, in dialogue with and shaped by their histories and communities, are also actively constructing the meaning of their own experiences.

Nancy Sommers exemplifies Murray's point in "Between the Drafts." Standing back and critiquing the way she positioned herself within her earlier work, Sommers now sees that earlier self as a "bloodless academic creating taxonomies, creating a hierarchy of student writers and experienced writers, and never asking myself how I was being displaced from my own work." In contrast, twelve years later, Sommers presents both her work and herself, her voice now shaping the dialogue with others, neither submerged nor silenced but present and aware of the interplay.

Such a broadened and contextualized understanding of composing processes, of course, leaves ample room for further inquiry. Researchers of composing have only begun to investigate, for example, the ways student writers choose to participate in the discourses of the communities in which they find themselves (Clark and Weidenhaupt, 1992; Sternglass, 1988), the ways teachers respond to, intervene in, challenge and support the work of students (Prior, 1991; Walvoord and McCarthy, 1991), and the ways composing is shaped by issues of difference (Lunsford and Ede, 1990; Tedesco, 1991). These and other context-sensitive studies require enormous investments of time and energy. It may be, in fact, that such work will most usefully be conducted by teams of researchers, since the agenda is broad, and composing, while a major feature, is often only one aspect of literate activity under study.

Academic writing is not, however, our only source of sophisticated understanding of what it means to compose. The reflections in *The Writing Life* by author Annie Dillard awaken in readers a sense of what makes composing so exciting and essential a human act. Excerpts from *Writing for Your Life* by novelist Deena Metzger begin to explore why. Both authors speak for an aspect of composing often overlooked in academic research: the sense that a writer can create, out of all that has come before, something new. Dillard, writing metaphorically, and Metzger, more concretely, speak for the fear evoked and the fearlessness called for by such an act of creation. For both know that during composing one composes both a work and a self, and both are speaking not only to academics and teachers but also to all those who wish to write.

Similarly, the final two essays in this volume speak to writers within and outside the academy. Since 1970 when it first appeared, William Stafford's "A Way of Writing" has often been anthologized. Stafford writes knowingly of his own writing process and of the value, for any writer, of receptivity, of waiting quietly and paying attention to whatever comes. In his view, writing is not reserved for an elite few but is available to all as "one of the great, free human activities." Brenda Ueland concurs. I close with her to underscore the point she makes, one she understood in 1938, long before we began our academic study of writing processes: that the shining moment we pursue in our ever-sophisticated studies and inquiries belongs ultimately and always to all of us, who by virtue of being human are necessarily readers, writers, thinkers—composers—shapers of meaning.

What Shines in the Shining Moment?

What does it mean to compose? How do we, as observers of composing processes, make sense of what we see? And what is it we are actually composing? A piece of writing? A life's work? Ourselves? The essays I have chosen to include in this volume mirror my own interest in these questions. While throughout much of this introduction I have traced how thinking and methodology within composing research have evolved, to conclude I want to highlight a few aspects which have remained the same and the perspective on research I most value.

First, in the work I respect, writers and what they do are at the center of inquiry. The focus is on what actually occurs as people write and how they make sense of what they are doing. In choosing such a focus, we grant human action central importance and enact the belief that looking closely at individuals can be a primary starting point for understanding them and their worlds.

But we must also ask, who is creating this understanding and from what frame of reference? The early work on composing, my own included, proceeded as if researchers could stand outside their research, observe a group of writers at work, document what they were doing, examine transcripts and tapes to determine patterns of behavior, and then report findings in scholarly language devoid of personal preferences.

Later on, it became obvious to many of us that such a stance was already imbued with preferences, most notably the theory that knowledge can and ought to be created with little or no reference to its creator. Such a stance implied that researchers could observe and report their observations without any concern that their personal predilections might be implicated in the construction of what they were reporting.

Yet when we enter a setting with the purpose of coming to understand how others act and make sense of the world, we have a hand in shaping the material. What we attend to, what emerges as important, which contextual factors we consider relevant and which, wittingly or not, we ignore, all influence how reality appears to us. And so, in this view, research findings are composed too, by the individual hand of the researcher and by whatever influences have trained that hand and won its allegiance.

As a result, the work I have increasingly come to value in composition research turns back on itself enough to take the researcher's shaping role into account. The integrity of such work rests not so much on a lifeless detachment from the phenomena being studied as on the author's vital engagement, and on a faithful rendering of what has been observed, including the author's revealing, as much as possible, his or her own impact on what has been seen and said.

When conducting such inquiries, researchers begin, then, not with an hypothesis to test but with a readiness to pay close attention to the phenomena at hand. They begin by observing writers and readers, teachers and tutors, parents and children as they go about the work of creating and constructing literate lives. They enter the contexts in which these people live and attempt to understand what is occurring from the inside, turning themselves as much as possible into participant-observers, recognizing that they can only come to understand others' frames of reference if they, too, enter those frames. Once having done so, they may then convey what they have learned through writing, by attempting to bring to life the people they have come to know and the particularities of their living.

Consequently, the writing I value in composition research resembles the writing I value in literature, complete with careful descriptions that take me inside the phenomena, that, through the slow piling up of detail, show me a person's actions and suggest what such actions might mean.

I am not suggesting, however, that the act of turning research data into finished prose is or should be the same as writing fiction. While both may benefit from an author's attempt to render lived experiences, only researchers are bound to record as accurately as they can what is before them and then to engage in careful sifting and sorting to determine how best to make sense of what they have seen. In fact, once they discern the human contours of what they have set out to describe, once they have a sense of the patterns and regularities and the ways the individuals they have looked to understand construct their lives, researchers find themselves faced with another composing task: fashioning what they have come to see into a text that will convey their understanding to others.

There is, then, underlying my preferences in research, a particular theory of learning at work, namely that we come to understand deeply and fully by attending to what is before us in slow and careful ways, whether we are studying ourselves or others, whether we are studying finished texts or those in the process of being written, whether those texts are school-based or professional, literary, artistic or musical; and that when we attend in slow and careful ways, we can compose our way to new understandings.

To understand in this view is to attend to the phenomenon before us in such a way that we let it speak, both to and with us. This method is not a solitary one; it establishes dialogue first at the most intuitive level, so that we come to know, deeply and intimately, by letting the situations we study speak to us through our living in their midst. Only then can we hope to give voice to what we have both seen and entered and make it come alive for those who read our renderings.

In the broadest sense, then, composing is something we all do: the students and parents and writers and teachers who serve as subjects of our research and those of us who write the research itself. It is what each of us is engaged in when we shape our understanding of life through the writing we do. And it is what can continue to light our way in composition studies for it illuminates what makes this inquiry still so intriguing and so rich: that only human beings have this capacity to look and see more, to create new texts and new work and in the creating compose our way to new understandings and new selves.

The Composing Process: Review of the Literature

by Janet Emig

Most of the data about the composing process occur as three broad types. First there are accounts concerning established writers, chiefly of imaginative, but also of factual, works such as the scientific essay and the historical monograph. These accounts take three forms: (a) description by a writer of his own methods of working; (b) dialogue, usually in the form of correspondence, between a writer and a highly attuned respondent, such as a fellow writer or a gifted editor; and (c) analysis by professional critics or fellow writers of the evolution of a given piece of writing, from sources tapped to revision undertaken and completed. Second, there are dicta and directives about writing by authors and editors of rhetoric and composition texts and handbooks. Third, there is research dealing with the whole or some part of what has been called, globally, "the creative process"; or with a particular kind of creative behavior—the act of writing among adolescents.

These descriptions of the composing process present certain difficulties as sources of data. (1) The data are unsystematic: they do not deal with part or all of the composing process according to any shared set of strategies. (2) The statements provided by different sources of data contradict one another—more they are often unique, even idiosyncratic. (3) Very few of the sources deal in adequate theoretical or empirical depth with how students of school age write. They answer very few of the following major and interesting questions about students as writers:

If the context of student writing—that is, community milieu, school, family—affects the composing process, in what ways does it do so, and why?

What are the resources students bring to the act of writing?

If there are specifiable elements, moments, and stages in the composing process of students, what are these? If they can be differentiated, how? Can certain portions be usefully designated by traditional nomenclature, such as planning, writing, and revising? Are

---

Reprinted from *The Composing Process of Twelfth Graders*, NCTE, 1971. Copyright 1971 by the National Council of Teachers of English. Reprinted with permission.

elements organized linearly in the writing process? recursively? in some other manner? How do these elements, moments, and stages in the composing process relate to one another?

If there is a phenomenon "prewriting," how can it be characterized?

What is a plan for a piece of writing? When and why do students have or not have a plan?

Under what conditions—physical, psychic—do students start to write?

If writing is essentially a selection among certain sorts of options—lexical, syntactic, rhetorical—what governs the choices students make?

What psychological factors affect or accompany portions of the writing process? What effects do they have? What is a block in writing (other than dysgraphia)? When and why do students have blocks? How can they be overcome?

Under what conditions do students stop work on a given piece of writing?

If all, or certain kinds of, writing within schools differs from all, or certain kinds of, writing outside schools, how do they differ and why?

If there are modes of school writing, how can these be differentiated? If the mode in which a piece is written affects the process of writing, or the process the mode, how?

What is the press of such variables as the reading of others' writing and the personal intervention of others upon any portion or upon the totality of the writing process?

Accounts By and About Established Writers

On the established writer as a useful source of data about writing, an investigator can say simply with the novelist Peter de Vries, "Don't ask the cow to analyze milk";[1] or he can examine this source.

If he does, he finds that writers' comments on how they write assume many modes. Occasionally, prose writers and poets write about their writing within their novels, short stories and poems: James Joyce in *Portrait of the Artist as a Young Man*, Thomas Mann in "Tonio Kröger," and Wordsworth in "The Prelude" are examples. In addition, they write about their own writing in diaries, journals, note-books, letters, prefaces to their own and to others' works, essays, full-length critical studies, autobiographical sketches and full-

---

[1] Peter de Vries, Interview from *Counterpoint*, compiled and edited by Roy Newquist, p. 147.

length self-studies, and interviews recorded in print, on record, and on film.[2]

As the range of modes chosen suggests, writers describe their methods of working and their attitudes toward writing for different reasons. With modes where the writer's audience is initially and perhaps ultimately himself—as in diaries, journals, and notebooks not written for publication, and in certain kinds of letters—the writer is usually concerned with working out a specific problem in the evolution of a specific piece of writing. These modes are expressive: they represent a private forum where to paraphrase E.M. Forster, a writer can discover how he thinks or feels about a matter by seeing what he has said. Self-discovery, compression or partiality of expression, immediacy, and uniqueness of stimulus characterize descriptions in these modes.

With modes such as the critical essay and the extended autobiography, an audience other than oneself must be acknowledged. Consequently, amenities aiding an audience are observed: accounts are more formal in diction and in organization, and more elaborated. These accounts also tend to be retrospective affairs, and consequently reportorial in approach.

By their quite different natures, these two basic sets of modes present different kinds of difficulty as data. Descriptions in the expressive mode are frankly idiosyncratic: they purport to be true only for an N of 1—a single writer who is pursuing, particularly if he is a major writer, a unique problem. Perhaps the most powerful contemporary expression of the problem of uniqueness are these lines from "East Coker" by T.S. Eliot:

> So here I am, in the middle way, having had twenty years—
> Twenty years largely wasted, the years of *l'entre deux guerres*—
> Trying to learn to use words, and every attempt
> Is a wholly new start, and a different kind of failure
> Because one has only learnt to get the better of words
> . . . .
> . . . a new beginning, a raid on the inarticulate
> . . . .
> In the general mess of imprecision of feeling,
> Undisciplined squads of emotion.[3]

Descriptions in modes involving an audience other than oneself present other kinds of difficulties. Since these accounts are retrospective, a possible

---

[2] Exemplars of writers' accounts in these modes, in the order mentioned in the text, are: Virginia Woolf, *A Writer's Diary, Being Extracts from the Diary of Virginia Woolf*, ed. Leonard Woolf; Katherine Mansfield, *Journal of Katherine Mansfield*, ed. J. Middleton Murry; Gerard Manley Hopkins, *The Notebooks and Papers of Gerard Manley Hopkins*, ed. Humphry House; John Keats, *The Selected Letters of John Keats*, ed. Lionel Trilling; Henry James, *The Art of the Novel, Critical Prefaces by Henry James*, ed. Richard P. Blackmuir; Elizabeth Bowen, "Notes on Making a Novel," *Collected Impressions*; E.M. Forster, *Aspects of the Novel*; F. Scott Fitzgerald, *The Crack-Up*, ed. Edmund Wilson, pp. 69-84; J. Paul Sartre, *The Words*, trans. Bernard Frechtman; *Writers at Work: The Paris Review Interviews I*, ed. Malcolm Cowley; Dylan Thomas, "An Evening with Dylan Thomas," Caedmon Recording No. 1157; "Creative Person, W. H. Auden," National Educational Television (NET) telecast, April 17, 1967.

[3] T.S. Eliot, "East Coker," *Four Quartets*. Copyright 1943 by Harcourt Brace Jovanovich, Inc. and Faber and Faber Ltd. Used by permission.

difficulty with such data is the high probability of the inaccuracy of the account, incurred in part by the time-lag between the writing and the description of that writing.

A second, related difficulty is that not only are accounts *post hoc* affairs, most of those published are by writers who work almost exclusively in the imaginative modes and who have been rewarded by publisher and public for their fictive endeavors. One thinks of D.H. Lawrence's comment in *Studies in Classic American Literature* that all of the old American artists were hopeless liars: that only their art-speech was to be trusted as an accurate revelation of their thoughts and feelings; and he wonders if the observation may not justly be extended to imaginative writers of all nationalities and all eras when they talk about their methods of writing.[4]

In a recent interview the poet-critic John Ciardi speaks directly of this matter:

> *N* [Roy Newquist, the interviewer]: If you would, I'd like you to read a few of your poems and comment on them—how they happened to be written, perhaps, or what you were driving at.
>
> *Ciardi*: You're asking for lies. It's inevitable. I've been asked to do this over and over again, and lies come out.
>
> Let me put it this way. The least a poem can be is an act of skill. An act of skill is one in which you have to do more things at one time than you have time to think about. Riding a bike is an act of skill. If you stop to think of what you're doing at each of the balances, you'd fall off the bike. Then someone would come along and ask you to rationalize what you thought you were doing. Well, you write a poem. And somebody comes along and asks you to rationalize what you thought you were doing. You pick out a theme and you're hung with trying to be consistent with the theme you've chosen. You have to doubt every explanation.
>
> Nobody has worked harder than Valéry, the French poet, in trying to explain how he produced certain poems. He answers with every qualification in the world—touching this and that but ultimately lying. You have to end up lying. You know that you had something in your mind, but you can never get it straight.[5]

In addition to unintentional lies, some writers very openly admit they try to throw interviewer and public off the scent, usually because they fear any conscious, explicit probing into their methods of work will, to use Hemingway's verb, "spook" their writing. In the recorded interviews granted by such writers they are usually quite frank about their reluctance to discuss

---

[4] D. H. Lawrence, *Studies in Classic American Literature*, p. 11.

[5] John Ciardi, Interview from *Counterpoint*, compiled and edited by Roy Newquist, pp. 122-23. Copyright 1964 by Rand McNally & Company. Used by permission.

their actual methods of work.

Finally, both kinds of accounts share a difficulty: they focus upon the feelings of writers about the difficulties of writing—or not writing—almost to the exclusion of an examination of the act itself. A very wide survey of writers' accounts reveals this preoccupation: Nelson Algren, Arnold Bennett, Joseph Conrad, Simone de Beauvoir, Guy de Maupassant, F. Scott Fitzgerald, E.M. Forster, Andre Gide, John Keats, Norman Mailer, Katherine Mansfield, Jean Paul Sartre, Robert Louis Stevenson, Leo Tolstoi, Mark Van Doren, H.G. Wells, and Virginia Woolf are but some of the writers for whom this generalization holds true.[6]

Perhaps one of the best-known and dramatic examples of this preoccupation with writing difficulties is Virginia Woolf in *A Writer's Diary*. Although she makes occasional allusion to formal problems in her novels and even in the diary itself, she writes constantly about her feelings, usually negative, about the evolution of her works and about their critical reception by a coterie of friends-and-critics. She finds sustaining her energies after beginning her novels an especial source of difficulty. Here, for example, are excerpts describing her struggles with *Jacob's Room*:

> My mind turned by anxiety, or other cause, from its scrutiny of blank paper, is like a lost child—wandering the house, sitting on the bottom step to cry.
>
> (December 5, 1919)[7]

and

> It is worth mentioning, for future reference, that the creative power which bubbles so pleasantly in beginning a new book quiets down after a time, and one goes on more steadily. Doubts creep in. Then one becomes resigned. Determination not to give in, and the sense of an impending shape keep one at it more than anything. I'm a little anxious. How am I to bring off this conception? Directly one gets to work one is like a person walking, who has seen the country stretching out before. I want to write nothing in this book that I don't enjoy writing. Yet writing is always difficult.
>
> (May 29, 1923)[8]

---

[6] H.E.F. Donohue, *Conversations with Nelson Algren; The Journals of Arnold Bennett*, ed. Frank Swinnerton; Joseph Conrad, *The Mirror of the Sea and A Personal Record*, ed. Morton Dauwen Zabel; Simone de Beauvoir, *The Prime of Life*, trans. Peter Green; Guy de Maupassant, "Preface to *Pierre et Jean*," *The Life Work of Henry Rene Guy de Maupassant*; F. Scott Fitzgerald, *The Crack-Up*; E.M. Forster, *Writers at Work: The Paris Review Interviews*, II; Andre Gide, *The Journals of Andre Gide*, trans. Justin O'Brien; John Keats, *Selected Letters*; Norman Mailer, *Advertisements for Myself*; Katherine Mansfield, *Journal*; Jean Paul Sartre, *The Words*; Robert Louis Stevenson, *Essays in the Art of Writing*; Leo Tolstoi, *Talks with Tolstoi: Tolstoi and His Problems*, trans. Aylmer Maude; Mark Van Doren, *Autobiography*; H.G. Wells, *Experiment in Autobiography; Discoveries and Conclusions of a Very Ordinary Brain (Since 1866)*.

[7] Virginia Woolf, *A Writer's Diary*, ed. Leonard Woolf, p. 21. Used by permission of Harcourt Brace Jovanovich, the Hogarth Press, and the author's literary estate.

[8] *Ibid.*, p. 25.

The limitation in referring to these forms of data exclusively, then, is that they focus on partial phenomena. They often describe brilliantly the context, the affective milieu of the writing act; but the act itself remains undescribed.

Dialogue Between Writer and Attuned Respondent

A second form of data about the composing process is the dialogue, usually in the form of correspondence about an imaginative work in progress, between a writer and a highly attuned respondent, such as a fellow artist or a skilled editor. In the first category, possibly one of the best-known technical correspondences is that between Gerard Manley Hopkins and Robert Bridges during the second half of the nineteenth century. Their letters, written over a period of twenty-four years from 1865 to 1889, often deal with formal problems each encountered in individual poems, with technical criticism of each other's poetry, and with their evolving theories of rhythm and versification.[9]

Understandably, correspondence between a writer and his editor, when not mercantile, is usually technical. In American letters perhaps the best-known correspondence in this category is that between the novelist Thomas Wolfe and Maxwell Perkins, his editor at Charles Scribner's publishing house.[10] A second, more recent example is the correspondence between the critic Malcolm Cowley and William Faulkner detailing the history of the Viking Portable Library edition of Faulkner's works.[11]

Inherently interesting as this form of data is, it, too, has limited value for a full inquiry into writing because it does not deal with the total process; rather, it focuses on only one part of the process, the revision specific to a given piece of work—for example, Hopkins' problems with "The Wreck of the Deutschland," or Wolfe's, with *Look Homeward, Angel.* Indeed, this specificity may be its major limitation in that the observations on these acts of revision may therefore be imperfectly generalizable.

Analyses By Others of Evolutions of Certain Pieces of Writing

Another form of data about writing is analysis of the evolution of a piece of writing by someone other than the author. Sometimes the analysts are fellow writers, as with Henry James's study of Hawthorne or John Berryman's of Stephen Crane. Sometimes the analysts are critics, as with Josephine Bennett's study, *The Evolution of "The Faerie Queene,"* and Butt and Tillotson's study, *Dickens at Work.*

These analysts focus upon different moments in the evolution of certain

---

[9] *The Letters of Gerard Manley Hopkins to Robert Bridges*, ed. Claude Colleer Abbott.
[10] *The Letters of Thomas Wolfe*, ed. Maxwell Perkins.
[11] Malcolm Cowley, *The Faulkner-Cowley File: Letters and Memories, 1944-1962.*

pieces. For some, focus is upon the early stages—sources read and recorded in notebooks and other accounts by the writer that later resonate in a work; for others, focus is upon the later stages—upon revisions, changes the writer makes in drafts that lead to, or even follow, initial publication.

Perhaps the best-known example of focus upon the early, upon what might even be called the prewriting, activities of the writer, is *The Road to Xanadu* by John Livingston Lowes, in which Lowes traces the sources through Coleridge's labyrinthine and cryptic note-book allusions to his reading for every aspect of "Kubla Khan" and "The Rime of the Ancient Mariner," from individual word choice to total thematic organization.

Although there is probably no one analysis of a prose work that holds the critical esteem of Lowes's analysis, a representative study is Jerome Beaty's *Middlemarch, From Notebook to Novel*. Focussing on chapter 81 as exemplar, Beaty juxtaposes his own direct analyses of Eliot's process of composing with accounts by her husband, John Cross; her publisher, John Blackwood; a biographer, Joan Bennett; and by the author herself. He finds a dissonance between his analyses and all other accounts which state or imply that Eliot wrote the scene between Dorothea and Rosamond in a "stroke of creative genius" with little prefiguring and less revision.*

Beaty's analyses of Eliot's notebook entries reveal that she planned for this chapter as she planned for other chapters in the novel:

> The plans for Chapter 81 are not particularly detailed—there was no attempt to sketch the stages of the conversation or the form of the dialogue—but then no chapter in *Middlemarch* was planned in that manner; it was not George Eliot's way. But it was planned for. All the motives and events, for example, are in the notebook that Dorothea has returned out of pity. That Rosamond is "wrought upon" by this pity of love, and that she tells Dorothea that it is Dorothea Will loves.[13]

His studies of the manuscript also reveal that not only was chapter 81 revised, "this chapter was more heavily revised than most of the others in *Middlemarch*, and revised in almost all its aspects: timing, content, point of view, characterization, tone, and outcome."[14]

Beaty concludes his analysis of chapter 81:

> Writing, to George Eliot, was not an unpremeditated outpouring; neither was it a mechanical following of detailed blueprint. It was a

---

*Beaty attributes the statements, at least by Cross and Eliot herself, to a shared belief in the Romantic notion of inspiration prevalent in the nineteenth century, even into the Victorian period:
  "Their best work . . . was written without premeditation, in a frenzy of inspiration Therefore it follows that revision and hard work are the signs of those who are less than geniuses."[12]

---

[12]Jerome Beaty, *Middlemarch, From Notebook to Novel: A Study of George Eliot's Creative Method.* Copyright 1960 by University of Illinois. Used by permission.
[13]*Ibid.*, pp. 110-11.
[14]*Ibid.*, p. 123.

process of evolution and of discovery.[15]

Whatever the motivation behind George Eliot's statements, the discrepancies between her description and Beaty's findings also serve to make suspect yet another writer's account as a valid source of data about his own process of writing, while at the same time suggesting the value of direct analysis of writers' notebooks and drafts as sources of information about the writing process.[16]

Other analysts have been interested instead in the process of revision or the transmutation of elements in original or early drafts into the burnished rightness of the final form. An early example in poetry criticism is M.R. Ridley's detailed examination of the drafts of certain poems by John Keats—specifically, "The Eve of St. Agnes" and the four major odes. More recent is *W.B. Yeats: The Later Poetry* by Thomas Parkinson, specifically chapter two, "Vestiges of Creation," and chapter four, "The Passionate Syntax." Studies of the revisions of prose works include Rudolf Arnheim's Poets at Work and an interesting casebook *Word for Word*, prepared by Wallace Hildick, in which are set forth for student examination "authors' alterations" by T.S. Eliot, D.H. Lawrence, Alexander Pope, Samuel Butler, Thomas Hardy, William Wordsworth, Henry James, William Blake, and Virginia Woolf.*

Literary critics have always studied style; in recent years scholars of style have made increasing use of linguistic analysis, often employing a computer. At times their cluster of techniques has been applied to works of disputed or shared authorship. Frederick Mosteller and David Wallace, for example, examined the Federalist Papers to ascertain whether John Jay or James Madison was the author of disputed passages, as well as what part Thomas Jefferson played in the revisions. In 1963, Bernard O'Donnell examined

---

*Certain themes emerge from a reading of these studies. One is the primacy of artifact over nature as stimulus to imaginative writing. What the writer has read seems more crucial than whatever is meant by direct confrontations with nature and other kinds of experience. This thesis has also been propounded for painters and other artists by Andre Malraux in *Les Voix du Silence*.

A second awareness is the validity of a distinction made by Stephen Spender in his essay "The Making of a Poem" between Mozartians and Beethovians. In her essay "The Uses of the Unconscious in Composing," this investigator elaborated Spender's distinctions:

> The Morzartian is one who can instantaneously arrange encounters with his unconscious; he is one in whom the creative self leads a constant and uninterrupted life of its own, serene to surface disturbances, oblivious of full upper activity—coach-riding, concert-giving, bill-paying. The Mozartian can "plunge the greatest depths of his own experience by the tremendous effort of a moment" and surface every time with a finished pearl—a Cosi Fan Tutte, a Piano Concerto in C Major.
>
> The Beethovian, on the other hand, is the agonizer, the evolutionizer. Scholars studying his first notes to a quartet or a symphony, as Spender points out, are astounded by their embryonic clumsiness. The creative self in a Beethovian is not a plummeting diver, but a plodding miner who seems at times to scoop south with his bare bands. To change the metaphor, for the Beethovian, composing is not unlike eating an artichoke—pricks and inadequate rewards in our tedious leaf-by-leaf spiraling toward the delectable heart.[16]

---

[15]*Ibid*, p. 125.

[16]Janet Emig, "The Uses of the Unconscious in Composing," *College Composition and Communication* (February 1964), p. 11.

Stephen Crane's posthumously published novel, *The O'Ruddy*, to ascertain what parts of the work were actually written by Crane and what parts by the reporter who completed the novel.

Computer analysis of style has also been employed to make a comparative examination of grammatical and lexical elements in authors' styles. J.B. Carroll, for example, attempted by factor analysis to delineate "the basic dimensions on which style varied"; and he demonstrated that the style of Mickey Spillane and F. Scott Fitzgerald varied along certain specifiable dimensions. Boder showed that the verb-adjective quotient was a significant index of stylistic differences among professional and student writers. There are certain general computer programs for handling language data, such as Iker and Harway's work with content analysis, and Stone and Boles's *General Inquirer Program*.

Although in these linguistic studies the process of writing is sometimes purportedly under scrutiny, to this writer's knowledge none of the investigators has yet attempted to develop generalizations from their studies of specific works and authors. They have not attempted, in other words, to delineate the, even a, writing process or to ascertain whether the process has constant characteristics across writers. Rather, they have been concerned with product- rather than process-centered research.

Rhetoric and Composition Texts and Handbooks

Another possible source of data about the composing process is the rhetoric or composition text which gives students dicta and directives about how to speak and write. The best-known classical rhetorics are of course Plato, Aristotle, Cicero, and Quintilian. These have provided the models for theory, and applications, down the centuries. Contemporary examples of rhetoric texts include Francis X. Connolly's *A Rhetoric Casebook*, Leo Rockas's *Models of Rhetoric*, and Martin, Ohmann and Wheatley's *The Logic and Rhetoric of Exposition*.

Composition handbooks—a more recent development—also give dicta and directives; but, unlike most of the rhetoric texts, they cite no substantiation for them. (See, for example, Warriner's handbook). The authors and editors of these texts neither state nor imply that they have tapped any of the following possible sources of data, if not substantiation: (a) introspection into their own processes of writing; (b) accounts by and about professional writers; and (c) accounts of and about secondary students, the audience to whom their advice is purportedly directed.

In America, beginning probably with John Walker's *A Teacher's Assistant in English Composition* (1803), composition texts served a different audience from that of rhetoric texts: whereas the rhetoric text was designed to help prepare young men of the upper classes for the pulpit, bar, and public forum, the composition text was designed to help younger students of both sexes in the middle and lower classes achieve a basic written literacy. In his survey of the rhetorical tradition Edward P.J. Corbett notes these differences in the two approaches to teaching writing:

> Rhetoric courses in the schools gradually assumed a new
> orientation—the study of the four forms of discourse: exposition,
> argumentation, description, and narration. The virtues that were
> stressed in this approach to composition were unity, coherence, and
> emphasis. Style continued to engage some attention, but the focus
> shifted from the schemes and tropes to a concern for diction (which
> gradually deteriorated into a neurotic concern for "correct usage") and
> for syntax (which, under the popular handbooks, became a rather
> negative approach to "correct grammar"). The study of the paragraph
> concentrated on the topic sentence and the various ways of
> developing the topic sentence to achieve maximum unity, coherence,
> and emphasis.[17]

The characterization these texts convey of the composing process is of a
quite conscious, wholly rational—at times, even mechanical—affair with
many of the components for a piece of discourse extrinsic to the speaker or
writer. For example, *inventio*, the first *division* of classical rhetoric, does not
refer to the writer's finding within his own experience the sources of his
discourse; it refers rather to discovering, in the universe outside, the *topoi*, or
"the set of sources available . . . in my argument."[18] The organization of a
piece of writing, particularly a speech, is, if one believes Cicero and others,
fixed by a traditional schema consisting of six parts: exordium, narrative,
partition, confirmation, repetition, peroration. A speaker or writer does not
evolve a mode of organization that is indigenous to a specific content: he
follows instead the six-part outline.

How the writer feels about the subject matter and how his feelings may
influence what he writes—the affective dimension—are not really considered
in these texts. The notion that there might be a press of personality upon all
components of the process is not present. This is not a criticism of the
classical texts; it is an historical comment. The rhetorical tradition is simply,
in its major works, significantly prior to the development of psychology with
its interests in introspection and theories of personality development. Because
they do not consider the possible effect of a writer's personality upon the
process, however, rhetoric and composition texts are not a useful source of
data for most of the questions posed earlier in this chapter.

Theory of the Creative Process

Research is a third source of data that might provide a theoretical base or
a methodological model for this inquiry. The two modes examined in this

---

[17]From *Classical Rhetoric for the Modern Student* by Edward P.J. Corbett, p. 566. Copyright © 1965 by
Oxford University Press, Inc. Used by permission.
[18]*Essays on Rhetoric*, ed. Dudley Bailey, p. 82.

section are (1) theoretical studies of what is called globally, "the creative process," and (2) pieces of empirical research dealing with the writing of adolescents.

In *The Art of Thought* (1926) Graham Wallas typologizes creative thought as a four-stage process—a delineation that persists, with occasional shifts and changes of terms and categories, into the present literature. Wallas credits Helmholtz, the German physicist, with first describing three stages in the process; the fourth Wallas adds along with descriptive terms for all four stages:

> We can . . . roughly dissect out a continuous process, with a beginning and a middle and an end of its own. . . . Helmholtz, . . . speaking in 1891 at a banquet on his seventieth birthday, described the way in which his most important new thoughts had come to him. He said that after previous investigation of the problem "in all directions . . . happy ideas come unexpectedly without effort, like an inspiration. So far as I am concerned, they have never come to me when my mind was fatigued, or when I was at my working table. . . . They came particularly readily during the slow ascent of wooded hills on a sunny day." Helmholtz here gives us three stages in the formation of a new thought. The first in time I shall call Preparation, the stage during which the problem was 'investigated . . . in all directions'; the second is the stage during which he was not consciously thinking about the problem, which I shall call Incubation; the third, consisting of the appearance of the 'happy idea' together with the psychological events which immediately preceded and accompanied that appearance, I shall call Illumination.
>
> And I shall add a fourth stage, of Verification, which Helmholtz does not here mention . . . in which both the validity of the idea was tested, and the idea itself was reduced to exact form.[19]

Many students of creativity as well as creators across modes—painting, composing—share this view of the creative process. Writing, for example, which can be regarded as a species of creative behavior, is often described in quite similar terms. In his introduction to *Writers at Work: The Paris Review Interviews*, Malcolm Cowley describes the composing process shared by the short-story writers and novelists interviewed:

> There would seem to be four stages in the composition of a story. First comes the germ of the story, then the period of more or less conscious meditation, then the first draft, and finally the revision, which may be simply "pencil work," as John O'Hara calls it—that is, minor changes in wording—or may lead to writing several drafts and

---

[19]Graham Wallas, *The Art of Thought*, pp. 79-81. Copyright 1926 by Harcourt Brace Jovanovich. Used by permission.

what amounts to a new work.[20]

In the process of writing, revision seems to occupy the same place that verification holds in scientific and mathematical inquiries.

Another view of the specific poetic process as a sequence of *five* (perhaps six) aligned stages is presented by the psychologist R.N. Wilson in his essay "Poetic Creativity, Process and Personality":

> A rough paradigm of the stages of poetic creativity would include at least the following elements: the selective perception of the environment; the acquisition of technique; the envisioning of combinations and distillations; elucidation of the vision; and the end of the poem and its meaning to the poet.[21]

This sequence differs from Wallas's chiefly in regarding the acquisition of technique as an element in the process (it is probable the acquisition of technique is regarded instead as a requisite *to* the process by Wallas and others); and in its concern with the end of the process, a later element than "elucidation" which for Wilson includes revision, Wallas's fourth stage, and the contemplation of the product.

In the literature there are perhaps only two markedly different characterizations of creation as something other than a process of several aligned stages. One characterization represents it as the tension generated between a single or multiple set of opposing variables; the second, as the point or moment of intersection between two disparate modes or fields of endeavor.

The earliest description of creation as the tension generated between a single set of polarities is probably Plato's dialogue *Ion*, with the movement of the artist between frenzy (divine inspiration) and formulation. The best-known is perhaps Freud's interpretation of creativity, in "The Relation of the Poet to Day-Dreaming" (1908) and "Leonardo da Vinci and a Memory of His Childhood" (1910), as the tension between the unconscious and conscious activities of the mind. In *Neurotic Distortion of the Creative Process*, L. S. Kubie also dichotomizes the activities of the mind during creation; but he suggests that creative behaviors emanate from the preconscious rather than the unconscious portion of the mind. Kubie describes the distinctive features of preconscious processes as

> their automatic and subtle recordings of multiple perceptions, their automatic recall, their multiple analogic and overlapping linkages, and their direct connections to the autonomic processes which underlie affective states.[22]

In his essay "The Conditions of Creativity" (1962), Jerome Bruner

---

[20]Malcolm Cowley, *Writers at Work, The Paris Review Interviews*. Copyright 1961 by the Viking Press, Inc. and Martin Secker & Warburg Limited. Used by permission.

[21]R.N. Wilson, "Poetic Creativity, Process and Personality," *Psychiatry* (1954), pp. 163-76.

[22]L.S. Kubie, *Neurotic Distortion of the Creative Process*, pp. 44-45.

describes creation as the tension produced among a multiple set of "antimonies."[23] These are detachment and commitment, passion and decorum, freedom from and domination by the artifact, deferral and immediacy, and conflicting identities within the creator. Creators are at once "disengaged from that which exists conventionally" and "engaged deeply in what they construct to replace it"; urgently vital in artistic impulse and courteous and formal in artistic expression; separated from the object and bored enough by creating it to put off completion until the psychologically appropriate time; and involved through their creation in "working out of conflict and coalition within the set of identities that compose" their personality.[24]

Another markedly different characterization of creativity is proffered by Arthur Koestler in his massive study, *The Act of Creation* (1964). Koestler describes creation, not as the outcome of a series of aligned stages nor as the result of tension between "antimonies," but rather as the intersection of two disparate "matrices." "Matrix" he defines as "any ability, habit, or skill, any pattern of ordered behavior governed by a *'code'* of fixed rules."[25] In Koestler's view, creation is "bisociative"; that is, the creator perceives "a situation or event in two habitually incompatible associative contexts."[26] Humor, literary creation, and scientific discovery are examples Koestler gives of bisociative activity.

Viewed singly, these three delineations of creation may seem descriptions of fact. Juxtaposed, however, they reveal their hypothetical nature. That there are data supporting all three sets of hypotheses suggests there may be processes of creation with quite different profiles or typographies. Indeed, there is the strong possibility that other delineations are equally valid.

Empirical Research About Adolescent Writing

Most pieces of empirical research on the adolescent writer focus upon the product(s) rather than upon the process(es) of their writing and, consequently, do not provide an appropriate methodology for a process-centered inquiry. Of the 504 studies written before 1963 that are cited in the bibliography of *Research in Written Composition*, only two deal even indirectly with the process of writing among adolescents.*

---

*These are the unpublished dissertations. "Proposals for the Conduct of Written Composition Activities in the Secondary School Inherent in an Analysis of the Language Composition Act" by Lester Angene and "Factors Affecting Regularity of the Flow of Words during Written Composition" by John A. Van Bruggen. Angene looks only at finished student themes: any examples and statements involving the process of writing he draws from a sample of professional writers and from analysis of the writing act in one composition handbook, written by his advisor. Van Bruggen's emphasis, as the title of his study makes clear, is the physical rate at which a sample of eighty-four junior high school students write— more specifically, how often and how fast they actually place pen to paper (actually stylus to electric disc) in the production of their themes. The process of writing, beyond this series of physical contacts between pen and paper, remains unexamined.

---

[23] Jerome Bruner, "The Conditions of Creativity," *On Knowing: Essays for the Left Hand.*
[24] *Ibid.*
[25] Arthur Koestler, *The Act of Creation*, p. 38.
[26] *Ibid.*, p. 95.

Two recent American studies which focus upon process rather than upon product of composition are "The Sound of Writing" by Anthony Tovatt and Ebert L. Miller and *Pre-Writing: The Construction and Application of Models for Concept Formation in Writing* by D. Gordon Rohman and Albert O. Wiecke.

Tovatt's study proceeds from the premise that "we write with our ears" and that if students can "hear" what they are writing, they can transmute satisfactory patterns of written discourse. In the first experimental year of the study (1964-65) thirty ninth-grade students, matched with a control class, were given the OAV (oral-aural-visual) stimuli approach to writing. As one of the two most significant—or at least unique—features of the experiment, the students used tape-recorders equipped with audio-active headsets so that they could hear themselves electronically as they composed. A second was that the teacher provided a constant role-model as writer by composing in the presence of the experimental class until they "eventually accept[ed] the fact good writing is achieved through sustained labor in three basic stages: prewriting, writing, and rewriting."[27]

Tovatt reports these findings:

> The OAV stimuli procedures demonstrated in the first year a general superiority over a conventional approach in increasing student abilities in writing, reading, listening, and language usage. However, rating of compositions from the control and experimental classes was inconclusive in establishing the superiority of either approach.[28]

In the study by Rohman and Wiecke, the investigators divide the writing process into three stages: "prewriting," "writing," and "rewriting." They focus upon prewriting—which they define as "the stage of discovery in process when a person assimilates 'his subject' to himself"—because prewriting "is crucial to the success of any writing that occurs later" and "is seldom given the attention it consequently deserves."[29]

In a project involving three sections of a sophomore-level course in expository writing at Michigan State University in 1964, the investigators sought "(1) to isolate and describe the principle of this assimilation and (2) to devise a course that would allow students to imitate its dynamics."[30]

The principle of the assimilation, they decided, is the conversion of an "event" into an "experience," to use the words of novelist Dorothy S. Sayers. The three means they employed were (1) the keeping of a journal, (2) the practice of some principles derived from the religious meditation, and (3) the

---

[27]Anthony Tovatt and Ebert L. Miller, "The Sound of Writing," *Research in the Teaching of English* (Fall 1967), pp. 182-83.

[28]*Ibid.*, pp. 187-88.

[29]D. Gordon Rohman and Albert O. Wiecke, *Pre-Writing: The Construction and Application of Models for Concept Formation in Writing*, Michigan State University, 1964, USOE Cooperative Research Project No. 2174, p. 103.

[30]*Ibid.*, p. 30.

use of the analogy. The essays produced after a one-semester course with the emphasis on assimilation "showed a statistically significant superiority [one set, at the .05 level; one set, at the .01 level] to essays produced in control sections."[31]

Both the Tovatt-Miller and the Rohman-Wiecke studies are experiments in instruction: that is, systematic group interventions are introduced to effect a change in students' behavior as they write. The purpose of the present inquiry, on the other hand, is to attempt to describe how student writers usually or typically behave as they write with minimal direct intervention by the investigator. In other words, the Tovatt-Miller and the Rohman-Wiecke studies are efforts to instruct or teach; this inquiry is an effort to describe. Nevertheless, as two of the few serious efforts extant to examine writing in process for adolescent writers, they deserve acknowledgment and explication.

Conflicting Data

Among these three major sources of data there is often disagreement. Writers' accounts and composition texts, for example, present a powerful instance of the phenomenon noted at the beginning of this chapter—one set of sources that contradict or are often directly contradicted by another. Here, for example, are two accounts of how the writing process proceeds:

(1) A good writer puts words together in correct, smooth sentences, according to the rules of standard usage. He puts sentences together to make paragraphs that are clear and effective, unified and well developed. Finally, he puts paragraphs together into larger forms of writing—essays, letters, stories, research papers.

In practice, as you know from your own experience, a writer begins with a general plan and ends with details of wording, sentence structure, and grammar. First, he chooses the *subject* of his composition. Second, he tackles the *preparation* of his material, from rough ideas to final outline. Third, he undertakes the writing itself, once again beginning with a rough form (the first draft) and ending with a finished form (the final draft) that is as nearly perfect as he can make it.

These three basic stages of composition are almost always the same for any form of writing. Each of the three stages proceeds according to certain definite steps, listed below in order.

a. Choosing and limiting the subject	1. Subject
b. Assembling materials	
c. Organizing materials	2. Preparation
d. Outlining	

---

[31]*Ibid.*, p. 181.

e. Writing the first draft   3. Writing
f. Revising
g. Writing the final draft[32]

(2) You will write . . . if you will write without thinking of the result
in terms of a result, but think of the writing in terms of discovery,
which is to say the creation must take place between the pen and the
paper, not before in a thought, or afterwards in a recasting. Yes,
before in a thought, but not in careful thinking. It will come if it is
there and if you will let it come, and if you have anything you will
get a sudden creative recognition. You won't know how it was, even
what it is, but it will be creation if it came out of the pen and out of
you and not out of an architectural drawing of the thing you are
doing . . . I can tell how important it is to have that creative
recognition. You cannot go into the womb to form the child; it is there
and makes itself and comes forth whole—and there it is and you have
made it and felt it, but it has come itself—and that is creative
recognition. Of course you have a little more control over your
writing than that; you have to know what you want to get; but when
you know that, let it take you and if it seems to take you off the track
don't hold back, because that is perhaps where instinctively you want
to be and if you hold back and try to be always where you have been
before, you will go dry.[33]

The first of these comes from Warriner's *English Grammar and Composition*, 11, one volume of a very widely used series of composition handbooks.
The second is by the writer Gertrude Stein. Clearly, the statements are almost
antithetical: according to Stein, writing is an act of discovery emanating "out
of the pen and out of you" while Warriner's suggests writing is a tidy,
accretive affair that proceeds by elaborating a fully pre-conceived and
formulated plan.

Statements in composition texts and handbooks also differ from those of
established writers in discussion of what might be called specific components
in the writing process. Take this same matter of planning, for example. The
quotation above from Warriner's handbook unequivocally states that a writer
always makes an outline before "writing," regardless of the mode of writing.

In 1964 this investigator collected data from professional writers
regarding their planning practices. Responding to a questionnaire about their
planning practices were the following professional and academic writers: Max
Bluestone, Reuben Brower, Jerome Bruner, John B. Carroll, John Ciardi,
Kenneth Lynn, Raven I. McDavid, Harold Martin, Theodore Morrison, Henry

---

[32]John E. Warriner, Joseph Mersand, and Francis Griffith, *English Grammar and Composition*, *11*, pp.
379-80. Copyright 1958 by Harcourt Brace Jovanovich. Used by permission.
[33]John Hyde Preston, "A Conversation," *Atlantic Monthly* (August 1935), p. 189. Reprinted by permission
of Harold Ober Associates Incorporated. Copyright 1935 by John Hyde Preston.

Olds, James K. Robinson, Israel Scheffler, Clifford Shipton, B.F. Skinner, Priscilla Tyler, and Mark Van Doren.[34]

The data from these questionnaires belie the textbook generalization that all writers make written outlines for all forms of writing they do. Indeed, the data suggest there is great diversity and individuality in planning practices, at least among this sample of writers.

In the sample four of the sixteen writers—J.B. Carroll, James K. Robinson, Israel Scheffler, and B.F. Skinner—proceed as the texts state all writers do. That is, they make a rough outline, then an elaborated one complete with full sentences, indentations, and numbering and lettering of items. For these writers the outline seems to represent the major act in the writing process, as B.F. Skinner makes clear:

> When I begin to think of a developed paper or a book, I turn almost immediately to outlines. These grow in detail, almost to the point of producing the final prose.

And James K. Robinson notes the usefulness of the elaborated outline not only for himself but also for his students:

> I found both for myself and for students whom I have had in Freshman English that the sentence outline is most satisfactory since it forces one to make definite statements that will enable one to test logical relationships or developments in the paper to be written. It goes a step beyond words or phrases in planning.

Israel Scheffler also produces an outline that structures, as well as fully pre-figures, the final piece of writing:

> . . . The outline is as detailed as I can make it, with different systems of numbering and lettering, plus indentation, to reveal subordination and other relationships among the items. The main items I try to spell out as full sentences or short paragraphs, the subordinate items as sentences, clauses, or simply tags to indicate examples or other points. I worry about parallelism of items with parallel position in the outline, as well as subordination of other items.

> Normally, the outline does not cover all the details of the eventual draft, but I do want it to give the main structure of the whole in as explicit form as I can get it at the beginning.

---

[34]Respondents to a questionnaire devised and distributed July 1964 by Janet Emig were: Max Bluestone, University of Massachusetts, Boston; Reuben Brower, Harvard University; Jerome Bruner, Harvard University; John B. Carroll, Harvard University; John Ciardi, poet, Poetry Editor, *Saturday Review*; Kenneth Lynn, Harvard University; Raven I. McDavid, University of Chicago; Harold Martin, President, Union College; Theodore Morrison, novelist, Harvard University; Henry Olds, Harvard Graduate School of Education; James K. Robinson, University of Cincinnati; Israel Scheffler, Harvard University; Clifford Shipton, Director, American Antiquarian Society, Worcester, Massachusetts; B.F. Skinner, Harvard University; Priscilla Tyler, Harvard University; Mark Van Doren, poet, Columbia University.

The majority in the group take what might be called a middle position toward planning—that is, they make some kind of informal outline adapted to their individual styles of working and to the mode of the piece involved. Kenneth Lynn jots down in phrase form a sequence of items he plans to use, observing some system of identation. Harold Martin sets down phrases without any particular order, then groups these "for meaningful relationships," and finally marks "1-2-3 for order": he finds no value to "IA, la." Theodore Morrison calls the plan he makes for his novels "a quick conspectus": he uses "heads as a reminder of where I am going."

Members of this middle group seem to be against any plan that totally pre-figures a piece of writing. Their shared reason is aptly set forth by Max Bluestone:

> The rough scheme [his form of plan] is a map to the territory of my thoughts. The map is never precise, first because the territory has not been thoroughly explored and second because writing is in itself the discovery of new territory. I usually anticipate discovery in the act of composition.

Contradicting another statement in Warriner's, writers in the sample who work in more than one mode proceed differently in different genres. Poetry seems to be a genre for which no outlines or elaborated plans are ever made, at least by the writers of poetry in this sample—Max Bluestone, John Ciardi, and Mark Van Doren.

Max Bluestone, Theodore Morrison, and Mark Van Doren, novelists and short story writers in the sample, also note for these modes they seldom make elaborate written outlines. They would seem to agree with the novelist Eileen Bassing about the use of the outline in fiction.

> *N* [Roy Newquist]: Could you outline your working procedures? Perhaps it's best to refer directly—if only roughly—to the production of *Home before Dark* and *Where's Annie?*
>
> *Bassing*: I'm glad you said "roughly" because I don't think I could give you a precise outline of any particular thing I write. I very much admire writers who can work from a neat, orderly outline, and I always feel that my method can only be called "chaotic." The complete outline isn't for me.
>
> I do have a shadowy outline in my mind—as I did in *Home before Dark*, for example. I knew what I wanted to say, and I knew a great deal about my central character. Once you have the chracter you're pretty well started, . . .
>
> . . . The outline, again [with her novel *Where's Annie?*] was very shadowy—I had the beginning, a kind of middle, a scene here and there, and maybe the end. . . .
>
> *N*: In other words you don't really work from an outline at the beginning. You work from an idea, or some characters, and write a

first draft—then make an outline and write it again. Is that right?

Bassing: Yes.

N: Isn't that a very unusual way of working?

Bassing: Is it? I don't think so.[35]

The single mode of exposition then is the only mode cited by this sample for which outlines are produced with any degree of regularity, and then only by some of these writers.

The data from the questionnaire also suggest that a second generalization of rhetoric texts and manuals about planning is not valid, at least for this sample of writers—that is, all planning precedes all writing as all writing precedes all revising. The metaphor implied in these accounts about the writing process is linear: each "stage" is monolithic and holds a fixed position in a lock-step chronological process. There are, in other words, no major recursive features in the writing process.

All writers in the sample state they do engage in some form of planning prior to the production of a piece of sustained discourse: for Reuben Brower and Jerome Bruner this takes the form of conversation with friends. They also state or imply, however, that they continue to plan and to adapt and revise previously written plans as the piece evolves. Theodore Morrison makes a conspectus "at such times as seem necessary or seem to offer help." Some of the writers even make written plans or outlines as part of their revising. Max Bluestone states that if he is revising "something that has lain fallow," he might make a revised outline as well, one that "usually has to do with compression and elaboration of the version before me." Clearly, for these authors the so-called "stages" of writing are not fixed in an inexorable sequence. Rather, they occur and reoccur throughout the process. These data then make suspect the straight line which rhetoric texts imply as an appropriate metaphor for the writing process.*

This discrepancy then between these two forms of data—the statements made about writing in composition texts and handbooks and statements by professional writers—make suspect the validity of one form, if not both forms, of data.

Another dissonance occurs between the statements made about the practice and value of outlining in composition texts, manuals, and textbooks and the actual practices of able secondary students as examined by empirical

---

*An aside: there is almost perfect unanimity among authors in the sample that whatever training in formal outlining they received in school has no influence on their current planning practices. Mark Van Doren and Jerome Bruner put it mildly: "Formal training seemed artificial and didn't interest me."

Others react more strongly: "Such procedures have helped me not at all." (Kenneth Lynn) "It was forced upon me and I did what I had to do, but I resist such outlining as a destruction. It seems to imply that one may complete his thought process in the outline and then merely go for 'style' in the writing. Nonsense. The writing and the thinking are inseperable [*sic*]. Any other assumption can only produce hack-work." (John Ciardi).

---

[35]Eileen Bassing, Interview from *Counterpoint*, compiled and edited by Roy Newquist. Copyright 1964 by Rand McNally & Company. Used by permission.

research. Modern rhetoric and composition texts, as the quotation above from Warriner's handbook suggests, present the formal outline as a customary prelude to student writing, at least in the mode of exposition.

In a pilot study conducted in 1964, this investigator examined two assumptions behind the generalization on outlining presented in Warriner's handbook. The first assumption is descriptive: student writers do organize by outlining. The second is normative: to assure the most skillfully organized theme, student writers should organize by formal outlining. These assumptions were treated as hypotheses and examined in the following ways.

If assumption one is true, if student writers do organize by outlining, it seemed logical to believe that superior student writers would use outlining in organizing a group of expository themes whether they were directed to or not. The only data that would yield such information were the total written evolutions of a number of student themes, from first recorded act through final submitted draft. To acquire such data, the investigator asked an eleventh-grade high honors English class of twenty-five students to save and to submit, with the final drafts of all expository themes written during an eight-week period, all written actions they performed in the course of writing these themes.

The students were given no directives about how these themes were to be organized. When one student asked, during the explanation about saving all materials, if the investigator expected to find outlines with every theme, the investigator said she had no set expectations about what she would find; she wanted only to have everything produced in the course of writing them, whatever these materials happened to be.

During the eight-week period the students submitted (as part or all of five writing assignments) 109 expository themes together with all written actions that preceded the final drafts. Of these, 40 themes (or 36.7 percent) were accompanied by a plan, defined here as any schema related to the composition of the theme, prior to that theme. Of these plans, nine (or 8.3 percent) qualified as formal outlines by what are, conventionally, the minimal criteria for formality: numbers or letters precede the items, and there is at least one level of indentation. The remaining 91.7 percent were atypical according to the generalization set forth in Warriner's handbook. To conclude from these very scant data that the students from whom these themes were collected typically or customarily do not outline formally for more than eight percent of the themes they write, much more that *all* secondary students do not, is, of course, unwarranted. These data however shed additional doubt upon the validity of the generalization in the rhetoric and composition texts.

The second assumption in the teaching of the outline, that the writing of a formal outline assures a more successfully organized theme, was examined in the following way: perhaps the most common means of determining the success of organization of a theme is by teacher evaluation, specifically, by the grade given the theme. If the writing of an outline prior to the writing of the theme assures superior organization, it would seem to follow that the student theme which had been preceded by an outline would rank higher by

Table 1

Types of Outlines Accompanying 109 Expository Themes Written
By 25 Eleventh Grade Students

Theme Assignment	Total Number of Expository Themes Written	Total Number of Outlines	Number of Informal Outlines	Number of Formal Outines
1.	25	15	9	6
2.	14	6	6	0
3.	23	6	5	1
4.	22	4	3	1
5.	25	9	8	1
Total	109	40	31	9

teacher evaluation than the theme which had not.

To test this hypothesis, three independent judges who were experienced teachers of English were asked to grade, from the total of 109 themes submitted, a sample of 20; 9 of which had been accompanied by outlines—4 formal, 5 informal—and 11 of which had not. The judges were not told to what category any theme belonged. They were asked to evaluate each theme solely on the basis of its organization.*

After the three judges evaluated all 20 themes and submitted their grades, the grades were coded according to whether that theme was accompanied by a formal outline, by an informal outline, or by no outline at all. These data, analyzed by a program of covariant analysis, revealed no correlation between the presence or absence of any outline and the grade a student receives evaluating how well organized that theme is.

Conclusion

Some of the data presented in this chapter contribute either useful methodological or theoretical models for this inquiry.

The technique of the interview found in the accounts of professional writers is scarcely unique to this form of data; but as one helpful means for eliciting information from student writers, it will also be employed in this inquiry. The provocative and rich responses to certain kinds of questions,

---

* To assure that the judges would be evaluating what constituted good organization according to the same set of criteria, the investigator asked them to draw up a list on which they all agreed and on which they would base their grades. What constituted to each of them an *A*, *B*, and *C* was also informally discussed, and the judges agreed that an *A* should represent fufillment of all criteria; *B* most of them; and *C*, some.

especially those posed in the *Paris Review* interviews, recommend such questions as those on prewriting be asked in this study as well.

Although, as the brief review of rhetoric and composition texts revealed, these data do not provide generative category-systems, several of the theories of creativity do. Examples include the attenuation of the poetic or creative process suggested by R.N. Wilson, particularly the notions that the "selective perception of the environment" and the contemplation of a product and its "meaning" represent components to describe if they apply to the composing process of students. The four-stage description of the process delineated by Helmholtz, Wallas, and Cowley will serve as the center of the delineation of the writing process in this study.

An Examination of the Writing Processes of Seven-Year-Old Children

by Donald H. Graves

The complexity of the writing process and the interrelationships of its components have been underestimated by researchers, teachers, and other educators, because writing is an organic process that frustrates approaches to explain its operation. Three major "Needs for Research" summaries in the last eleven years reflect specific concern for dealing with the issue of complexity (Braddock, 1963; Parke, 1960; Meckel, 1963). All three recommend extensive investigation of developmental issues, issues that focus much more on individual differences than on the "procedural-methodological" matters which have historically received research emphasis.

A review of research since the summaries indicates that most efforts have focused on correlative studies or the examination of the effects of single or multivariate interventions. The data from these separate studies make it difficult to produce a sound, organic understanding of what is even involved in the writing process. Furthermore, only two studies seem to have involved the actual observation of the behaviors of writers while they are in the process of writing. One of these studies (Emig, 1969) involved the composing processes of twelfth graders and the other (Holstein, 1970) was primarily concerned with the use of metaphor by fifth-grade children.

This investigation was undertaken to explore the writing processes and related variables of a group of seven-year-old children. Through the gathering of data in a case study procedure, an analysis of broad samples of writing, and the naturalistic observation of children while writing in two types of classroom environments, formal and informal, the study sought to avoid both a fragmentary approach and teacher intervention. From this study a profile of writing in the early years emerges sufficient in depth and scope to make effective research hypotheses and recommendations.

In recent years new focus has come to the case study approach as a means to investigation of the variables involved in new areas of research. Indeed, the case study approach in the field of comparative research is most often recommended when entering virgin territory in which little has been investigated. Because of a lack of studies on the writing process or the actual

Reprinted from *Research in the Teaching of English* (Winter 1975). Copyright 1975 by the National Council of Teachers of English. Reprinted with permission.

observation of children while actually writing, the use of the case study to investigate the writing processes of children was considered as one of the appropriate methodologies.

The emphasis in this report of the study of the writing processes of seven-year-old children will be placed on a detailed description of the procedures used, and the conclusions and hypotheses formulated from the findings. This was done because the complexity and extent of the actual findings from case studies, small and large groups precluded their reporting in short space.

Procedures

The Sample

Two formal and two informal second level (second grade) classrooms in a middle class community were chosen for the principal focus of a five-month investigation. The classrooms selected met specific criteria that identified them as being either formal or informal. These criteria concerned the degree to which children were able to function without specific directions from the teacher and the amount of choice children had in determining their learning activities.

Figure 1 depicts the makeup of the sample for the different phases of data gathering in the study. The First Phase involved ninety-four children (forty-eight boys and forty-six girls) with a mean age of seven years and six months at the beginning of the study. In Phase II fourteen seven-year-old children (eight boys and six girls) from each of the four rooms were observed while they were writing. In Phase III, seventeen seven-year-old children (nine boys and eight girls) from each of the four rooms were interviewed as to their views of their own writing and concepts of the "good writer." Finally, in Phase IV, eight children (six boys and two girls), two from each of the four classrooms, were chosen for case study investigation. The eight children selected were considered by teachers and administrators as representative of "normal" seven-year-old children; thus pupils of unusually high intellectual capacity and those with learning or emotional problems were excluded.

Data Collection Procedures

Throughout the data collection period from the first week of December, 1972, to the middle of April, 1973, the primary emphasis was placed on gathering case study data on two children in each of the four environments. Secondary emphasis was placed on gathering data from larger groups in the same four classrooms. Data were collected from: (1) the logging of five categories of information secured from the writing of ninety-four children; 1,635 writings were logged for theme, type of writing, number of words, use of accompanying art, and teacher comments; (2) the naturalistic observation of fourteen children while they were writing in their classrooms; (3) the interviewing in four different sessions of the eight case study children as to their views of their own writing and of seventeen children as to their concepts of "a good writer"; (4) the gathering of full case study data about eight

Phase IV—Case Study
Michael
N-1

Phase III—Interviews
Interviews on children's views of
their own writing and concept of
the "good writer."
N-17

Phase II—The Writing Episode
The observation of fifty-three writing
episodes.
N-14

Phase I—The Writing Folder

1. Thematic choices of children
2. Writing frequency
3. Types of writing (assigned—unassigned)

N-94

Formal Classrooms		Informal Classrooms	
Room A N-24	Room B N-25	Room C N-24	Room D N-21

Figure 1: Study Phases and Procedures

children through parent interviews, testing, assembling of educational-developmental history, and observing the children in several environments. The purpose of this form of data gathering and reporting was to provide a range of cross-validation of data to support the findings and, thus, to add power to the research recommendations and instructional hypotheses posed. This approach made it possible to follow findings from the several larger settings to an individual case and, conversely, from the case and/or small group findings to all-class profiles and to the entire group of seven-year-old children studied.

Phase One: The Writing Folder

Writing folders were kept by all children in each of the four classrooms in the study. The purposes of having all children keep a writing folder were the following:

1. to reduce focus on the eight children chosen for case study work;
2. to provide background data of a total classroom nature in order to view the writing of the eight children with greater objectivity;
3. to assess the general writing habits of the children in terms of writing frequency, assigned-unassigned writing, use of illustrations accompanying writing, writing length, and the thematic interests of children.

The definition of writing that was employed to determine paper selection was as follows:

> Any writing intended to be at least a sentence unit that was completely composed by the child.

Teachers distinguished between two types of writing—assigned or unassigned—when they reviewed the writing folders. Assigned was defined as writing that children were required to attempt and for which completion was expected. Unassigned writing was defined as unrequired writing. In this situation the child chose on his own initiative to write. There was no expectation by the teacher that specific work would be completed. Thus the child made choices as to mode, length of writing, and the disposition of the writing product.

Phase Two: Writing Process Observation (The Writing Episode)

In this stage of the investigation, fifty-three writing episodes of fourteen seven-year-old children (mean age—7:7), made up of eight boys and six girls from all of the four rooms were observed. Writing of the children in the episodes was observed within the classroom in order to gain a more valid view of their writing processes. Writing episodes were not structured by the researcher. Rather, recordings of the children's writing behaviors were made when they chose to initiate writing in assigned or unassigned work. For this reason, approximately 250 hours were spent observing children while waiting for them to enter into a writing episode.

Within each of the four environments two children were chosen as case studies. These eight children were the prime focus of classroom observation. Because these cases were not always engaged in writing, were absent, or were working with the teacher, it was possible to record some of the writings of other children in the rooms. Twelve of the fifty-three writing episodes recorded were from six children who were not case studies.

There is more to a writing episode than the children's act of composing and writing down words. The observation of writing at only one point in time limits an analysis of the writing process and may result in conclusions which overlook important variables. Therefore, a single writing episode was considered to consist of three phases of observation: prewriting, composing and postwriting. Definitions of these phases and the factors in each phase for which data were obtained are given.

Prewriting phase. This phase immediately precedes the writing of the child. Examples of factors related to writing observed in this phase were the contribution of room stimuli to thematic choice, art work behaviors, and discussions with other persons.

Composing phase. This phase begins and ends with the actual writing of the message. Examples of phase factors were spelling, resource use, accompanying language, pupil interactions, proofreadings, re-readings, interruptions, erasures, and teacher participation.

Postwriting phase. This phase refers to all behaviors recorded following the completion of writing the message.

Examples of these behaviors were product disposition, approval solicitation, material disposition, proofreading, and contemplation of the finished product.

Recording of the Episode

Whenever the researcher noted that a child was structuring materials for a writing episode, he moved close to the child and usually seated himself directly in front of his desk or table. Although the researcher was viewing the child's work in the upside-down position, it was the best location to record behaviors accompanying the writing episode. In this way the child's body posture, use of overt language, and rereading could be better observed.

For many children drawing was a major step in the prewriting phase. Michael, the case study chosen for reporting, apparently needed to draw before he was able to write in the composing phase. As he drew he would talk, often making appropriate sound effects to go along with the figure being drawn at the moment. While drawing the dinosaur referred to in Table I, Michael made growling noises to simulate the dinosaur's presence. To aid the recording of such data the observer reproduced the drawing, at the same time numbered each operation to indicate the sequence in which the picture evolved. Notable behaviors that accompanied each step were also recorded.

As soon as Michael completed his drawing, he started to write about information contained in the picture. At this juncture he began the composing phase. The researcher immediately recorded the time in the center column (Table I). When the child completed his writing the time was also recorded at the bottom of the column. In this way, the length of time the child was engaged in the composing phase could be computed.

The procedure for recording behaviors in the composing phase are contained in Table I. The left column records exactly what Michael wrote. The sequence of the writing and significant acts are indicated by the numerals. Since specific behaviors were noted from time to time by the observer as the writing was done, reference is made to these by circled numerals, with explanations of them given in the right column. For example, the circled eleven in the left column is explained following the eleven in the right column. That is, as Michael wrote dinosaur, he copied the word from the dictionary. Other behaviors were recorded during the composing phase and noted in the right hand column. To assist the summary of these behaviors,

Table I

Example of a Writing Episode

A whale is eating the
  1   2   3   4   5
men. A   dinosaur is
6 7 8 ⑨⑩ ⑪   12
triing to eat the whale.
 13 14 15 16   17 ⑱
  A dinosaur is frowning
⑲⑳ ㉑ 22   23 ㉔
a tree at the lion. and
㉕ 26 27 28 29 30 31 32
the cavman too. the men
33   34   35 ㊱ 37 38
are killed. The dinosaur
39 40 41 42   43
killed the whale. The
44   45   46 47 49
         ㊽
cavmen live is the roks.
  50   51 52 53 54 55 ㊴
	10:12
	R
	
	IU
	R
	
	RR
	OV
	OV
	IS
	
	RR
	RR
	
	RR
	10:20
		9—Gets up to get dictionary. Has
		    the page with pictures of
		    animals.
		
		10—Teacher announcement.
		11—Copies from dictionary and
		    returns book to side of room.
		
		18—Stops, rubs eyes.
		19—Rereads from 13 to 19.
		20—Voices as he writes.
		21—Still voicing.
		24—Gets up to sharpen pencil and
		    returns.
		25—Rereads from 20 to 25.
		36—Rereads to 36. Lost starting
		    point.
		48—Puts away paper, takes out
		    again.
		56—Rereads outloud from 49 to
		    56.

KEY: 1-2-3-4—Numerals indicate writing sequence. ④—Item explained in comment column on the right. ////—erasure or proofreading. T—Teacher involvement; IS—Interruption Solicited; IU—Interruption Unsolicited; RR—Reread; PR—Proofread; DR—Works on drawing; R—Resource use. Accompanying Language: OV—Overt; WH—Whispering; F—Forms letters and words; M—Murmuring; S—No overt language visible.

lettered symbols were placed in the center column from the key below to indicate the classification of the child's behaviors in the episode. For example, in the center column opposite the numeral twenty in the right column, the symbol "OV" was recorded. This symbol indicates that in step twenty Michael voiced words as he was writing them.

In the key at the bottom of the page in Table I the range of behaviors monitored when a child engaged in a writing episode was listed. Teacher involvement (T) was any form of teacher interaction with a child during his writing episode. Interruptions (IS-IU) were monitored for their effect on the continuance of the child's writing. Two other behaviors, rereadings and proofreadings (RR and PR), were important indices of other writing habits. Rereadings were the child's rescanning of writing composed prior to the current word being written whereas proofreading was defined as an adjustment of a previously composed writing operation. In a number of instances children would adjust a picture to go with a new idea in the text

(DR). The use of resources to aid writing (R) such as word banks, phonic charts, etc. were recorded during the observations. Finally, the range and type of language used to accompany the actual writing were recorded. This language behavior ranged from full voicing (overt—OV) to the absence of any visible or aural indication of accompanying language (covert—S).

From time to time the researcher would intervene and elicit information from the child as he was engaged in a writing episode. The purpose of this procedure was to gain understanding of the child's rationale for a previous operation or insight into his strategies for future operations. The type of intervention varied with the phase of the episode. Examples of interventions and their settings and objectives are shown in Table II. Although there were many types of interventions they were infrequently employed to minimize the observer's effect on the child's writing.

Phase Three: Interviews

Two types of interviews were used to record children's views of their own writing and writing in general. The first included individual conversations with the eight case study children about the writing in their folders. The purpose in employing the writing folder interview was to gain a profile of the child's view of his own writing. This profile was constructed from the child's rating of papers from his folder, the rationales for such ratings, and his responses to other statements and questions about the papers. In the interview the child was asked to rate writings in his folder from best to poorest and to state a rationale for his choice of the best paper. The second interview consisted of asking questions as to the child's conception of what good writers needed to be able to do in order to write well. The questions were asked of seventeen children, seven of whom were the case study children.

Phase Four: Case Study (Michael)

At the conclusion of the data gathering, a decision was made to report only one case study, Michael, but to use all of the writing observations and interviews of the other cases, as well as the additional information gathered on other children in the four classrooms. The procedures used for gathering case study data involved all of those used in the first three phases, plus additional procedures unique to case study research. The additional procedures were the interviewing of parents throughout the study, the individual administration of test batteries in reading, intelligence, and language; the gathering of the child's educational-developmental history, and the extended observation of the child in areas other than writing at home and in school.

Conclusions

The findings in this study led to conclusions in five areas: learning environments, sex differences in writing, developmental factors and the writing process, the case study, Michael, and the procedures used in the study.

These conclusions are reported below.

Table II
Examples of Interventions Made By Observer During Writing Episodes

Phase in Episode	Setting at Time of Intervention	Observer's Objective	Observer's Questions or Statements
Prewriting Phase	1. The child was about to start drawing his picture.	1. To determine how much the drawing contributes to the writing.	1. "Tell me what you are going to write about when you finish your drawing."
	2. The child has finished his drawing.	2. To determine how much the drawing contributes to the writing.	2. "Tell me what you are going to write about now that you have finished your drawing."
	3. The child has finished his drawing.	3. To determine in less direct fashion how the drawing contributes to the writing.	3. "Tell me about your drawing."
Composing Phase	1. The child is about to start writing.	1. To determine the range of writing ideas possessed before child writes.	1. "Tell me what you are going to write about."
	2. The child attempts to spell a word.	2. To determine the child's understanding of the resources available for spelling help.	2. "That seems to be a hard one. How can you figure out how to spell it? Tell me all the different ways you can figure out how to spell it."
	3. The child has written three to four sentences.	3. To determine the range of ideas possessed after the child has started writing.	3. "Tell me what you are going to write about next. Tell me how your story is going to end."
Postwriting Phase	1. The child is starting to put his paper away.	1. To check the child's oral reading in relation to the actual words written by the child.	1. "Would you please read outloud what you have just written."
	2. The child is starting to put his paper away.	2. To check the child's feelings or value judgments about work that has been completed.	2. Question series: "Which sentence do you like best? Tell me about it." "Is there anything you would change to make it better?" "Pick out two words that you felt were the most difficult to write."

Learning Environments

Since the study distinguished two types of environments, conclusions relative to writing in each are possible. These are the following:

1. Informal environments give greater choice to children. When children are given choice as to whether they write or not and as to what to write, they write more and in greater length than when specific writing assignments are given.
2. Results of writing done in the informal environments demonstrate that children do not need motivation or supervision in order to write.
3. The formal environments seem to be more favorable to girls in that they write more, and to greater length, than do boys whether the writing is assigned or unassigned.
4. The informal environments seem to favor boys in that they write more than girls in assigned or unassigned work.
5. In either environment, formal or informal, unassigned writing is longer than assigned writing.
6. An environment that requires large amounts of assigned writing inhibits the range, content, and amount of writing done by children.
7. The writing developmental level of the child is the best predictor of writing process behaviors and therefore transcends the importance of environment, materials and methodologies in influence on children's writing.

Sex Differences in Writing

Differences in boys and girls were examined in three areas: writing frequency, thematic choice, and their concept of the "good writer." Warranted conclusions relative to these appear to be the following:

1. Girls write longer products than do boys in either formal or informal environments.
2. Boys from either learning environment write more unassigned writing than do girls. Unassigned writing seems to provide an incentive for boys to write about subjects not normally provided in teacher-assigned work. Teachers do not normally assign work that includes themes from secondary and extended territory, the areas most used by boys in unassigned writing. (Secondary territory is defined as the metropolitan area beyond the child's home and school. Expanded territory is defined as the area beyond the secondary, which would include current events, history and geography on a national and world scale.)
3. Boys seldom use the first person form in unassigned writing, especially the *I* form, unless they are developmentally advanced.
4. Boys write more about themes identified as in secondary and

extended geographical territories than do girls. The only girls who write in these areas are those who are more developmentally advanced than others.

5. Girls write more about primary territory, which is related to the home and school, than do boys.
6. Boys are more concerned than are girls with the importance of spacing, formation of letters, and neatness in expressing their concept of "the good writer."
7. Girls stress more prethinking and organizational qualities, feelings in characterizations, and give more illustrations to support their judgments than do boys in expressing their concept of "the good writer."

Developmental Factors and the Writing Process

Such factors as a child's sex, the use of language, and problem solving behaviors, all of which have developmental roots, are involved as a child writes and interacts in various ways to produce two distinctive types of writers, identified by this study as *reactive* and *reflective*. These characteristics and behaviors are summarized in the following statements:

1. *Reactive:* Children who were identified as reactive showed erratic problem solving strategies, the use of overt language to accompany prewriting and composing phases, isolation that evolved in action-reaction couplets, proofreading at the word unit level, a need for immediate rehearsal in order to write, rare contemplation or reviewing of products, characterizations that exhibited general behaviors similar to their own, a lack of a sense of audience when writing, and an inability to use reasons beyond the affective domain in evaluating their writing.
2. *Reflective:* Children who were identified as reflective showed little rehearsal before writing, little overt language to accompany writing, periodic rereadings to adjust small units of writing at the word or phrase level, growing sense of audience connect with their writing, characterizations that exhibit general behaviors similar to their own in the expression of feelings, and the ability to give examples to support their reasons for evaluating writing.

The reactive writer was most often a boy and the reflective writer was most often a girl. The reactive and reflective writers, however, were each composite profiles of a general type of child. Identification of either the reactive or the reflective writer was not dependent on the observation of a single behavioral trait. Rather, the characteristics exist in varying degrees in all children, and can emerge under different types of writing conditions, but they gain greater visibility when viewed at the extremes of the high and low ends of a developmental continuum. The identification of a cluster of traits over a period of time from any one behavioral type (reactive or reflective) can be useful in predicting other writing behaviors of children and thereby be of assistance to teachers in adjusting instruction to their needs.

The Case Study, Michael

The chief conclusion drawn from the case study of Michael was that many variables contribute in unique ways at any given point in the process of writing. Although the contributions of these variables were specific to each child, the identification of them appears to be transferable to the study of the writing of other children. Table III reports several factors identified as contributing to various components of Michael's writing and writing processes. Findings from the case study data made it possible to chart the

Table III
General Contribution of Specific Variables To Michael's Writing and Writing Processes

	Family and Home	Teacher Room D	Michael Developmental	Peers (Kevin)
Writing Cause	Family is generally supportive of his work. Gives Michael encourage-ment with his drawing. Provides Michael with extra ma-terials for drawing and writing at home.	Provides mostly positive feedback Provides help with self-direction. Provides freedom of choice, time, and activity.	Writes in order to draw. Writes in order to play.	Boys write up a joint project. Kevin makes suggestion to write.
Thematic Origin	King Arthur, sports, ghosts and witches, camping and hunting, fires and explo-sions	Apollo 17, groundhogs, whales	Secondary and extended territorial use. Use of third person male, no females. Little use of first person. Need to express aggression	Mutual interests: Kevin: "Let's write about fires." Request for Michael to draw and write on a subject to help Kevin with ideas and drawing models.

Table III *(continued)*

	Family and Home	Teacher Room D	Michael Developmental	Peers (Kevin)
Writing Process— Prewriting Phase	Rehearses for ideas in family discussions. Provided materials and encouragement for drawing. Draws at home.	Provides materials that permit art work before writing. Provides freedom to discuss materials and content.	Needs to draw to rehearse ideas for writing. Interested primarily in drawing. Exhibits action-reaction style of drawing ideas. Demonstrates playing behaviors with sound effects.	Two boys discuss what they will draw.
Writing Process— Composing Phase	Vocabulary backgrounds. Speech interference problems.	Teaching of: spelling reading punctuation proofreading. Provision of resources: Phonic charts Pictionaries Word blanks.	Generally reactive behaviors. Letter reversal problems. Speech interference problems. Speech interference with spelling. Speech interference with writing syntax.	Minimal contribution to ideation. Some spelling assistance. Affects pace and structure by saying to Michael, "Hurry up, let's paint."
Writing Process— Post-Writing Phase	Unknown.	Attempts to teach proofreading.	Quickly disposes of writing product by placing in folder or desk.	Kevin sometimes is in a hurry for Michael to do another activity and may subvert proofreading.

influence of four main variables on factors identified as important in the process of writing. In Table III the influence of four main variables, family and home, teacher—room D, Michael's developmental characteristics, and a peer, Kevin, can be viewed in relation to their effect on such writing process factors as writing cause, thematic origin of writing, prewriting, composing, and postwriting. Each of these variables should be viewed in relation to its influence on the writing process. For example, in investigating what causes Michael to write, one can view specific contributions of a positive nature from the family and home, the teacher, the satisfaction of personal need, and the support of Kevin. Any one of these factors alone, or in combination with others, could be the cause of Michael's choosing to draw and then write.

The influence of these variables on the thematic origin factor can be both direct and indirect. Examples of a direct factor in Table III is seen in the home's influence on Michael's writing about King Arthur, sports, ghosts and witches. An example of a multiple, and less direct, origin is seen in Michael's drawing in the prewriting phase. Michael may draw because of Kevin's suggestion, extra time given by the teacher, a desire to express a favorite theme, or the need to prepare ideas for writing. Thus, the following conclusions appear to be significant concerning the case study.

1. At any given point in a writing episode, many variables, most of them unknown at the time of composing, contribute to the writing process.
2. Children write for unique reasons, employ highly individual coping strategies, and view writing in ways peculiar to their own person. In short, the writing process is as variable and unique as the individual's personality.

Procedures Used in the Study

Because the use of the case study combined with data gathering from both large and small groups produced particularly striking findings, a number of conclusions related to the procedure are warranted. First, the case study is an effective means of making visible those variables that contribute to a child's writing. Through the unity of one child's life, the constant focus in observation, interviewing, and testing makes it possible to hypothesize concerning the variables that contribute to the child's writing. In a broad interventive-type inquiry involving many children such speculation would not have been possible. Many of the variables discussed in larger group findings became apparent as a result of the intensive case study. In this sense case studies serve principally as surveying expeditions for identifying the writing territories needing further investigation. Some of the areas identified through case study and reported in larger group findings are the following:

1. The use of first and third person reported in thematic choices.
2. The identification of secondary and extended territoriality reported in thematic choices.

3. The identification of the prewriting, composing, and postwriting phases in the writing episode.
4. The identification of the components making up profiles for assessing developmental levels of children

Whereas the case study contributed to the identification of variables in the larger group data gathering activities, large-group data provided a means for additional testing of the suitability of certain research hypotheses and directions. For example, large-group data were of assistance in analyzing the case study findings in the following areas:

1. Combining all of the fifty-three writing episodes made it possible to develop and hypothesize about the range and relationship of the developmental variables deemed significant to the writing process.
2. The larger group data confirmed the significance of assigned and unassigned writing and thereby contributed to the recognition of the need to pursue the area with the case study children.
3. The larger group data made it possible to view the differences in boys' and girls' writing shown in the case studies with greater objectivity. Writing frequencies, thematic choices, use of assigned and unassigned writing, and responses to the question on the "good writer" in larger groups are examples of these differences which were observed.

Questions To Be Researched

The main purpose of this study was to formulate instructional and research hypotheses concerning children's writing. The most significant of these hypotheses grouped into related categories appear to be the following:

Assigned and Unassigned Writing
1. If given the opportunity in an environment providing the freedom to exercise choice in activities, will children produce more writings on their own than if the teacher gives specific assigned tasks?
2. Will unassigned writing be longer than assigned writing, show greater thematic diversity, and be used more by boys than girls?
3. Will boys in comparison with girls, exhibit distinctive choices with respect to the use of primary, secondary and extended territory as well as first, second, and third person in their writing?
4. Will a survey of teacher-assigned writing in the primary years show that girls are favored through the assigning of topics chiefly concerned with primary territory?

Concepts of the "Good Writer"
5. Will distinctive responses to the "good writer" question be noted with respect to: boys and girls in general, those rated high and low

developmentally, and specific writing strengths and limitations of the respondents?

Developmental Factors

6. Will two distinct groups of seven-year-old children be judged high and low developmentally as a result of the demonstration of consistent behaviors related to writing in the following categories: word writing rate, length of proofreading unit during writing, concept of an audience who may read their papers, spelling errors, rereadings, proofreading after writing, range and complexity of ideas expressed before writing, and in reasons expressed in rating their own writing?

General Factors

7. Will general behaviors exhibited by the child in his writing episodes be determined principally by his developmental level and be changed only slightly by the classroom environment?

Needed Research Directions

To date the need for developmental studies related to children's writing has been virtually ignored. Direct contact and extended observation of the children themselves are necessary to reach conclusions relating to developmental variables involving the behaviors of children. In fields such as psychiatry, child development, or anthropology, the investigation of behaviors would be unthinkable without the direct observation of the persons to be studied.

With the exception of a few studies, researchers have been removed from the direct observation of children at the time of their writing. Furthermore, the scope of even the direct observation at the time of writing needs to expand to include other behaviors in the environment. Such studies, however, cannot be conducted without the successful development of procedures that effectively record the full-range of child behaviors in their natural environment.

In order to improve both procedures and study scope, future research in writing should continue to explore the feasibility of the case study method. Further studies are needed to investigate the developmental histories of different types of children in relation to writing and the writing process. In a profession where there is a basic commitment to the teaching and understanding of the individual child, it is ironic that research devoted to the full study of single individuals is so rare.

References

Braddock, Richard, Lloyd-Jones, Richard, and Schoer, Lowell. *Research in Written Composition.* Champaign, Illinois, NCTE, 1963.

Emig, Janet A., "Component of the Composing Process Among Twelfth Grade Writers." Unpublished doctoral dissertation, Harvard University, 1969.

Holstein, Barbara I. "Use of Metaphor to Induce Innovative Thinking in Fourth Grade Children." Unpublished doctoral dissertation, Boston University, 1970.

Meckel, Henry C. "Research on Teaching Composition," *Handbook of Research on Teaching*, American Education Research Association, Chicago: Rand, McNally and Co., 1963.

Parke, Margaret B. "Composition in Primary Grades," *Children's Writing: Research in Composition and Related Skills*, Champaign, Illinois, National Council of Teachers of English, 1961.

The Composing Processes of Unskilled College Writers

by Sondra Perl

This paper presents the pertinent findings from a study of the composing processes of five unskilled college writers (Perl, 1978). The first part summarizes the goals of the original study, the kinds of data collected, and the research methods employed. The second part is a synopsis of the study of Tony, one of the original five case studies. The third part presents a condensed version of the findings on the composing process and discusses these findings in light of current pedagogical practice and research design.

Goals of the Study

This research addressed three major questions: (1) How do unskilled writers write? (2) Can their writing processes be analyzed in a systematic, replicable manner? and (3) What does an increased understanding of their processes suggest about the nature of composing in general and the manner in which writing is taught in the schools?

In recent years, interest in the composing process has grown (Britton, 1975; Burton, 1973; Cooper, 1974; Emig, 1967, 1971). In 1963, Braddock, Lloyd-Jones, and Schoer, writing on the state of research in written composition, included the need for "direct observation" and case study procedures in their suggestions for future research (pp. 24, 31-32). In a section entitled "Unexplored Territory," they listed basic unanswered questions such as, "What is involved in the act of writing?" and "Of what does skill in writing actually consist?" (p. 51). Fifteen years later, Cooper and Odell (1978) edited a volume similar in scope, only this one was devoted entirely to issues and questions related to research on composing. This volume in particular signals a shift in emphasis in writing research. Alongside the traditional, large-scale experimental studies, there is now widespread recognition of the need for works of a more modest, probing nature, works that attempt to elucidate basic processes. The studies on composing that have been completed to date are precisely of this kind; they are small-scale studies, based on the systematic observation of writers engaged in the process of

Reprinted from *Research in the Teaching of English*, December 1979. Copyright 1979 by the National Council of Teachers of English. Used with permission.

writing (Emig, 1971; Graves, 1973; Mischel, 1974; Pianko 1977; Stallard, 1974).

For all of its promise, this body of research has yet to produce work that would insure wide recognition for the value of process studies of composing. One limitation of work done to date is methodological. Narrative descriptions of composing processes do not provide sufficiently graphic evidence for the perception of underlying regularities and patterns. Without such evidence, it is difficult to generate well-defined hypotheses and to move from exploratory research to more controlled experimental studies. A second limitation pertains to the subjects studied. To date no examination of composing processes has dealt primarily with unskilled writers. As long as "average" or skilled writers are the focus, it remains unclear as to how process research will provide teachers with a firmer understanding of the needs of students with serious writing problems.

The present study is intended to carry process research forward by addressing both of these limitations. One prominent feature of the research design involves the development and use of a meaningful and replicable method for rendering the composing process as a sequence of observable and scorable behaviors. A second aspect of the design is the focus on students whose writing problems baffle the teachers charged with their education.

Design of the Study

This study took place during the 1975-76 fall semester at Eugenio Maria de Hostos Community College of the City University of New York. Students were selected for the study on the basis of two criteria: writing samples that qualified them as unskilled writers and willingness to participate. Each student met with the researcher for five 90-minute sessions (see Table 1). Four sessions were devoted to writing with the students directed to compose aloud, to externalize their thinking processes as much as possible, during each session. In one additional session, a writing profile on the students' perceptions and memories of writing was developed through the use of an open-ended interview. All of the sessions took place in a soundproof room in the college library. Throughout each session, the researcher assumed a noninterfering role.

The topics for writing were developed in an introductory social science course in which the five students were enrolled. The "content" material they were studying was divided into two modes: extensive, in which the writer was directed to approach the material in an objective, impersonal fashion, and reflexive, in which the writer was directed to approach similar material in an affective, personalized fashion. Contrary to Emig's (1971) definitions, in this study it was assumed that the teacher was always the audience.

Data Analysis

Three kinds of data were collected in this study: the students' written

Table 1
Design of the Study

	SESSION 1 (s1)	SESSION 1 (s1)	SESSION 3 (s3)	SESSION 4 (s4)	SESSION 5 (s5)
Mode	Extensive	Reflexive		Extensive	Reflexive
Topic	Society & Culture	Society & Culture	Interview: Writing Profile	Capitalism	Capitalism
Directions	Students told to compose aloud; no other directions given	Students told to compose aloud; no other directions given		Students told to compose aloud; also directed to talk out ideas before writing	Students told to compose aloud; also directed to talk out ideas before writing

products, their composing tapes, and their responses to the interview. Each of these was studied carefully and then discussed in detail in each of the five case study presentations. Due to limitations of space, this paper will review only two of the data sets generated in the study.

Coding the Composing Process

One of the goals of this research was to devise a tool for describing the movements that occur during composing. In the past such descriptions have taken the form of narratives which detail, with relative precision and insight, observable composing behaviors; however, these narratives provide no way of ascertaining the frequency, relative importance, and place of each behavior within an individual's composing process. As such, they are cumbersome and difficult to replicate. Furthermore, lengthy, idiosyncratic narratives run the risk of leaving underlying patterns and regularities obscure. In contrast, the method created in this research provides a means of viewing the composing process that is:

1. Standardized—it introduces a coding system for observing the composing process that can be replicated;
2. Categorical—it labels specific, observable behaviors so that types of composing movements are revealed;
3. Concise—it presents the entire sequence of composing movements on one or two pages;

4. Structural—it provides a way of determining how parts of the process relate to the whole; and
5. Diachronic—it presents the sequences of movements that occur during composing as they unfold in time.

In total, the method allows the researcher to apprehend a process as it unfolds. It lays out the movements or behavior sequences in such a way that if patterns within a student's process or among a group of students exist, they become apparent.

The Code

The method consists of coding each composing behavior exhibited by the student and charting each behavior on a continuum. During this study, the coding occurred after the student had finished composing and was done by working from the student's written product and the audiotape of the session. It was possible to do this since the tape captured both what the student was saying and the literal sound of the pen moving across the page. As a result, it was possible to determine when students were talking, when they were writing, when both occurred simultaneously, and when neither occurred.

The major categorical divisions in this coding system are talking, writing, and reading; however, it was clear that there are various kinds of talk and various kinds of writing and reading operations, and that a coding system would need to distinguish among these various types. In this study the following operations were distinguished:

1. General planning [PL]—organizing one's thoughts for writing, discussing how one will proceed.
2. Local planning [PLL]—talking out what idea will come next.
3. Global planning [PLG]—discussing changes in drafts.
4. Commenting [C]—sighing, making a comment or judgment about the topic.
5. Interpreting [I]—rephrasing the topic to get a "handle" on it.
6. Assessing [A(+); A(-)]—making a judgment about one's writing; may be positive or negative.
7. Questioning [Q]—asking a question.
8. Talking leading to writing [T→W]—voicing ideas on the topic, tentatively finding one's way, but not necessarily being committed to or using all one is saying.
9. Talking and writing at the same time [TW]—composing aloud in such a way that what one is saying is actually being written at the same time.
10. Repeating [re]—repeating written or unwritten phrases a number of times.
11. Reading related to the topic:
    a. Reading the directions $[R_D]$
    b. Reading the question $[R_Q]$
    c. Reading the statement $[R_S]$

12. Reading related to one's own written product:
    a. Reading one sentence or a few words [R^a]
    b. Reading a number of sentences together [R$^{a\text{-}b}$]
    c. Reading the entire draft through [R^{w1}]
13. Writing silently [W]
14. Writing aloud [TW]
15. Editing [E]
    a. adding syntactic markers, words, phrases, or clauses [Eadd]
    b. deleting syntactic markers, words, phrases, or clauses [Edel]
    c. indicating concern for a grammatical rule [Egr]
    d. adding, deleting, or considering the use of punctuation [Epunc]
    e. considering or changing spelling [Esp]
    f. changing the sentence structure through embedding, coordination or subordination [Ess]
    g. indicating concern for appropriate vocabulary (word choice) [Ewc]
    h. considering or changing verb form [Evc]
16. Periods of silence [s]

By taking specific observable behaviors that occur during composing and supplying labels for them, this system thus far provides a way of analyzing the process that is categorical and capable of replication. In order to view the frequency and the duration of composing behaviors and the relation between one particular behavior and the whole process, these behaviors need to be depicted graphically to show their duration and sequence.

The Continuum

The second component of this system is the construction of a time line and a numbering system. In this study, blank charts with lines like the following were designed:

```
- - - -  - - - - -  - - - - -  - - - -  - - - - -  - - - -  - - - -
    10         20        30        40         50         60        70
```

A ten-digit interval corresponds to one minute and is keyed to a counter on a tape recorder. By listening to the tape and watching the counter, it is possible to determine the nature and duration of each operation. As each behavior is heard on the tape, it is coded and then noted on the chart with the counter used as a time marker. For example, if a student during prewriting reads the directions and the question twice and then begins to plan exactly what she is going to say, all within the first minute, it would be coded like this:

Prewriting

R$_D$R$_Q$R$_D$R$_Q$PLL

10

If at this point the student spends two minutes writing the first sentence, during which time she pauses, rereads the question, continues writing, and then edits for spelling before continuing on, it would be coded like this:

$$
\overbrace{\underset{20}{\text{TW}_1/s/R_Q} \quad \text{TW}_1 \text{ [Esp] TW}_1}^{1}
$$

$$
\begin{array}{cc}
20 & 30
\end{array}
$$

At this point two types of brackets and numbering systems have appeared. The initial sublevel number linked with the TW code indicates which draft the student is working on. TW_1 indicates the writing of the first draft; TW_2 and TW_3 indicate the writing of the second and third drafts. Brackets such as [Esp] separate these operations from writing and indicate the amount of time the operation takes. The upper-level number above the horizontal bracket indicates which sentence in the written product is being written and the length of the bracket indicates the amount of time spent on the writing of each sentence. All horizontal brackets refer to sentences, and from the charts it is possible to see when sentences are grouped together and written in a chunk (adjacent brackets) or when each sentence is produced in isolation (gaps between brackets). (See Appendix for sample chart.)

The charts can be read by moving along the time line, noting which behaviors occur and in what sequence. Three types of comments are also included in the charts. In bold-face type, the beginning and end of each draft are indicated; in lighter type-face, comments on the actual composing movements are provided; and in the lightest type-face, specific statements made by students or specific words they found particularly troublesome are noted.

From the charts, the following information can be determined:

1. the amount of time spent during prewriting;
2. the strategies used during prewriting;
3. the amount of time spent writing each sentence;
4. the behaviors that occur while each sentence is being written;
5. when sentences are written in groups or "chunks" (fluent writing);
6. when sentences are written in isolation (choppy or sporadic writing);
7. the amount of time spent between sentences;
8. the behaviors that occur between sentences;
9. when editing occurs (during the writing of sentences, between sentences, in the time between drafts);
10. the frequency of editing behavior;
11. the nature of the editing operations; and
12. where and in what frequency pauses or periods of silence occur in the process.

The charts, or *composing style sheets* as they are called, do not explain what students wrote but rather *how* they wrote. They indicate, on one page, the sequences of behavior that occur from the beginning of the process to the end. From them it is possible to determine where and how these behaviors fall into patterns and whether these patterns vary according to the mode of discourse.

It should be noted that although the coding system is presented before the analysis of the data, it was derived from the data and then used as the basis for generalizing about the patterns and behavioral sequences found within each student's process. These individual patterns were reported in each of the five case studies. Thus, initially, a style sheet was constructed for each writing session on each student. When there were four style sheets for each student, it was possible to determine if composing patterns existed among the group. The summary of results reported here is based on the patterns revealed by these charts.

Analyzing Miscues in the Writing Process

Miscue analysis is based on Goodman's model of the reading process. Created in 1962, it has become a widespread tool for studying what students do when they read and is based on the premise that reading is a psycho-linguistic process which "uses language, in written form, to get to the meaning" (Goodman, 1973, p. 4). Miscue analysis "involves its user in examining the observed behavior of oral readers as an interaction between language and thought, as a process of constructing meaning from a graphic display" (Goodman, 1973, p. 4). Methodologically, the observer analyzes the mismatch that occurs when readers make responses during oral reading that differ from the text. This mismatch or miscueing is then analyzed from Goodman's "meaning-getting" model, based on the assumption that "the reader's preoccupation with meaning will show in his miscues, because they will tend to result in language that still makes sense" (Goodman, 1973, p. 9).

In the present study, miscue analysis was adapted from Goodman's model in order to provide insight into the writing process. Since students composed aloud, two types of oral behaviors were available for study: encoding processes or what students spoke while they were writing and decoding processes or what students "read"[1] after they had finished writing. When a discrepancy existed between encoding or decoding and what was on the paper, it was referred to as miscue.

For encoding, the miscue analysis was carried out in the following manner:

1. The students' written products were typed, preserving the original style and spelling.

---

[1] The word "read" is used in a particular manner here. In the traditional sense, reading refers to accurate decoding of written symbols. Here it refers to students' verbalizing words or endings even when the symbols for those words are missing or only minimally present. Whenever the term "reading" is used in this way, it will be in quotation marks.

2. What students said while composing aloud was checked against the written products; discrepancies were noted on the paper wherever they occurred.
3. The discrepancies were categorized and counted.

Three miscue categories were derived for encoding:

1. Speaking complete ideas but omitting certain words during writing.
2. Pronouncing words with plural markers or other suffixes completely but omitting these endings during writing.
3. Pronouncing the desired word but writing a homonym, an approximation of the word or a personal abbreviation of the word on paper.

For decoding, similar procedures were used, this time comparing the words of the written product with what the student "read" orally. When a discrepancy occurred, it was noted. The discrepancies were then categorized and counted.

Four miscue categories were derived for decoding:

1. "Reading in" missing words or word endings;
2. Deleting words or word endings;
3. "Reading" the desired word rather than the word on the page;
4. "Reading" abbreviations and misspellings as though they were written correctly.

A brief summary of the results of this analysis appears in the findings.

Synopsis of a Case Study

Tony was a 20-year-old ex-Marine born and raised in the Bronx, New York. Like many Puerto Ricans born in the United States, he was able to speak Spanish, but he considered English his native tongue. In the eleventh grade, Tony left high school, returning three years later to take the New York State high school equivalency exam. As a freshman in college, he was also working part-time to support a child and a wife from whom he was separated.

Behaviors

The composing style sheets provide an overview of the observable behaviors exhibited by Tony during the composing process. (See Appendix for samples of Tony's writing and the accompanying composing style sheet.) The most salient feature of Tony's composing process was its recursiveness. Tony rarely produced a sentence without stopping to reread either a part or the whole. This repetition set up a particular kind of composing rhythm, one that was cumulative in nature and that set ideas in motion by its very repetitiveness. Thus, as can be seen from any of the style sheets, talking led to writing which led to reading which led to planning which again led to writing.

The style sheets indicated a difference in the composing rhythms exhibited in the extensive and reflexive modes. On the extensive topics there was not only more repetition within each sentence but also many more pauses and repetitions between sentences, with intervals often lasting as long as two minutes. On the reflexive topics, sentences were often written in groups, with fewer rereadings and only minimal time intervals separating the creation of one sentence from another.

Editing occurred consistently in all sessions. From the moment Tony began writing, he indicated a concern for correct form that actually inhibited the development of ideas. In none of the writing sessions did he ever write more than two sentences before he began to edit. While editing fit into his overall recursive pattern, it simultaneously interrupted the composing rhythm he had just initiated.

During the intervals between drafts, Tony read his written work, assessed his writing, planned new phrasings, transitions or endings, read the directions and the question over, and edited once again.

Tony performed these operations in both the extensive and reflexive modes and was remarkably consistent in all of his composing operations. The style sheets attest both to this consistency and to the densely packed, tight quality of Tony's composing process—indeed, if the notations on these sheets were any indication at all, it was clear that Tony's composing process was so full that there was little room left for invention or change.

Fluency

Table 2 provides a numerical analysis of Tony's writing performance. Here it is possible to compare not only the amount of time spent on the various composing operations but also the relative fluency. For Sessions 1 and 2 the data indicate that while Tony spent more time prewriting and writing in the extensive mode, he actually produced fewer words. For Sessions 4 and 5, a similar pattern can be detected. In the extensive mode, Tony again spent more time prewriting and produced fewer words. Although writing time was increased in the reflexive mode, the additional 20 minutes spent writing did not sufficiently account for an increase of 194 words. Rather, the data indicate that Tony produced more words with less planning and generally in less time in the reflexive mode, suggesting that his greater fluency lay in this mode.

Strategies

Tony exhibited a number of strategies that served him as a writer whether the mode was extensive or reflexive. Given any topic, the first operation he performed was to focus in and narrow down the topic. He did this by rephrasing the topic until either a word or an idea in the topic linked up with something in his own experience (an attitude, an opinion, an event). In this way he established a connection between the field of discourse and himself and at this point he felt ready to write.

Table 2
Tony: Summary of Four Writing Sessions
(Time in Minutes)

EXTENSIVE MODE

s1 TW$_1$		
Drafts	Words	Time
		Prewriting: 7.8
W1	132	18.8
W2	170	51.0
Total	302	Total composing: 91.2*

s4 T→W		
Drafts	Words	Time
		Prewriting: 8.0
W1	182	29.0
W2	174	33.9
Total	356	Total composing: 82.0*

REFLEXIVE MODE

s2 TW$_1$		
Drafts	Words	Time
		Prewriting: 3.5
W1	165	14.5
W2	169	25.0
W3	178	24.2
Total	512	Total composing: 76.0*

s5 T→W		
Drafts	Words	Time
		Prewriting: 5.7
W1	208	24.0
W2	190	38.3
W3	152	20.8
Total	550	Total composing: 96.0*

*Total composing includes time spent on editing and rereading, as well as actual writing.

Level of Language Use

Once writing, Tony employed a pattern of classifying or dividing the topic into manageable pieces and then using one or both of the divisions as the basis for narration. In the four writing sessions, his classifications were made on the basis of economic, racial, and political differences. However, all of his writing reflected a low level of generality. No formal principles were used to organize the narratives nor were the implications of ideas present in the essay developed.

In his writing, Tony was able to maintain the extensive/reflexive distinction. He recognized when he was being asked directly for an opinion and when he was being asked to discuss concepts or ideas that were not directly linked to his experience. However, the more distance between the topic and himself, the more difficulty he experienced, and the more repetitive his process became. Conversely, when the topic was close to his own experience, the smoother and more fluent the process became. More writing was produced, pauses were fewer, and positive assessment occurred more often. However, Tony made more assumptions on the part of the audience in the reflexive mode. When writing about himself, Tony often did not stop to explain the context from which he was writing; rather, the reader's understanding of the context was taken for granted.

Editing

Tony spent a great deal of his composing time editing. However, most of this time was spent proofreading rather than changing, rephrasing, adding, or evaluating the substantive parts of the discourse. Of a total of 234 changes made in all of the sessions, only 24 were related to changes of content and included the following categories:

1. Elaborations of ideas through the use of specification and detail;
2. Additions of modals that shift the mood of a sentence;
3. Deletions that narrow the focus of a paper;
4. Clause reductions or embeddings that tighten the structure of a paper;
5. Vocabulary choices that reflect a sensitivity to language;
6. Reordering of elements in a narrative;
7. Strengthening transitions between paragraphs;
8. Pronoun changes that signal an increased sensitivity to audience.

The 210 changes in form included the following:

Additions	19	Verb changes	4
Deletions	44	Spelling	95
Word choice	13	Punctuation	35
Unresolved problems		89	

The area that Tony changed most often was spelling, although, even after completing three drafts of a paper, Tony still had many words misspelled.

Miscue Analysis

Despite continual proofreading, Tony's completed drafts often retained a look of incompleteness. Words remained misspelled, syntax was uncorrected or overcorrected, suffixes, plural markers, and verb endings were missing, and often words or complete phrases were omitted.

The composing aloud behavior and the miscue analysis derived from it provide one of the first demonstrable ways of understanding how such seemingly incomplete texts can be considered "finished" by the student. (See Table 3 for a summary of Tony's miscues.) Tony consistently voiced complete sentences when composing aloud but only transcribed partial sentences. The same behavior occurred in relation to words with plural or marked endings. However, during rereading and even during editing, Tony supplied the missing endings, words, or phrases and did not seem to "see" what was missing from the text. Thus, when reading his paper, Tony "read in" the meaning he expected to be there which turned him into a reader of content rather than form. However, a difference can be observed between the extensive and reflexive modes, and in the area of correctness Tony's greater strength lay in the reflexive mode. In this mode, not only were more words produced in less time (1,062 vs. 658), but fewer decoding miscues occurred (38 vs. 46), and fewer unresolved problems remained in the text (34 vs. 55).

When Tony did choose to read for form, he was handicapped in another way. Through his years of schooling, Tony learned that there were sets of rules to be applied to one's writing, and he attempted to apply these rules of form to his prose. Often, though, the structures he produced were far more complicated than the simple set of proofreading rules he had at his disposal. He was therefore faced with applying the rule partially, discarding it, or attempting corrections through sound. None of these systems was completely helpful to Tony, and as often as a correction was made that improved the discourse, another was made that obscured it.

Summary

Finally, when Tony completed the writing process, he refrained from commenting on or contemplating his total written product. When he initiated writing, he immediately established distance between himself as writer and his discourse. He knew his preliminary draft might have errors and might need revision. At the end of each session, the distance had decreased if not entirely disappeared. Tony "read in" missing or omitted features, rarely perceived syntactic errors, and did not untangle overly embedded sentences. It was as if the semantic model in his head predominated, and the distance with which he entered the writing process had dissolved. Thus, even with his concern for revision and for correctness, even with the enormous amount of time he invested in rereading and repetition, Tony concluded the composing process with unresolved stylistic and syntactic problems. The conclusion here is not that Tony can't write, or that Tony doesn't know how to write, or that Tony needs to learn more rules: Tony is a writer with a highly consistent and deeply embedded recursive process. What he needs are teachers who can interpret

Table 3
Tony—Miscue Analysis

ENCODING

	Speaking complete ideas but omitting certain words during writing	Pronouncing words with plural markers or other suffixes completely but omitting these endings during writing	Pronouncing the desired word but writing a homonym, an approximation of the word or a personal abbreviation of the word on paper	Total
S1	1	4	11	16
S2	8	0	14	22
S4	4	0	16	20
S5	3	1	15	19
	16	5	56	77

DECODING

	Reading in missing words or word endings	Deleting words or word endings	Reading the desired word rather than the word on the page	Reading abbreviations and misspellings as though they were written correctly	Total
S1	10	1	1	15	27
S2	5	1	2	10	18
S4	3	3	0	13	19
S5	7	1	2	10	20
	25	6	5	48	84

that process for him, who can see through the tangles in the process just as he sees meaning beneath the tangles in his prose, and who can intervene in such a way that untangling his composing process leads him to create better prose.

Summary of the Findings

A major finding of this study is that, like Tony, all of the students studied displayed consistent composing processes; that is, the behavioral subsequences prewriting, writing, and editing appeared in sequential patterns that were recognizable across writing sessions and across students.

This consistency suggests a much greater internalization of process than has ever before been suspected. Since the written products of basic writers often look arbitrary, observers commonly assume that the students' approach is also arbitrary. However, just as Shaughnessy (1977) points out that there is "very little that is random . . . in what they have written" (p. 5), so, on close observation, very little appears random in *how* they write. The students observed had stable composing processes which they used whenever they were presented with a writing task. While this consistency argues against seeing these students as beginning writers, it ought not necessarily imply that they are proficient writers. Indeed, their lack of proficiency may be attributable to the way in which premature and rigid attempts to correct and edit their work truncate the flow of composing without substantially improving the form of what they have written. More detailed findings will be reviewed in the following subsections which treat the three major aspects of composing: prewriting, writing, and editing.

Prewriting

When not given specific prewriting instructions, the students in this study began writing within the first few minutes. The average time they spent on prewriting in sessions 1 and 2 was four minutes (see Table 4), and the planning strategies they used fell into three principal types:

1. Rephrasing the topic until a particular word or idea connected with the student's experience. The student then had "an event" in mind before writing began.
2. Turning the large conceptual issue in the topic (e.g., equality) into two manageable pieces for writing (e.g., rich vs. poor; black vs. white).
3. Initiating a string of associations to a word in the topic and then developing one or more of the associations during writing.

When students planned in any of these ways, they began to write with an articulated sense of where they wanted their discourse to go. However, frequently students read the topic and directions a few times and indicated that they had "no idea" what to write. On these occasions, they began writing without any secure sense of where they were heading, acknowledging only that they would "figure it out" as they went along. Often their first sentence was a rephrasing of the question in the topic which, now that it was in their own handwriting and down on paper in front of them, seemed to enable them to plan what ought to come next. In these instances, writing led to planning which led to clarifying which led to more writing. This sequence of planning and writing, clarifying and discarding, was repeated frequently in all of the sessions, even when students began writing with a secure sense of direction. Although one might be tempted to conclude that these students began writing prematurely and that planning precisely what they were going to write ought to have occurred before they put pen to paper, the data here suggest:

Table 4
Overview of All Writing Sessions

| | PREWRITING TIME* | | | | TOTAL WORDS / TOTAL COMPOSING TIME | | | | EDITING CHANGES | | UNRESOLVED PROBLEMS | MISCUES DURING READING |
	S1	S2	S4	S5	S1	S2	S4	S5	Content	Form		
Tony	7.8	3.5	8.0	5.7	302 / 91.2	512 / 76.0	356 / 82.0	550 / 96.0	24	210	89	84
Dee	2.5	2.9	5.0	5.0	409 / 55.5	559 / 65.0	91 / 24.5	212 / 29.0	7	24	40	32
Stan	3.5	4.3	14.8	14.7	419 / 62.0	553 / 73.1	365 / 73.0	303 / 68.0	13	49	45	55
Lueller	2.0	1.5	4.0	13.0	518 / 90.8	588 / 96.8	315 / 93.0	363 / 77.8	2	167	143	147
Beverly	5.5	7.0	32.0	20.0	519 / 79.0	536 / 80.3	348 / 97.4	776 / 120.0	21	100	55	30

*Due to a change in the prewriting directions, only Sessions 1 and 2 are used to calculate the average time spent in prewriting.

1. that certain strategies, such as creating an association to a key
   word, focusing in and narrowing down the topic, dichotomizing
   and classifying, can and do take place in a relatively brief span of
   time; and
2. that the developing and clarifying of ideas is facilitated once
   students translate some of those ideas into written form. In other
   words, seeing ideas on paper enables students to reflect upon,
   change and develop those ideas further.

Writing

Careful study revealed that students wrote by shuttling from the sense of
what they wanted to say forward to the words on the page and back from the
words on the page to their intended meaning. This "back and forth"
movement appeared to be a recursive feature: at one moment students were
writing, moving their ideas and their discourse forward; at the next they were
back-tracking, rereading, and digesting what had been written.

Recursive movements appeared at many points during the writing process.
Occasionally sentences were written in groups and then reread as a "piece" of
discourse; at other times sentences and phrases were written alone, repeated
until the writer was satisfied or worn down, or rehearsed until the act of
rehearsal led to the creation of a new sentence. In the midst of writing, editing
occurred as students considered the surface features of language. Often
planning of a global nature took place: in the midst of producing a first draft,
students stopped and began planning how the second draft would differ from
the first. Often in the midst of writing, students stopped and referred to the
topic in order to check if they had remained faithful to the original intent, and
occasionally, though infrequently, they identified a sentence or a phrase that
seemed, to them, to produce a satisfactory ending. In all these behaviors, they
were shuttling back and forth, projecting what would come next and doubling
back to be sure of the ground they had covered.

A number of conclusions can be drawn from the observations of these
students composing and from the comments they made: although they
produced inadequate or flawed products, they nevertheless seemed to
understand and perform some of the crucial operations involved in composing
with skill. While it cannot be stated with certainty that the patterns they
displayed are shared by other writers, some of the operations they performed
appear sufficiently sound to serve as prototypes for constructing two major
hypotheses on the nature of their composing processes. Whether the following
hypotheses are borne out in studies of different types of writers remains an
open question:

1. Composing does not occur in a straightforward, linear fashion. The
   process is one of accumulating discrete bits down on the paper and
   then working from those bits to reflect upon, structure, and then
   further develop what one means to say. It can be thought of as a
   kind of "retrospective structuring"; movement forward occurs only

after one has reached back, which in turn occurs only after one has some sense of where one wants to go. Both aspects, the reaching back and the sensing forward, have a clarifying effect.

2. Composing always involves some measure of both construction and discovery. Writers construct their discourse inasmuch as they begin with a sense of what they want to write. This sense, as long as it remains implicit, is not equivalent to the explicit form it gives rise to. Thus, a process of constructing meaning is required. Rereading or backward movements become a way of assessing whether or not the words on the page adequately capture the original sense intended. Constructing simultaneously affords discovery. Writers know more fully what they mean only after having written it. In this way the explicit written form serves as a window on the implicit sense with which one began.

Editing

Editing played a major role in the composing processes of the students in this study (see Table 5). Soon after students began writing their first drafts, they began to edit, and they continued to do so during the intervals between drafts, during the writing of their second drafts and during the final reading of papers.

While editing, the students were concerned with a variety of items: the lexicon (i.e., spelling, word choice, and the context of words); the syntax (i.e., grammar, punctuation, and sentence structure); and the discourse as a whole (i.e., organization, coherence, and audience). However, despite the students' considered attempts to proofread their work, serious syntactic and stylistic problems remained in their finished drafts. The persistence of these errors may, in part, be understood by looking briefly at some of the problems that arose for these students during editing:

Rule Confusion

(1) All of the students observed asked themselves, "Is this sentence [or feature] correct?" but the simple set of editing rules at their disposal was often inappropriate for the types of complicated structures they produced. As a result, they misapplied what they knew and either created a hypercorrection or impaired the meaning they had originally intended to clarify; (2) The students observed attempted to write with terms they heard in lectures or class discussions, but since they were not yet familiar with the syntactic or semantic constraints one word placed upon another, their experiments with academic language resulted in what Shaughnessy (1977, p. 49) calls, "lexical transplants" or "syntactic dissonances"; (3) The students tried to rely on their intuitions about language, in particular the sound of words. Often, however, they had been taught to mistrust what "sounded" right to them, and they were unaware of the particular feature in their speech codes that might need to be changed in writing to match the standard code. As a result, when they attempted corrections by sound, they became confused, and they began to

Table 5
Editing Changes

	Tony	Dee	Stan	Lueller	Beverly	Totals
Total number of words produced	**1720**	**1271**	**1640**	**1754**	**2179**	**8564**
Total form	210	24	49	167	100	550
Additions	19	2	10	21	11	63
Deletions	44	9	18	41	38	150
Word choice	13	4	1	27	6	51
Verb changes	4	1	2	7	12	26
Spelling	95	4	13	60	19	191
Punctuation	35	4	5	11	14	69
Total content	24	7	13	2	21	67

have difficulty differentiating between what sounded right in speech and what needed to be marked on the paper.

Selective Perception

These students habitually reread their papers from internal semantic or meaning models. They extracted the meaning they wanted from the minimal cues on the page, and they did not recognize that outside readers would find those cues insufficient for meaning.

A study of Table 6 indicates that the number of problems remaining in the students' written products approximates the number of miscues produced during reading. This proximity, itself, suggests that many of these errors persisted because the students were so certain of the words they wanted to have on the page that they "read in" these words even when they were absent; in other words, they reduced uncertainty by operating as though what was in their heads was already on the page. The problem of selective perception, then, cannot be reduced solely to mechanical decoding; the semantic model from which students read needs to be acknowledged and taken into account in any study that attempts to explain how students write and why their completed written products end up looking so incomplete.

Egocentricity

The students in this study wrote from an egocentric point of view. While they occasionally indicated a concern for their readers, they more often took the reader's understanding for granted. They did not see the necessity of making their referents explicit, of making the connections among their ideas apparent, of carefully and explicitly relating one phenomenon to another, or

Table 6
The Talk-Write Paradigm Miscues—Decoding Behaviors

	Tony	Dee	Stan	Lueller	Beverly	Totals
Unresolved problems	**89**	**40**	**45**	**143**	**55**	**372**
"Reading in" missing words or word endings	25	13	11	44	11	104
Deleting words or word endings	6	2	4	14	9	35
"Reading" the desired word rather than the word on the page	5	6	18	15	8	52
"Reading" abbreviations and misspellings as though they were written correctly	48	11	22	74	2	157
	84	32	55	147	30	348

of placing narratives or generalizations within an orienting, conceptual framework.

On the basis of these observations one may be led to conclude that these writers did not know how to edit their work. Such a conclusion must, however, be drawn with care. Efforts to improve their editing need to be based on an informed view of the role that editing already plays in their composing processes. Two conclusions in this regard are appropriate here:

1. Editing intrudes so often and to such a degree that it breaks down the rhythms generated by thinking and writing. When this happens the students are forced to go back and recapture the strands of their thinking once the editing operation has been completed. Thus, editing occurs prematurely, before students have generated enough discourse to approximate the ideas they have, and it often results in their losing track of their ideas.

2. Editing is primarily an exercise in error-hunting. The students are prematurely concerned with the "look" of their writing; thus, as soon as a few words are written on the paper, detection and correction of errors replaces writing and revising. Even when they begin writing with a tentative, flexible frame of mind, they soon become locked into whatever is on the page. What they seem to lack as much as any rule is a conception of editing that includes

flexibility, suspended judgment, the weighing of possibilities, and the reworking of ideas.

Implications for Teaching and Research

One major implication of this study pertains to teachers' conceptions of unskilled writers. Traditionally, these students have been labeled "remedial," which usually implies that teaching ought to remedy what is "wrong" in their written products. Since the surface features in the writing of unskilled writers seriously interfere with the extraction of meaning from the page, much class time is devoted to examining the rules of the standard code. The pedagogical soundness of this procedure has been questioned frequently,[2] but in spite of the debate, the practice continues, and it results in a further complication, namely that students begin to conceive of writing as a "cosmetic" process where concern for correct form supersedes development of ideas. As a result, the excitement of composing, of constructing and discovering meaning, is cut off almost before it has begun.

More recently, unskilled writers have been referred to as "beginners," implying that teachers can start anew. They need not "punish" students for making mistakes, and they need not assume that their students have already been taught how to write. Yet this view ignores the highly elaborated, deeply embedded processes the students bring with them. These unskilled college writers are not beginners in a *tabula rasa* sense, and teachers err in assuming they are. The results of this study suggest that teachers may first need to identify which characteristic components of each student's process facilitate writing and which inhibit it before further teaching takes place. If they do not, teachers of unskilled writers may continue to place themselves in a defeating position: imposing another method of writing instruction upon the students' already internalized processes without first helping students to extricate themselves from the knots and tangles in those processes.

A second implication of this study is that the composing process is now amenable to a replicable and graphic mode of representation as a sequence of codable behaviors. The composing style sheets provide researchers and teachers with the first demonstrable way of documenting how individual students write. Such a tool may have diagnostic as well as research benefits. It may be used to record writing behaviors in large groups, prior to and after instruction, as well as in individuals. Certainly it lends itself to the longitudinal study of the writing process and may help to elucidate what it is that changes in the process as writers become more skilled.

A third implication relates to case studies and to the theories derived from

---

[2] For discussions on the controversy over the effects of grammar instruction on writing ability, see the following: Richard Braddock, Richard Lloyd-Jones, and Lowell Schoer, *Research in Written Composition* (Urbana, Ill.: National Council of Teachers of English, 1963); Frank O'Hare, *Sentence Combining* (NCTE Research Report No. 15, Urbana, Ill.: National Council of Teachers of English, 1973); Elizabeth F. Haynes, "Using Research in Preparing to Teach Writing," *English Journal* 1978, 67, 82-89.

them. This study is an illustration of the way in which a theoretical model of the composing process can be grounded in observations of the individual's experience of composing. It is precisely the complexity of this experience that the case study brings to light. However, by viewing a series of cases, the researcher can discern patterns and themes that suggest regularities in composing behavior across individuals. These common features lead to hypotheses and theoretical formulations which have some basis in shared experience. How far this shared experience extends is, of course, a question that can only be answered through further research.

A final implication derives from the preponderance of recursive behaviors in the composing processes studied here, and from the theoretical notion derived from these observations: retrospective structuring, or the going back to the sense of one's meaning in order to go forward and discover more of what one has to say. Seen in this light, composing becomes the carrying forward of an implicit sense into explicit form. Teaching composing, then, means paying attention not only to the forms or products but also to the explicative process through which they arise.

Appendix
Composing Style Sheet

Name: Tony   Mode: Extensive TW₁   Date: October 31, 1975

Session: 1   Topic: Society & Culture   Time: 11:00 AM - 12:30 PM

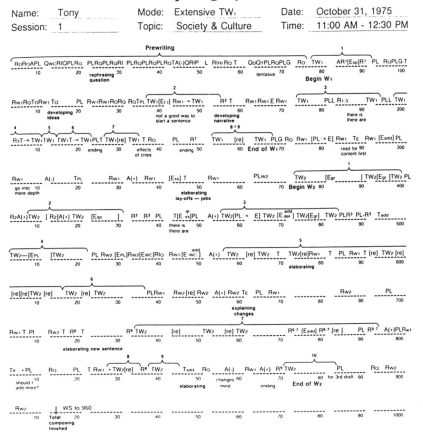

Writing Sample

Tony
Session 1
W1

All men can't be consider equal in a America base on financial situation.[1] Because their are men born in rich families that will never have to worry about any financial difficulties.[2]

         are   may

And then theyre / ~~the~~ another type of Americans that is born to a poor family and alway / have some kind of fina—difficulty.[3] Espeicaly nowadays in New York city With the bugdit Crisis and all   If he is able

/   .[4] ~~He may~~ be able To get a job.[5] But are now he lose the job just as easy as he got it[6] So when he loses his job he'll have to try to get some fina—assistance.[7]

                                                 here

∧ Then he'll probley have even more fin—diffuicuty.[8] So right /   you can't see that In Ameriᴀn, all men are not create equal in the fin—sense.[9]

Writing Sample

Tony
Session 1
W2

All men can not be consider equal in America base on financial situations.[1] Because their are men born in rich families that will never have to worry about any financial ~~diffiuel~~ diffuliculties.[2]

                the

And then they're are / another type of amersicans that are born to a poor famitly.[3] And This

                  may

is the type of Americans that ~~will~~/   alway have some kind of financial diffuliculty.[4] Espeical today ~~today the~~ in new york The way the city has fallen ~~has fallen~~ into fin—debt.[5] It has become

                          working

such a big crisis for the /   ~~people~~ people, in the[6] If the working man is able to find a job,

           with the   the   ~~is~~

espeicaly ~~for~~ /   ~~city a~~ city The way ~~the way~~   city / fin—sitionu is set up now, ~~h~~He'll probley lose the job a whole lot faster than what he got it.[7] When he loses his job he'll ~~p~~ have even more fin—difficulty.[8] And then he'll be force to got to the city for some fini—assi—.[9] So right here you can see that all men in America are not create equal in the fin—sense.[10]

References

Braddock, R., Lloyd-Jones, R., & Schoer, L. *Research in written composition.* Urbana, Ill.: National Council of Teachers of English, 1963.

Britton, J., Burgess, T., Martin, N., McLeod, A., & Rosen, H. *The development of writing abilities* (11-18). London: Macmillan Education Ltd., 1975.

Burton, D. L. Research in the teaching of English: The troubled dream. *Research in the Teaching of English,* 1973, 1, 160-187.

Cooper, C. R. Doing research/reading research. *English Journal,* 1974, 63, 94-99.

Cooper, C. R., & Odell, L. (Eds.) *Research on composing: Points of departure.* Urbana, Ill.: National Council of Teachers of English, 1978.

Emig, J. A. On teaching composition: Some hypotheses as definitions. *Research in the Teaching of English,* 1967, 1, 127-135.

Emig, J. A. *The composing processes of twelfth graders.* Urbana, Ill.: National Council of Teachers of English, 1971. (Research Report No. 13) (Ed. D. Dissertation, Harvard University, 1969).

Goodman, K. S. (Ed.) *Miscue analysis: Applications to reading instruction.* Urbana, Ill.: NCTE and ERIC, 1973.

Graves, D. H. Children's writing: Research directions and hypotheses based upon an examination of the writing process of seven year old children (Doctoral dissertation, State University of New York at Buffalo, 1973). *Dissertation Abstracts International,* 1974, 34, 6255A.

Haynes, E. F. Using research in preparing to teach writing. *English Journal,* 1978, 67, 82-89.

Mischel, T. A case study of a twelfth-grade writer. *Research in the Teaching of English,* 1974, 8, 303-314.

O'Hare, F. *Sentence-combining: Improving student writing without formal grammar instruction.* Urbana, Ill.: National Council of Teachers of English, 1973. (Research Report No. 15).

Perl, S. *Five writers writing: Case studies of the composing processes of unskilled college writers.* Unpublished doctoral dissertation, New York University, 1978.

Pianko, S. *The composing acts of college freshmen writers.* Unpublished Ed.D. dissertation, Rutgers University, 1977.

Shaughnessy, M. P. *Errors and expectations: A guide for the teacher of basic writing.* New York: Oxford University Press, 1977.

Stallard, C. K. An analysis of the writing behavior of good student writers. *Research in the Teaching of English,* 1974, 8, 206-218.

The Cognition of Discovery:
Defining a Rhetorical Problem

by Linda Flower and John R. Hayes

Metaphors give shape to mysteries, and traditionally we have used the metaphor of *discovery* to describe the writer's creative process. Its broad meaning has sheltered many intellectual styles ranging from classical invention to modern heuristics such as tagmemics to self-exploratory modes such as Pre-Writing. Furthermore, *discovery* carries an implicit suggestion that, somewhere in the mind's recesses or in data outside the mind, there is something waiting to be discovered, and that writing is a way to bring that something out. However, if we try to use this metaphor to teach or analyze the creative process itself, we discover its limitations.[1]

First of all, because *discovery* emphasizes the rather glamorous experience of "Eureka, now I see it," it obscures the fact that writers don't find meanings, they *make* them. A writer in the act of discovery is hard at work searching memory, forming concepts, and forging a new structure of ideas, while at the same time trying to juggle all the constraints imposed by his or her purpose, audience, and language itself.[2] Discovery, the event, and its product, new insights, are only the end result of a complicated intellectual process. And it is this process we need to understand more fully.

There is a second, practical reason for teachers to probe this metaphor. The notion of discovery is surrounded by a mythology which, like the popular myth of romantic inspiration, can lead writers to self-defeating writing strategies. The myth of discovery implies a method, and this method is based on the premise that hidden stores of insight and ready-made ideas exist, buried in the mind of the writer, waiting only to be "discovered." Or they are to be found in books and data if only the enterprising researcher knows where to look. What does one do when a ready-made answer can't be found in external sources? The myth says, "look to your own experience." But what

Reprinted from *College Composition and Communication* (February 1980). Copyright 1980 by the National Council of Teachers of English. Used with permission.

[1] This research was partially supported by a grant from the National Institute of Education, Department of Health, Education, and Welfare, Grant NIE G780195.

[2] Linda Flower and John R. Hayes, "The Dynamics of Composing: Making Plans and Juggling Constraints," in *Cognitive Processes in Writing,* ed. Lee Gregg and Erwin Steinberg (Hillsdale, NJ: Lawrence Erlbaum, in press); Linda Flower and John R. Hayes, "Problem Solving Strategies and the Writing Process," *College English,* 39 (Dec. 1977), 449-461.

happens when a writer on this internal voyage of discovery still can't "find" something to say because his or her "ideas" as such are not actually formed? What is there to "discover" if only confused experience and conflicting perceptions are stored in a writer's memory? The mythology of discovery doesn't warn the writer that he or she must often build or create new concepts out of the raw material of experience; nor does it tell the writer how to do it. And yet, this act of *creating* ideas, not finding them, is at the heart of significant writing.

When an attempt at this literal discovery fails, as it often must, it leads inexperienced writers to an unnecessary defeat. Fluent writers are affected by the myth of discovery in another way. As Nancy Sommers has shown, many seem to equate the successful discovery of something to say (i.e., the "flow" of stored ideas) with successful writing, whether that flow is appropriate to the rhetorical situation or not.[3] The myth of discovery, as many of us see it in students, leads the poor writer to give up too soon and the fluent writer to be satisfied with too little.

Discovery, then, is a perplexing notion. On the one hand, it metaphorically describes an intellectual process we want to teach. On the other hand, the metaphor and mythology of discovery itself often distort our vision of that process. This paper attempts to probe the cognition of discovery, the process itself, by studying the way writers initiate and guide themselves through the act of making meaning.

Our approach has been to study writing as a problem-solving, cognitive process. From a psychological point of view, people have a "problem" whenever they are at some point "A" and wish to be at another point "B"; for example, when they have a new insight into *Hamlet*, but have yet to write the paper that will explain it. Their problem-solving process is the thinking process they use to get to point "B," the completed paper. That process might involve many intellectual skills including open, exploratory procedures, such as free writing and day dreaming. But it is important to remember that this process is not a creative accident.

In this study we wanted to explore the problem-solving or discovery process that produces new insight and new ideas. So we started with what many feel to be the most crucial part of that process—the act of finding or defining the problem to be "solved." As Ann Berthoff says, "A shortcoming of most of our students [is] they do not easily recognize particular problems [that need to be solved] because they do not have a method for, that is, a means of formulating critical questions."[4]

This shortcoming turns out to be critical because people only solve the problem they give themselves to solve. The act of formulating questions is sometimes called "problem-finding," but it is more accurate to say that writers

---

[3] Nancy I. Sommers, "Revision Strategies of Student Writers and Experienced Writers," MLA Convention, New York, 28 Dec. 1978.
[4] Ann E. Berthoff, "Towards a Pedagogy of Knowing," *Freshman English News,* 7 (Spring 1978), 4.

build or represent such a problem to themselves, rather than "find" it. A rhetorical problem in particular is never merely a given: it is an elaborate construction which the writer creates in the act of composing. We wanted to see how writers actually go about building this inner, private representation.

There are a number of reasons why this act of constructing an image of one's rhetorical problem is worth study. First, it helps explain why writing, like other creative thinking, can be so utterly unpredictable. Even though a teacher gives 20 students the same assignment, *the writers themselves create the problem they solve.* The reader is not the writer's only "fiction." Furthermore, the act of problem-finding is a critical part of general creativity in both the arts and sciences. Because people only solve the problems they give themselves, the act of representing the problem has a dramatic impact on performance. James Britton saw this with bewildered or unmotivated children, with their strange notions of what the teacher wanted, as did Sondra Perl working with adult basic writers. People simply rewrite an assignment or a situation to make it commensurate with their own skills, habits, or fears.[5] Although writing texts generally ignore this part of the writing process,[6] our work suggests that it may be one of the most critical steps the average writer takes.

The first part of this paper, then, will describe our method for studying the cognitive process by which people represent the rhetorical problem. Then we will present a model of the rhetorical problem itself, that is, a description of the major elements writers could consider in building such an image. Finally, we will use this model of the possible as a basis for comparing what good and poor writers actually do.

Studying Cognitive Processes

The research question we posed for ourselves was this: if discovery is an act of making meaning, not finding it, in response to a *self-defined problem* or goal, how does this problem get defined? Specifically, we wanted to answer three questions:

1. What aspects of a rhetorical problem do people actively represent to themselves? For example, do writers actually spend much time analyzing their audience, and if so, how do they do it?
2. If writers do spend time developing a full representation of their problem, does it help them generate new ideas?
3. And finally, are there any significant differences in the way good and poor writers go about this task?

---

[5] James Britton et al., *The Development of Writing Abilities (11-18)* (London: Macmillan, 1975); Sondra Perl, "Five Writers Writing: Case Studies of the Composing Process of Unskilled College Writers," Diss. New York University, 1978.

[6] Richard L. Larson, "The Rhetorical Act of Planning a Piece of Discourse." Beaver College Conference on Evaluation of Writing, Glenside, PA, October 1978.

In order to describe the problem definition process itself, we collected thinking-aloud protocols from both expert and novice writers. A protocol is a detailed record of a subject's behavior. Our protocols include a transcript of a tape recording made by writers instructed to verbalize their thinking process as they write, as well as all written material the writer produced. A typical protocol from a one-hour session will include four to five pages of notes and writing and 15 pages of typed transcript. The novice writers were college students who had gone to the Communication Skills Center for general writing problems such as coherence and organization. The expert writers were teachers of writing and rhetoric who had received year-long NEH fellowships to study writing. Each writer was given the following problem: "write about your job for the readers of *Seventeen* magazine, 13-14 year-old girls," and was asked to compose out loud into a tape recorder as he or she worked. They were told to verbalize everything that went through their minds, including stray thoughts and crazy ideas, but not to try to analyze their thought process, just to express it.

A Model of the Rhetorical Problem

From these protocols, we pulled together a composite picture or model of the rhetorical problem itself. This composite is shown in Figure 1, with

The Rhetorical Problem	
Elements of the Problem	Examples
THE RHETORICAL SITUATION	
Exigency or Assignment	"Write for Seventeen magazine; this is impossible."
Audience	"Someone like myself, but adjusted for twenty years."
THE WRITER'S OWN GOALS involving the	
Reader	"I'll change their notion of English teachers . . ."
Persona or Self	"I'll look like an idiot if I say . . ."
Meaning	"So if I compare those two attitudes . . ."
Text	"First we'll want an introduction."

Figure 1. Elements of the rhetorical problem writers represent to themselves in composing.

examples drawn from our writers' protocols. It is based on what the group of writers did and shows the basic elements of a writing problem which a given writer *could* actively consider in the process of composing, *if* he or she chose to. For example, the writer in the following excerpt is actively creating an image of himself or his *persona,* an image of what effect he might have on his reader, and an initial representation of a meaning or idea he might choose to develop, as the words in brackets indicate.

> Ah, in fact, that might be a useful thing to focus on, how a professor differs from . . . how a teacher differs from a professor, [meaning], and I see myself as a teacher, *[persona],* that might help them, my audience, to reconsider their notion of what an English teacher does. [effect on audience]

Taken as a whole, the *rhetorical problem* breaks into two major units. The first is the rhetorical *situation.* This situation, which is the writer's given, includes the audience and assignment. The second unit is the set of *goals* the writer himself creates. The four dominant kinds of goals we observed involved affecting the *reader,* creating a *persona* or voice, building a *meaning,* and producing a formal *text.* As you see, these turned out to closely parallel the four terms of the communication triangle: reader, writer, world, word. This parallel between communication theory and our study is a happy one, since protocol analysis lets us describe what writers actually do as they write, not just what we, as theorists, think they should do. And, as we will see, one of the major differences between good and poor writers will be how many aspects of this total rhetorical problem they actually consider and how thoroughly they represent any aspect of it to themselves.

This model of the rhetorical problem reflects the elements writers actively consider as they write. It accounts for the conscious representation going on as writers compose. But is that enough? Protocols yield a wealth of information available in no other way, but they are limited to those aspects of the problem the writer is able in some way to articulate. But in understanding a writer's process we can't ignore that rich body of inarticulate information Polanyi would call our "tacit knowledge." We think that much of the information people have about rhetorical problems exists in the form of *stored problem-representations.* Writers do no doubt have many such representations for familiar or conventional problems, such as writing a thank-you letter. Such a representation would contain not only a conventional definition of the situation, audience, and the writer's purpose, but might include quite detailed information about solutions, even down to appropriate tone and phrases. Experienced writers are likely to have stored representations of even quite complex rhetorical problems (e.g., writing a book review for readers of *The Daily Tribune)* if they have confronted them often before.

Naturally, if a writer has a stored representation that is fully adequate for the current situation, we wouldn't expect him to spend time building a new one. Achieving that kind of mental efficiency is what learning is all about. However, many writing problems, such as the one we gave our subjects, are unique and require a writer to build a *unique representation.* In such situations, we would expect a good writer to explore the problem afresh and to give conscious time and attention to building a unique representation. Therefore, in capturing the conscious representation of these unique problems, we feel we are likely to capture the critical part of the process. As it turned out, one of the most telling differences between our good and poor writers was the degree to which they created a unique, fully-developed representation of this unique rhetorical problem.

Our model or composite picture of the writer's rhetorical problem specifies two kinds of information writers represent to themselves: information about the rhetorical situation and information about the writer's own purpose and goals. We will discuss these two aspects of the rhetorical problem in order.

Representing a Rhetorical Situation

A *rhetorical situation* is the name we assign to the givens with which a writer must work, namely, the audience and assignment. Lloyd Bitzer's description of this situation as an exigency (e.g., assignment), an audience, and a set of constraints is a good description of what our subjects actually considered or represented to themselves.[7] (However, unlike Bitzer, we see this external situation as only part of a larger entity we call the rhetorical problem.)

The writer's initial analysis of the assignment and audience was usually brief. Most writers—both novice and expert—plunged quickly into generating ideas, but often returned to reconsider these givens later. For the novice writer, however, this re-examination of the *situation* often took the form of simply rereading the assignment, maybe two or three times, as if searching for a clue in it. A more intense form of this strategy was also observed by Perl, whose basic writers would read the assignment over and over until some key word struck an associative chord and reminded them of a topic on which they had something to say.[8] Although the novice writers in our study were actually analyzing the situation, they never moved beyond the sketchy, conventional representation of audience and assignment with which they started.

The good writers, by contrast, used their re-examination of the situation to add to their image of the audience or assignment. For example, this writer initially defined the audience as "someone like myself when I read—well, not like myself but adjusted for, well, twenty years later." Later in the protocol her image of the reader became significantly different:

> I feel a certain constraint knowing as I do the rather saccharine editorial policy. Perhaps I'm mistaken, but the last time I had my hair cut or something, I read it and they still seemed to be mostly looking

---

[7] Lloyd Bitzer, "The Rhetorical Situation," *Philosophy and Rhetoric,* 1 (Jan. 1968), 1-14.
[8] Perl, "Five Writers Writing."

at women as consumers of fashion and as consumers of men and really not as capable or interested in or likely to be drawn to an occupation like mine which is rather low paying and unglamorous and, ah, far from chic clothes.

As you can see, this writer is creating a sophisticated, complex image of a reader—half alter-ego, half fashion consumer—which she will have to deal with in the act of writing. No doubt it will be harder to write for such an audience than for a simple stereotype, but the final result is going to be more effective if she has indeed represented her audience accurately. We can imagine similar differences in two students' representations of an assignment such as "analyze *Hamlet.*" Let us assume that both writers have roughly equal bodies of knowledge stored in memory. One writer might draw on that knowledge to give herself detailed instructions, e.g., " 'analyze this play'; that means I should try to break it down into some kind of parts. Perhaps I could analyze the plot, or the issues in the play, or its theatrical conventions." This student is drawing on the experience and semantic knowledge which both students possess to create a highly developed image of how to analyze something (e.g., break it into parts) and how to analyze this play in particular (e.g., find the critical issues). Meanwhile, another writer might blithely represent the problem as "Write another theme and talk about *Hamlet* this time, in time for Tuesday's class. That probably means about two pages."

Representing One's Purpose and Goals

An audience and exigency can jolt a writer into action, but the force which drives composing is the writer's own set of goals, purposes, or intentions. A major part of defining the rhetorical problem then is representing one's own goals. As we might predict from the way writers progressively fill in their image of the audience, writers also build a progressive representation of their goals as they write.

We can break these goals into four groups. The first is focused on the effect the writer wants to have on the *reader*. These can range from quite ambitious global plans, such as "I'll change their image of English teachers," down to decisions about local effects, such as "make this sound plausible," or "make this seem immediate to their experience." At times the intention of the writer is to have a direct personal effect on the reader as a person. For example, one writer structured her paper in order to make her reader "remain in a state of suspension [about jobs] and remain in an attentive posture toward her own history, abilities, and sources of satisfaction." She wanted to make the reader "feel autonomous and optimistic and effective." At other times the goal is a more general one of making the reader simply see something or comprehend accurately a train of thought (e.g., "I've got to attract the attention of the reader," or "There needs to be a transition between those two ideas to be clear").

One of the hallmarks of the good writers was the time they spent thinking about how they wanted to affect a reader. They were clearly representing their rhetorical problem as a complex speech act. The poor writers, by contrast, often seemed tied to their topic. This difference matters because, in our study, one of the most powerful strategies we saw for producing new ideas throughout the composing process was planning what one wanted to do to or for one's reader.

A second kind of purpose writers represent to themselves involves the relationship they wish to establish with the reader. This relationship can also be described as the *persona,* projected self, or voice the writer wishes to create. This part of the problem representation is the least likely to appear in a protocol because writers are probably likely to draw on a stored representation of their *persona* even for unique problems. Furthermore, decisions about one's *persona* are often expressed by changes in word choice and tone, not by direct statements. Nevertheless, this is a part of a writer's goals or purpose which he or she must define in some way. In one writer this issue was directly broached three times. At the beginning of composing, she saw her role as that of a free-lance writer writing to a formula. But unfortunately

> my sense is that its a formula which I'm not sure I know, so I suppose what I have to do is invent what the formula might be, and then try to include events or occurrences or attitude or experiences in my own job that could be conveyed in formula. So let's see . . .

Clearly, her sense of her role as formula writer affects how she will go about writing this paper. But later this same writer revised her relationship with the reader and in so doing radically changed the rhetorical problem. She accused herself of taking the hypocritical voice of adulthood and set a new goal:

> I feel enormously doubtful of my capacity to relate very effectively to the audience that is specified and in that case, I mean, all I can do is, is just, you know, present myself, present my concepts and my message or my utterance in a kind of simple and straightforward and unpretentious way, I hope.

A third goal writers develop involves the writer's attempt to build a coherent network of ideas, to create *meaning.* All writers start, we assume, with a stored goal that probably says something like, "Explore what you know about this topic and write it down; that is, generate and express relevant ideas." We see evidence of this goal when writers test or evaluate what they've just said to see if it is related to or consistent with other ideas. Many of our writers never appeared to develop goals much more sophisticated than this generate-and-express goal, which, in its most basic form, could produce simply an interior monologue. However, some writers defined their meaning-making problem in more complex and demanding ways, telling themselves to focus on an important difference, to pursue an idea because it seemed challenging, or to step back and decide "more generally, how do I want to characterize my job." Perhaps the difference here is one of degree. At one end of a spectrum, writers are merely trying to express a network of ideas already formed and available in memory; at the other, writers are consciously attempting to probe for analogues and contradictions, to form new concepts, and perhaps even to restructure their old knowledge of the subject.

Finally, a fourth goal which writers represent involves the formal or conventional features of a written text. Early in composing, writers appear to make many basic decisions about their genre and set up goals such as "write an introduction first." Most college students no doubt have a great deal of information in their stored representation of the problem "write a short essay." However, once into the text, writers often expand their image of possibilities by considering unique features the text might include. For example, writers tell themselves to "fictionalize it," to "use a direct question," "try a rhetorical question," or "try to add a little example or little story here to flesh it out." In doing so, they set up goals based primarily on their knowledge of the conventions of writing and the features of texts. This may be one way in which extensive reading affects a person's ability to write: a well-read person simply has a much larger and richer set of images of what a text can look like. Goals such as these often have plans for reaching the goal built right into them. For example, when one of the expert writers decided to use a problem/solution format for the paper, he was immediately able to tap a pocket of stored plans for creating such a format. The convention itself specified just what to include. Furthermore, once he set up this familiar format as a goal, he saw what to do with a whole body of previously unorganized ideas.

Differences Among Writers

This six-part model of the rhetorical problem attempts to describe the major kinds of givens and goals writers could represent to themselves as they compose. As a model for comparison it allowed us to see patterns in what our good and poor writers actually did. The differences, which were striking, were these:

1. Good writers respond to *all* aspects of the rhetorical problem. As they compose they build a unique representation not only of their audience and assignment, but also of their goals involving the audience, their own *persona,* and the text. By contrast, the problem representations of the poor writers were concerned primarily with the features and conventions of a written text, such as number of pages or magazine format. For example, Figure 2 shows a vivid contrast between an expert and novice when we compare the way two writers represented their rhetorical problem in the first 60 lines of a protocol. The numbers are based on categorizing phrases and sentences within the protocol.

As you can see, the expert made reference to his audience or assignment 18 times in the first seven to eight minutes of composing, whereas the novice considered the rhetorical situation less than half that often. The most striking difference, of course, is in their tendency to represent or create goals for dealing with the audience. Finally, the column marked "Total" shows our expert writer simply spending more time than the novice in thinking about

	Analysis of rhetorical situation: Audience and Assignment	Analysis of goals				
		Audience	Self	Text	Meaning	Total
Novice	7	0	0	3	7	17
Expert	18	11	1	3	9	42

Figure 2. Number of times writer explicitly represented each aspect of the rhetorical problem in first 60 lines of protocol

and commenting on the rhetorical problem, as opposed to spending that time generating text.

2. In building their problem representation, good writers create a particularly rich network of goals for affecting their reader. Furthermore, these goals, based on affecting a reader, also helped the writer generate new ideas. In an earlier study we discovered that our experienced writers (a different group this time) generated up to 60 per cent of their new ideas in response to the larger rhetorical problem (that is, in response to the assignment, their audience, or their own goals). Only 30 per cent were in response to the topic alone. For example, a writer would say, "I'll want an introduction that pulls you in," instead of merely reciting facts about the topic, such as "As an engineer the first thing to do is . . ." In the poor writers the results were almost reversed: 70 per cent of their new ideas were statements about the topic alone without concern for the larger rhetorical problem.[9] All of this suggests that setting up goals to affect a reader is not only a reasonable act, but a powerful strategy for generating new ideas and exploring even a topic as personal as "my job."

As you might easily predict, plans for affecting a reader also give the final paper a more effective rhetorical focus. For example, one of the novice writers, whose only goals for affecting the audience were to "explain [his] job simply so it would appeal to a broad range of intellect," ended up writing a detailed technical analysis of steam turbulence in an electrical generator. The topic was of considerable importance to him as a future research engineer, but hardly well focused for the readers of *Seventeen*.

3. Good writers represent the problem not only in more breadth, but in depth. As they write, they continue to develop their image of the reader, the

---

[9] Linda Flower and John R. Hayes, "Process-Based Evaluation of Writing: Changing the Performance, Not the Product," American Educational Research Association Convention, San Francisco, 9 April 1979.

situation, and their own goals with increasing detail and specificity. We saw this in the writer who came back to revise and elaborate her image of her fashion-consuming reader. By contrast, poor writers often remain throughout the entire composing period with the flat, undeveloped, conventional representation of the problem with which they started.

The main conclusion of our study is this: good writers are simply solving a different problem than poor writers. Given the fluency we can expect from native speakers, this raises an important question. Would the performance of poor writers change if they too had a richer sense of what they were trying to do as they wrote, or if they had more of the goals for affecting the reader which were so stimulating to the good writers? People only solve the problems they represent to themselves. Our guess is that the poor writers we studied possess verbal and rhetorical skills which they fail to use because of their underdeveloped image of their rhetorical problem. Because they have narrowed a rhetorical act to a paper-writing problem, their representation of the problem doesn't call on abilities they may well have.

This study has, we think, two important implications, one for teaching and one for research. First, if we can describe how a person represents his or her own problem in the act of writing, we will be describing a part of what makes a writer "creative." A recent, long-range study of the development of creative skill in fine art showed some striking parallels between successful artists and our expert writers. This seven-year study, entitled *The Creative Vision: A Longitudinal Study of Problem-Finding in Art,* concluded that the critical ability which distinguished the successful artists was not technical skill, but what the authors called *problem-finding*—the ability to envision, pose, formulate, or create a new problematic situation.[10] Furthermore, in this experimental study of artists at work, the three behaviors which distinguished the successful artists were the breadth and depth of their exploration of the problem and their delay in reaching closure on the finished product. In this experiment the artists were given a studio equipped with materials and a collection of objects they might draw. The successful artists, like our expert writers, explored more of the materials before them and explored them in more depth, fingering, moving, touching, rearranging, and playing with alternatives, versus moving quickly to a rather conventional arrangement and sketch. Once drawing was begun, the artists' willingness to explore and reformulate the problem continued, often until the drawing was nearly completed. Similarly, our successful writers continued to develop and alter their representation of the problem throughout the writing process. This important study of creativity in fine art suggested that problem-finding is a talent, a cognitive skill which can lead to creativity. The parallels between these two studies suggest that problem-finding in both literature and art is

---

[10]Jacob W. Getzels and Mihaly Csikszentmihalyi, *The Creative Vision: A Longitudinal Study of Problem Finding in Art* (New York: John Wiley and Sons, 1976).

related not only to success, but in some less well defined way to "creativity" itself.

Other studies in the psychology of creativity make this link between creative thinking and problem-solving processes more explicit.[11] Many "creative" breakthroughs in science and the arts are not the result of finding a better technical solution to an old problem (e.g., the disease-producing influence of evil spirits), but of seeing a new problem (e.g., the existence of germs). In many cases, the solution procedure is relatively straightforward once one has defined the problem. For example, Virginia Woolf's *The Waves* or Van Gogh's impressionistic landscapes are less a technical feat than an act of imagining a new problem or set of goals for the artist.

We feel there are implications for exciting research in this area. This study has attempted to develop a model of the rhetorical problem as a guide to further research, and to describe three major differences between good and poor writers. But there is much we could learn about how people define their rhetorical problems as they write and why they make some of the choices they do.

The second implication we see in our own study is that the ability to explore a rhetorical problem is eminently teachable. Unlike a metaphoric "discovery," problem-finding is not a totally mysterious or magical act. Writers discover what they want to do by insistently, energetically exploring the entire problem before them and building for themselves a unique image of the problem they want to solve. A part of creative thinking is just plain thinking.

Exploring a topic alone isn't enough. As Donald Murray put it, "writers wait for signals" which tell them it is time to write, which "give a sense of closure, a way of handling a diffuse and overwhelming subject."[12] Many of the "signals" Murray described, such as having found a point of view, a voice, or a genre, parallel our description of the goals and plans we saw good writers making. If we can teach students to explore and define their own problems, even within the constraints of an assignment, we can help them to create inspiration instead of wait for it.

---

[11] John R. Hayes, *Cognitive Psychology: Thinking and Creating* (Homewood, IL: Dorsey Press, 1978); M. Wertheimer, *Productive Thinking* (New York: Harper and Row, 1945).
[12] Donald M. Murray, "Write Before Writing," *College Composition and Communication,* 29 (Dec. 1978), 375-381.

Revision Strategies of Student Writers and Experienced Adult Writers

by Nancy Sommers

Although various aspects of the writing process have been studied extensively of late, research on revision has been notably absent. The reason for this, I suspect, is that current models of the writing process have directed attention away from revision. With few exceptions, these models are linear; they separate the writing process into discrete stages. Two representative models are Gordon Rohman's suggestion that the composing process moves from prewriting to writing to rewriting and James Britton's model of the writing process as a series of stages described in metaphors of linear growth, conception—incubation—production.[1] What is striking about these theories of writing is that they model themselves on speech: Rohman defines the writer in a way that cannot distinguish him from a speaker ("A writer is a man who . . . puts [his] experience into words in his own mind"—p. 15); and Britton bases his theory of writing on what he calls (following Jakobson) the "expressiveness" of speech.[2] Moreover, Britton's study itself follows the "linear model" of the relation of thought and language in speech proposed by Vygotsky, a relationship embodied in the linear movement "from the motive which engenders a thought to the shaping of the thought, *first* in inner speech, *then* in meanings of words, *and finally* in words" (quoted in Britton, p. 40). What this movement fails to take into account in its linear structure— "first . . . then . . . finally"—is the recursive shaping of thought by language; what it fails to take into account is *revision*. In these linear conceptions of the writing process revision is understood as a separate stage at the end of the process—a stage that comes after the completion of a first or second draft and one that is temporally distinct from the prewriting and writing stages of the process.[3]

Reprinted from *College Composition and Communication* (December 1980). Copyright 1980 by the National Council of Teachers of English. Reprinted with permission.

[1] D. Gordon Rohman and Albert O. Wlecke, "Pre-writing: The Construction and Application of Models for Concept Formation in Writing," Cooperative Research Project No. 2174, U.S. Office of Education, Department of Health, Education, and Welfare; James Britton, Anthony Burgess, Nancy Martin, Alex McLeod, Harold Rosen, *The Development of Writing Abilities (11-18)* (London: Macmillan Education, 1975).

[2] Britton is following Roman Jakobson, "Linguistics and Poetics," in T. A. Sebeok, *Style in Language* (Cambridge, Mass: MIT Press, 1960).

[3] For an extended discussion of this issue see Nancy Sommers, "The Need for Theory in Composition Research," *College Composition and Communication*, 30 (February, 1979), 46-49.

The linear model bases itself on speech in two specific ways. First of all, it is based on traditional rhetorical models, models that were created to serve the spoken art of oratory. In whatever ways the parts of classical rhetoric are described, they offer "stages" of composition that are repeated in contemporary models of the writing process. Edward Corbett, for instance, describes the "five parts of a discourse"—*inventio, dispositio, elocutio, memoria, pronuntiatio*—and, disregarding the last two parts since "after rhetoric came to be concerned mainly with written discourse, there was no further need to deal with them,"[4] he produces a model very close to Britton's conception *[inventio]*, incubation *[dispositio]*, production *[elocutio]*. Other rhetorics also follow this procedure, and they do so not simply because of historical accident. Rather, the process represented in the linear model is based on the irreversibility of speech. Speech, Roland Barthes says, "is irreversible":

> "A word cannot be retracted, except precisely by saying that one retracts it. To cross out here is to add: if I want to erase what I have just said, I cannot do it without showing the eraser itself (I must say: *'or rather . . .' 'I expressed myself badly . . .')*; paradoxically, it is ephemeral speech which is indelible, not monumental writing. All that one can do in the case of a spoken utterance is to tack on another utterance."[5]

What is impossible in speech is *revision:* like the example Barthes gives, revision in speech is an afterthought. In the same way, each stage of the linear model must be exclusive (distinct from the other stages) or else it becomes trivial and counterproductive to refer to these junctures as "stages."

By staging revision after enunciation, the linear models reduce revision in writing, as in speech, to no more than an afterthought. In this way such models make the study of revision impossible. Revision, in Rohman's model, is simply the repetition of writing; or to pursue Britton's organic metaphor, revision is simply the further growth of what is already there, the "preconceived" product. The absence of research on revision, then, is a function of a theory of writing which makes revision both superfluous and redundant, a theory which does not distinguish between writing and speech.

What the linear models do produce is a parody of writing. Isolating revision and then disregarding it plays havoc with the experiences composition teachers have of the actual writing and rewriting of experienced writers. Why should the linear model be preferred? Why should revision be forgotten, superfluous? Why do teachers offer the linear model and students accept it? One reason, Barthes suggests, is that "there is a fundamental tie between teaching and speech," while "writing begins at the point where speech

---

[4] *Classical Rhetoric for the Modern Student* (New York: Oxford University Press, 1965), p. 27.
[5] Roland Barthes, ''Writers, Intellectuals, Teachers,'' in *Image—Music—Text*, trans. Stephen Heath (New York: Hill and Wang, 1977), pp. 190-191.

becomes *impossible*."[6] The spoken word cannot be revised. The possibility of revision distinguishes the written text from speech. In fact, according to Barthes, this is the essential difference between writing and speaking. When we must revise, when the very idea is subject to recursive shaping by language, then speech becomes inadequate. This is a matter to which I will return, but first we should examine, theoretically, a detailed exploration of what student writers as distinguished from experienced adult writers *do* when they write and rewrite their work. Dissatisfied with both the linear model of writing and the lack of attention to the process of revision, I conducted a series of studies over the past three years which examined the revision processes of student writers and experienced writers to see what role revision played in their writing processes. In the course of my work the revision process was redefined as *a sequence of changes in a composition—changes which are initiated by cues and occur continually throughout the writing of a work.*

Methodology

I used a case study approach. The student writers were twenty freshmen at Boston University and the University of Oklahoma with SAT verbal scores ranging from 450-600 in their first semester of composition. The twenty experienced adult writers from Boston and Oklahoma City included journalists, editors, and academics. To refer to the two groups, I use the terms *student writers* and *experienced writers* because the principal difference between these two groups is the amount of experience they have had in writing.

Each writer wrote three essays, expressive, explanatory, and persuasive, and rewrote each essay twice, producing nine written products in draft and final form. Each writer was interviewed three times after the final revision of each essay. And each writer suggested revisions for a composition written by an anonymous author. Thus extensive written and spoken documents were obtained from each writer.

The essays were analyzed by counting and categorizing the changes made. Four revision operations were identified: deletion, substitution, addition, and reordering. And four levels of changes were identified: word, phrase, sentence, theme (the extended statement of one idea). A coding system was developed for identifying the frequency of revision by level and operation. In addition, transcripts of the interviews in which the writers interpreted their revisions were used to develop what was called a *scale of concerns* for each writer. This scale enabled me to codify what were the writer's primary concerns, secondary concerns, tertiary concerns, and whether the writers used the same scale of concerns when revising the second or third drafts as they used in revising the first draft.

---

[6] "Writers, Intellectuals, Teachers," p. 190.

Revision Strategies of Student Writers

Most of the students I studied did not use the terms *revision* or *rewriting*. In fact, they did not seem comfortable using the word *revision* and explained that revision was not a word they used, but the word their teachers used. Instead, most of the students had developed various functional terms to describe the type of changes they made. The following are samples of these definitions:

Scratch Out and Do Over Again. "I say scratch out and do over, and that means what it says. Scratching out and cutting out. I read what I have written and I cross out a word and put another word in; a more decent word or a better word. Then if there is somewhere to use a sentence that I have crossed out, I will put it there."

Reviewing. "Reviewing means just using better words and eliminating words that are not needed. I go over and change words around."

Reviewing. "I just review every word and make sure that everything is worded right. I see if I am rambling; I see if I can put a better word in or leave one out. Usually when I read what I have written, I say to myself, 'that word is so bland or so trite,' and then I go and get my thesaurus."

Redoing: "Redoing means cleaning up the paper and crossing out. It is looking at something and saying, no that has to go, or no, that is not right."

Marking Out: "I don't use the word rewriting because I only write one draft and the changes that I make are made on top of the draft. The changes that I make are usually just marking out words and putting different ones in."

Slashing and Throwing Out: "I throw things out and say they are not good. I like to write like Fitzgerald did by inspiration, and if I feel inspired then I don't need to slash and throw much out."

The predominant concern in these definitions is vocabulary. The students understand the revision process as a rewording activity. They do so because they perceive words as the unit of written discourse. That is, they concentrate on particular words apart from their role in the text. Thus one student quoted above thinks in terms of dictionaries, and, following the eighteenth century theory of words parodied in *Gulliver's Travels*, he imagines a load of things carried about to be exchanged. Lexical changes are the major revision activities of the students because economy is their goal. They are governed, like the linear model itself, by the Law of Occam's razor that prohibits logically needless repetition: redundancy and superfluity. Nothing governs speech more than such superfluities; speech constantly repeats itself precisely because spoken words, as Barthes writes, are expendable in the cause of communication. The aim of revision according to the students' own description is therefore to clean up speech; the redundancy of speech is unnecessary in writing, their logic suggests, because writing, unlike speech, can be reread. Thus one student said, "Redoing means cleaning up the paper and crossing out." The remarkable contradiction of cleaning by marking might, indeed, stand for student revision as I have encountered it.

The students place a symbolic importance on their selection and rejection of words as the determiners of success or failure for their compositions. When revising, they primarily ask themselves: can I find a better word or phrase? A more impressive, not so cliched, or less hum-drum word? Am I repeating the same word or phrase too often? They approach the revision process with what could be labeled as a "thesaurus philosophy of writing"; the students consider the thesaurus a harvest of lexical substitutions and believe that most problems in their essays can be solved by rewording. What is revealed in the students' use of the thesaurus is a governing attitude toward their writing: that the meaning to be communicated is already there, already finished, already produced, ready to be communicated, and all that is necessary is a better word "rightly worded." One student defined revision as "redoing"; "redoing" meant "just using better words and eliminating words that are not needed." For the students, writing is translating: the thought to the page, the language of speech to the more formal language of prose, the word to its synonym. Whatever is translated, an original text already exists for students, one which need not be discovered or acted upon, but simply communicated.[7]

The students list repetition as one of the elements they most worry about. This cue signals to them that they need to eliminate the repetition either by substituting or deleting words or phrases. Repetition occurs, in large part, because student writing imitates—transcribes—speech: attention to repetitious words is a manner of cleaning speech. Without a sense of the developmental possibilities of revision (and writing in general) students seek, on the authority of many textbooks, simply to clean up their language and prepare to type. What is curious, however, is that students are aware of lexical repetition, but not conceptual repetition. They only notice the repetition if they can "hear" it; they do not diagnose lexical repetition as symptomatic of problems on a deeper level. By rewording their sentences to avoid the lexical repetition, the students solve the immediate problem, but blind themselves to problems on a textual level; although they are using different words, they are sometimes merely restating the same idea with different words. Such blindness, as I discovered with student writers, is the inability to "see" revision as a process: the inability to "review" their work again, as it were, with different eyes, and to start over.

The revision strategies described above are consistent with the students' understanding of the revision process as requiring lexical changes but not semantic changes. For the students, the extent to which they revise is a function of their level of inspiration. In fact, they use the word *inspiration* to describe the ease or difficulty with which their essay is written, and the extent

---

[7] Nancy Sommers and Ronald Schleifer, "Means and Ends: Some Assumptions of Student Writers," *Composition and Teaching*, II (in press).

to which the essay needs to be revised. If students feel inspired, if the writing comes easily, and if they don't get stuck on individual words or phrases, then they say that they cannot see any reason to revise. Because students do not see revision as an activity in which they modify and develop perspectives and ideas, they feel that if they know what they want to say, then there is little reason for making revisions.

The only modification of ideas in the students' essays occurred when they tried out two or three introductory paragraphs. This results, in part, because the students have been taught in another version of the linear model of composing to use a thesis statement as a controlling device in their introductory paragraphs. Since they write their introductions and their thesis statements even before they have really discovered what they want to say, their early close attention to the thesis statement, and more generally the linear model, function to restrict and circumscribe not only the development of their ideas, but also their ability to change the direction of these ideas.

Too often as composition teachers we conclude that students do not willingly revise. The evidence from my research suggests that it is not that students are unwilling to revise, but rather that they do what they have been taught to do in a consistently narrow and predictable way. On every occasion when I asked students why they hadn't made any more changes, they essentially replied, "I knew something larger was wrong, but I didn't think it would help to move words around." The students have strategies for handling words and phrases and their strategies helped them on a word or sentence level. What they lack, however, is a set of strategies to help them identify the "something larger" that they sensed was wrong and work from there. The students do not have strategies for handling the whole essay. They lack procedures or heuristics to help them reorder lines of reasoning or ask questions about their purposes and readers. The students view their compositions in a linear way as a series of parts. Even such potentially useful concepts as "unity" or "form" are reduced to the rule that a composition, if it is to have form, must have an introduction, a body, and a conclusion, or the sum total of the necessary parts.

The students decide to stop revising when they decide that they have not violated any of the rules for revising. These rules, such as "Never begin a sentence with a conjunction" or "Never end a sentence with a preposition," are lexically cued and rigidly applied. In general, students will subordinate the demands of the specific problems of their text to the demands of the rules. Changes are made in compliance with abstract rules about the product, rules that quite often do not apply to the specific problems in the text. These revision strategies are teacher-based, directed towards a teacher-reader who expects compliance with rules—with pre-existing "conceptions"—and who will only examine parts of the composition (writing comments about those parts in the margins of their essays) and will cite any violations of rules in those parts. At best the students see their writing altogether passively through the eyes of former teachers or their surrogates, the textbooks, and are bound to the rules which they have been taught.

Revision Strategies of Experienced Writers

One aim of my research has been to contrast how student writers define revision with how a group of experienced writers define their revision processes. Here is a sampling of the definitions from the experienced writers:

Rewriting: "It is a matter of looking at the kernel of what I have written, the content, and then thinking about it, responding to it, making decisions, and actually restructuring it."

Rewriting. "I rewrite as I write. It is hard to tell what is a first draft because it is not determined by time. In one draft, I might cross out three pages, write two, cross out a fourth, rewrite it, and call it a draft. I am constantly writing and rewriting. I can only conceptualize so much in my first draft—only so much information can be held in my head at one time; my rewriting efforts are a reflection of how much information I can encompass at one time. There are levels and agenda which I have to attend to in each draft."

Rewriting: "Rewriting means on one level, finding the argument, and on another level, language changes to make the argument more effective. Most of the time I feel as if I can go on rewriting forever. There is always one part of a piece that I could keep working on. It is always difficult to know at what point to abandon a piece of writing. I like this idea that a piece of writing is never finished, just abandoned."

Rewriting: My first draft is usually very scattered. In rewriting, I find the line of argument. After the argument is resolved, I am much more interested in word choice and phrasing."

Revising: "My cardinal rule in revising is never to fall in love with what I have written in a first or second draft. An idea, sentence, or even a phrase that looks catchy, I don't trust. Part of this idea is to wait a while. I am much more in love with something after I have written it than I am a day or two later. It is much easier to change anything with time."

Revising: "It means taking apart what I have written and putting it back together again. I ask major theoretical questions of my ideas, respond to those questions, and think of proportion and structure, and try to find a controlling metaphor. I find out which ideas can be developed and which should be dropped. I am constantly chiseling and changing as I revise."

The experienced writers describe their primary objective when revising as finding the form or shape of their argument. Although the metaphors vary, the experienced writers often use structural expressions such as "finding a framework," "a pattern," or "a design" for their argument. When questioned about this emphasis, the experienced writers responded that since their first drafts are usually scattered attempts to define their territory, their objective in the second draft is to begin observing general patterns of development and deciding what should be included and what excluded. One writer explained, "I have learned from experience that I need to keep writing a first draft until I figure out what I want to say. Then in a second draft, I begin to see the structure of an argument and how all the various sub-arguments which are buried beneath the surface of all those sentences are related." What is described here is a process in which the writer is both agent and vehicle. "Writing," says Barthes, unlike speech, "develops like a seed, not a line,"[8] and like a seed it confuses beginning and end, conception and production. Thus, the experienced writers say their drafts are "not determined by time," that rewriting is a "constant process," that they feel as if (they) "can go on forever." Revising confuses the beginning and end, the agent and vehicle; it confuses, *in order to find*, the line of argument.

After a concern for form, the experienced writers have a second objective: a concern for their readership. In this way, "production" precedes "conception." The experienced writers imagine a reader (reading their product) whose existence and whose expectations influence their revision process. They have abstracted the standards of a reader and this reader seems to be partially a reflection of themselves and functions as a critical and productive collaborator—a collaborator who has yet to love their work. The anticipation of a reader's judgment causes a feeling of dissonance when the writer recognizes incongruities between intention and execution, and requires these writers to make revisions on all levels. Such a reader gives them just what the students lacked: new eyes to "review" their work. The experienced writers believe that they have learned the causes and conditions, the product, which will influence their reader, and their revision strategies are geared towards creating these causes and conditions. They demonstrate a complex understanding of which examples, sentences, or phrases should be included or excluded. For example, one experienced writer decided to delete public examples and add private examples when writing about the energy crisis because "private examples would be less controversial and thus more persuasive." Another writer revised his transitional sentences because "some kinds of transitions are more easily recognized as transitions than others." These examples represent the type of strategic attempts these experienced writers use to manipulate the conventions of discourse in order to communicate to their reader.

But these revision strategies are a process of more than communication; they are part of the process of *discovering meaning* altogether. Here we can see the importance of dissonance; at the heart of revision is the process by which writers recognize and resolve the dissonance they sense in their writing. Ferdinand de Saussure has argued that meaning is differential or "diacritical," based on differences between terms rather than "essential" or

---

[8] *Writing Degree Zero* in *Writing Degree Zero and Elements of Semiology,* trans. Annette Lavers and Colin Smith (New York: Hill and Wang, 1968), p. 20.

inherent qualities of terms. "Phonemes," he said, "are characterized not, as one might think, by their own positive quality but simply by the fact that they are distinct."[9] In fact, Saussure bases his entire *Course in General Linguistics* on these differences, and such differences are dissonant; like musical dissonances which gain their significance from their relationship to the "key" of the composition which itself is determined by the whole language, specific language (parole) gains its meaning from the system of language (langue) of which it is a manifestation and part. The musical composition—a "composition" of parts—creates its "key" as in an over-all structure which determines the value (meaning) of its parts. The analogy with music is readily seen in the compositions of experienced writers: both sorts of composition are based precisely on those structures experienced writers seek in their writing. It is this complicated relationship between the parts and the whole in the work of experienced writers which destroys the linear model; writing cannot develop "like a line" because each addition or deletion is a reordering of the whole. Explicating Saussure, Jonathan Culler asserts that "meaning depends on difference of meaning."[10] But student writers constantly struggle to bring their essays into congruence with a predefined meaning. The experienced writers do the opposite: they seek to discover (to create) meaning in the engagement with their writing, in revision. They seek to emphasize and exploit the lack of clarity, the differences of meaning, the dissonance, that writing as opposed to speech allows in the possibility of revision. Writing has spatial and temporal features not apparent in speech—words are recorded in space and fixed in time—which is why writing is susceptible to reordering and later addition. Such features make possible the dissonance that both provokes revision and promises, from itself, new meaning.

For the experienced writers the heaviest concentration of changes is on the sentence level, and the changes are predominantly by addition and deletion. But, unlike the students, experienced writers make changes on all levels and use all revision operations. Moreover, the operations the students fail to use—reordering and addition—seem to require a theory of the revision process as a totality—a theory which, in fact, encompasses the *whole* of the composition. Unlike the students, the experienced writers possess a nonlinear theory in which a sense of the whole writing both precedes and grows out of an examination of the parts. As we saw, one writer said he needed "a first draft to figure out what to say," and "a second draft to see the structure of an argument buried beneath the surface." Such a "theory" is both theoretical and strategical; once again, strategy and theory are conflated in ways that are literally impossible for the linear model. Writing appears to be more like a seed than a line.

Two elements of the experienced writers' theory of the revision process are the adoption of a holistic perspective and the perception that revision is a

---

[9] *Course in General Linguistics,* trans. Wade Baskin (New York, 1966), p. 119.
[10]Jonathan Culler, *Saussure* (Penguin Modern Masters Series; London: Penguin Books, 1976), p. 70.

recursive process. The writers ask: what does my essay as a *whole* need for form, balance, rhythm, or communication. Details are added, dropped, substituted, or reordered according to their sense of what the essay needs for emphasis and proportion. This sense, however, is constantly in flux as ideas are developed and modified; it is constantly "reviewed" in relation to the parts. As their ideas change, revision becomes an attempt to make their writing consonant with that changing vision.

The experienced writers see their revision process as a recursive process—a process with significant recurring activities—with different levels of attention and different agenda for each cycle. During the first revision cycle their attention is primarily directed towards narrowing the topic and delimiting their ideas. At this point, they are not as concerned as they are later about vocabulary and style. The experienced writers explained that they get closer to their meaning by not limiting themselves too early to lexical concerns. As one writer commented to explain her revision process, a comment inspired by the summer 1977 New York power failure: "I feel like Con Edison cutting off certain states to keep the generators going. In first and second drafts, I try to cut off as much as I can of my editing generator, and in a third draft, I try to cut off some of my idea generators, so I can make sure that I will actually finish the essay." Although the experienced writers describe their revision process as a series of different levels or cycles, it is inaccurate to assume that they have only one objective for each cycle and that each cycle can be defined by a different objective. The same objectives and sub-processes are present in each cycle, but in different proportions. Even though these experienced writers place the predominant weight upon finding the form of their argument during the first cycle, other concerns exist as well. Conversely, during the later cycles, when the experienced writers' primary attention is focused upon stylistic concerns, they are still attuned, although in a reduced way, to the form of the argument. Since writers are limited in what they can attend to during each cycle (understandings are temporal), revision strategies help balance competing demands on attention. Thus, writers can concentrate on more than one objective at a time by developing strategies to sort out and organize their different concerns in successive cycles of revision.

It is a sense of writing as discovery—a repeated process of beginning over again, starting out new—that the students failed to have. I have used the notion of dissonance because such dissonance, the incongruities between intention and execution, governs both writing and meaning. Students do not see the incongruities. They need to rely on their own internalized sense of good writing and to see their writing with their "own" eyes. Seeing in revision—seeing beyond hearing—is at the root of the word *revision* and the process itself; current dicta on revising blind our students to what is actually involved in revision. In fact, they blind them to what constitutes good writing altogether. Good writing disturbs: it creates dissonance. Students need to seek the dissonance of discovery, utilizing in their writing, as the experienced writers do, the very difference between writing and speech—the possibility of revision.

Rigid Rules, Inflexible Plans, and the Stifling of Language: A Cognitivist Analysis of Writer's Block

by Mike Rose

Ruth will labor over the first paragraph of an essay for hours. She'll write a sentence, then erase it. Try another, then scratch part of it out. Finally, as the evening winds on toward ten o'clock and Ruth, anxious about tomorrow's deadline, begins to wind into herself, she'll compose that first paragraph only to sit back and level her favorite exasperated interdiction at herself and her page: "No. You can't say that. You'll bore them to death."

Ruth is one of ten UCLA undergraduates with whom I discussed writer's block, that frustrating, self-defeating inability to generate the next line, the right phrase, the sentence that will release the flow of words once again. These ten people represented a fair cross-section of the UCLA student community: lower-middle-class to upper-middle-class backgrounds and high schools, third-world and Caucasian origins, biology to fine arts majors, C+ to A- grade point averages, enthusiastic to blasé attitudes toward school. They were set off from the community by the twin facts that all ten could write competently, and all were currently enrolled in at least one course that required a significant amount of writing. They were set off among themselves by the fact that five of them wrote with relative to enviable ease while the other five experienced moderate to nearly immobilizing writer's block. This blocking usually resulted in rushed, often late papers and resultant grades that did not truly reflect these students' writing ability. And then, of course, there were other less measurable but probably more serious results: a growing distrust of their abilities and an aversion toward the composing process itself.

What separated the five students who blocked from those who didn't? It wasn't skill; that was held fairly constant. The answer could have rested in the emotional realm—anxiety, fear of evaluation, insecurity, etc. Or perhaps blocking in some way resulted from variation in cognitive style. Perhaps, too, blocking originated in and typified a melding of emotion and cognition not unlike the relationship posited by Shapiro between neurotic feeling and neurotic thinking.[1] Each of these was possible. Extended clinical interviews

---

Reprinted from *College Composition and Communication* (December 1980). Copyright 1980 by the National Council of Teachers of English. Reprinted with permission.
[1] David Shapiro, *Neurotic Styles* (New York: Basic Books, 1965).

and testing could have teased out the answer. But there was one answer that surfaced readily in brief explorations of these students' writing processes. It was not profoundly emotional, nor was it embedded in that still unclear construct of cognitive style. It was constant, surprising, almost amusing if its results weren't so troublesome, and, in the final analysis, obvious: the five students who experienced blocking were all operating either with writing rules or with planning strategies that impeded rather than enhanced the composing process. The five students who were not hampered by writer's block also utilized rules, but they were less rigid ones, and thus more appropriate to a complex process like writing. Also, the plans these non-blockers brought to the writing process were more functional, more flexible, more open to information from the outside.

These observations are the result of one to three interviews with each student. I used recent notes, drafts, and finished compositions to direct and hone my questions. This procedure is admittedly non-experimental, certainly more clinical than scientific; still, it did lead to several inferences that lay the foundation for future, more rigorous investigation: (a) composing is a highly complex problem-solving process[2] and (b) certain disruptions of that process can be explained with cognitive psychology's problem-solving framework. Such investigation might include a study using "stimulated recall" techniques to validate or disconfirm these hunches. In such a study, blockers and non-blockers would write essays. Their activity would be videotaped and, immediately after writing, they would be shown their respective tapes and questioned about the rules, plans, and beliefs operating in their writing behavior. This procedure would bring us close to the composing process (the writers' recall is stimulated by their viewing the tape), yet would not interfere with actual composing.

In the next section I will introduce several key concepts in the problem-solving literature. In section three I will let the students speak for themselves. Fourth, I will offer a cognitivist analysis of blockers' and non-blockers' grace or torpor. I will close with a brief note on treatment.

Selected Concepts in Problem Solving: Rules and Plans

As diverse as theories of problem solving are, they share certain basic assumptions and characteristics. Each posits an *introductory period* during which a problem is presented, and all theorists, from Behaviorist to Gestalt to Information Processing, admit that certain aspects, stimuli, or "functions" of the problem must become or be made salient and attended to in certain ways if successful problem-solving processes are to be engaged. Theorists also believe that some conflict, some stress, some gap in information in these

---

[2] Barbara Hayes-Ruth, a Rand cognitive psychologist, and I are currently developing an information-processing model of the composing process. A good deal of work has already been done by Linda Flower and John Hayes (see p. 90 of this article) I have just received—and recommend—their "Writing as Problem Solving" (paper presented at American Educational Research Association, April, 1979).

perceived "aspects" seems to trigger problem-solving behavior. Next comes a *processing period,* and for all the variance of opinion about this critical stage, theorists recognize the necessity of its existence—recognize that man, at the least, somehow "weighs" possible solutions as they are stumbled upon and, at the most, goes through an elaborate and sophisticated information-processing routine to achieve problem solution. Furthermore, theorists believe—to varying degrees—that past learning and the particular "set," direction, or orientation that the problem solver takes in dealing with past experience and present stimuli have critical bearing on the efficacy of solution. Finally, all theorists admit to a *solution period,* an end-state of the process where "stress" and "search" terminate, an answer is attained, and a sense of completion or "closure" is experienced.

These are the gross similarities, and the framework they offer will be useful in understanding the problem-solving behavior of the students discussed in this paper. But since this paper is primarily concerned with the second stage of problem-solving operations, it would be most useful to focus this introduction on two critical constructs in the processing period: rules and plans.

Rules

Robert M. Gagné defines "rule" as "an inferred capability that enables the individual to respond to a class of stimulus situations with a class of perform-ances."[3] Rules can be learned directly[4] or by inference through experience.[5] But, in either case, most problem-solving theorists would affirm Gagné's dictum that "rules are probably the major organizing factor, and quite possibly the primary one, in intellectual functioning."[6] As Gagné implies, we wouldn't be able to function without rules; they guide response to the myriad stimuli that confront us daily, and might even be the central element in complex problem-solving behavior.

Dunker, Polya, and Miller, Galanter, and Pribram offer a very useful distinction between two general kinds of rules: algorithms and heuristics.[7] Algorithms are precise rules that will always result in a specific answer if

---

[3] *The Conditions of Learning* (New York: Holt, Rinehart and Winston, 1970), p. 193.
[4] E. James Archer, "The Psychological Nature of Concepts," in H. J. Klausmeier and C. W. Harris, eds., *Analysis of Concept Learning* (New York: Academic Press, 1966), pp. 37-44; David P. Ausubel, *The Psychology of Meaningful Verbal Behavior* (New York: Grune and Stratton, 1963); Robert M. Gagné, "Problem Solving," in Arthur W. Melton, ed., *Categories of Human Learning* (New York: Academic Press, 1964), pp. 293-317; George A. Miller, *Language and Communication* (New York: McGraw-Hill, 1951).
[5] George Katona, *Organizing and Memorizing* (New York: Columbia Univ. Press, 1940); Roger N. Shepard, Carl I. Hovland, and Herbert M. Jenkins, "Learning and Memorization of Classifications," *Psychological Monographs*, 75, No. 13 (1961) (entire No. 517); Robert S. Woodworth, *Dynamics of Behavior* (New York: Henry Holt, 1958), chs. 10-12.
[6] *The Conditions of Learning*, pp. 190-91.
[7] Karl Dunker, "On Problem Solving," *Psychological Monographs*, 58, No. 5 (1945) (entire No. 270); George A. Polya, *How to Solve It* (Princeton: Princeton University Press, 1945); George A. Miller, Eugene Galanter, and Karl H. Pribram, *Plans and the Structure of Behavior* (New York: Henry Holt, 1960).

applied to an appropriate problem. Most mathematical rules, for example, are algorithms. Functions are constant (e.g., pi), procedures are routine (squaring the radius), and outcomes are completely predictable. However, few day-to-day situations are mathematically circumscribed enough to warrant the application of algorithms. Most often we function with the aid of fairly general heuristics or "rules of thumb," guidelines that allow varying degrees of flexibility when approaching problems. Rather than operating with algorithmic precision and certainty, we search, critically, through alternatives, using our heuristic as a divining rod—"if a math problem stumps you, try working backwards to solution"; "if the car won't start, check x, y, or z, and so forth. Heuristics won't allow the precision or the certitude afforded by algorithmic operations; heuristics can even be so "loose" as to be vague. But in a world where tasks and problems are rarely mathematically precise, heuristic rules become the most appropriate, the most functional rules available to us: "a heuristic does not guarantee the optimal solution or, indeed, any solution at all; rather, heuristics offer solutions that are good enough most of the time."[8]

Plans

People don't proceed through problem situations, in or out of a laboratory, without some set of internalized instructions to the self, some program, some course of action that, even roughly, takes goals and possible paths to that goal into consideration. Miller, Galanter, and Pribram have referred to this course of action as a plan: "A plan is any hierarchical process in the organism that can control the order in which a sequence of operations is to be performed" (p. 16). They name the fundamental plan in human problem-solving behavior the TOTE, with the initial T representing a *test* that matches a possible solution against the perceived end-goal of problem completion. O represents the clearance to *operate* if the comparison between solution and goal indicates that the solution is a sensible one. The second T represents a further, post-operation, *test* or comparison of solution with goal, and if the two mesh and problem solution is at hand the person *exits* (E) from problem-solving behavior. If the second test presents further discordance between solution and goal, a further solution is attempted in TOTE-fashion. Such plans can be both long-term and global and, as problem solving is underway, short-term and immediate.[9] Though the mechanicality of this information-processing model renders it simplistic and, possibly, unreal, the central notion of a plan and an operating procedure is an important one in problem-solving theory; it at least attempts to metaphorically explain what earlier cognitive psychologists could

---

[8] Lyle E. Bourne, Jr., Bruce R. Ekstrand, and Roger L. Dominowski, *The Psychology of Thinking* (Engle-wood Cliffs, NJ.: Prentice-Hall, 1971).
[9] John R. Hayes, "Problem Topology and the Solution Process," in Carl P. Duncan, ed., *Thinking: Current Experimental Studies* (Philadelphia: Lippincott, 1967), pp. 167-81.

not—the mental procedures (see pp. 86-87) underlying problem-solving behavior.

Before concluding this section, a distinction between heuristic rules and plans should be attempted; it is a distinction often blurred in the literature, blurred because, after all, we are very much in the area of gestating theory and preliminary models. Heuristic rules seem to function with the flexibility of plans. Is, for example, "If the car won't start, try x, y, or z" a heuristic or a plan? It could be either, though two qualifications will mark it as heuristic rather than plan. (A) Plans subsume and sequence heuristic and algorithmic rules. Rules are usually "smaller," more discrete cognitive capabilities; plans can become quite large and complex, composed of a series of ordered algorithms, heuristics, and further planning "sub-routines." (B) Plans, as was mentioned earlier, include criteria to determine successful goal-attainment and, as well, include "feedback" processes—ways to incorporate and use information gained from "tests" of potential solutions against desired goals.

One other distinction should be made: that is, between "set" and plan. Set, also called "determining tendency" or "readiness,"[10] refers to the fact that people often approach problems with habitual ways of reacting, a predisposition, a tendency to perceive or function in one way rather than another. Set, which can be established through instructions or, consciously or unconsciously, through experience, can assist performance if it is appropriate to a specific problem,[11] but much of the literature on set has shown its rigidifying, dysfunctional effects.[12] Set differs from plan in that set represents a limiting and narrowing of response alternatives with no inherent process to shift alternatives. It is a kind of cognitive habit that can limit perception, not a course of action with multiple paths that directs and sequences response possibilities.

The constructs of rules and plans advance the understanding of problem solving beyond that possible with earlier, less developed formulations. Still, critical problems remain. Though mathematical and computer models move one toward more complex (and thus more real) problems than the earlier research, they are still too neat, too rigidly sequenced to approximate the stunning complexity of day-to-day (not to mention highly creative) problem-solving behavior. Also, information-processing models of problem-solving are built on logic theorems, chess strategies, and simple planning tasks. Even

---

[10]Hulda J. Rees and Harold E. Israel, "An Investigation of the Establishment and Operation of Mental Sets," *Psychological Monographs*, 46 (1925) (entire No. 210).

[11]Ibid.; Melvin H. Marx, Wilton W. Murphy, and Aaron J. Brownstein, "Recognition of Complex Visual Stimuli as a Function of Training with Abstracted Patterns," *Journal of Experimental Psychology*, 62 (1961), 456-60.

[12]James L. Adams, *Conceptual Blockbusting* (San Francisco: W. H. Freeman, 1974); Edward DeBono, *New Think* (New York: Basic Books, 1958); Ronald H. Forgus, *Perception* (New York: McGraw-Hill, 1966), ch. 13; Abraham Luchins and Edith Hirsch Luchins, *Rigidity of Behavior* (Eugene: Univ. of Oregon Books, 1959); N. R. F. Maier, "Reasoning in Humans. I. On Direction," *Journal of Comparative Psychology*, 10 (1920), 115-43.

Gagné seems to feel more comfortable with illustrations from mathematics and science rather than with social science and humanities problems. So although these complex models and constructs tell us a good deal about problem-solving behavior, they are still laboratory simulations, still invoked from the outside rather than self-generated, and still founded on the mathematico-logical.

Two Carnegie-Mellon researchers, however, have recently extended the above into a truly real, amorphous, unmathematical problem-solving process —writing. Relying on protocol analysis (thinking aloud while solving problems), Linda Flower and John Hayes have attempted to tease out the role of heuristic rules and plans in writing behavior.[13] Their research pushes problem-solving investigations to the real and complex and pushes, from the other end, the often mysterious process of writing toward the explainable. The latter is important, for at least since Plotinus many have viewed the composing process as unexplainable, inspired, infused with the transcendent. But Flower and Hayes are beginning, anyway, to show how writing generates from a problem-solving process with rich heuristic rules and plans of its own. They show, as well, how many writing problems arise from a paucity of heuristics and suggest an intervention that provides such rules.

This paper, too, treats writing as a problem-solving process, focusing, however, on what happens when the process dead-ends in writer's block. It will further suggest that, as opposed to Flower and Hayes' students who need more rules and plans, blockers may well be stymied by possessing rigid or inappropriate rules, or inflexible or confused plans. Ironically enough, these are occasionally instilled by the composition teacher or gleaned from the writing textbook.

"Always Grab Your Audience"—The Blockers

In high school, *Ruth* was told and told again that a good essay always grabs a reader's attention immediately. Until you can make your essay do that, her teachers and textbooks putatively declaimed, there is no need to go on. For Ruth, this means that beginning bland and seeing what emerges as one generates prose is unacceptable. The beginning is everything. And what exactly is the audience seeking that reads this beginning? The rule, or Ruth's use of it, doesn't provide for such investigation. She has an edict with no determiners. Ruth operates with another rule that restricts her productions as well: if sentences aren't grammatically "correct," they aren't useful. This keeps Ruth from toying with ideas on paper, from the kind of linguistic play that often frees up the flow of prose. These two rules converge in a way that pretty effectively restricts Ruth's composing process.

---

[13]"Plans and the Cognitive Process of Writing," paper presented at the National Institute of Education Writing Conference, June 1977; "Problem Solving Strategies and the Writing Process," *College English*, 39 (1977), 449-61. See also footnote 2.

The first two papers I received from *Laurel* were weeks overdue. Sections of them were well written; there were even moments of stylistic flair. But the papers were late and, overall, the prose seemed rushed. Furthermore, one paper included a paragraph on an issue that was never mentioned in the topic paragraph. This was the kind of mistake that someone with Laurel's apparent ability doesn't make. I asked her about this irrelevant passage. She knew very well that it didn't fit, but believed she had to include it to round out the paper. "You must always make three or more points in an essay. If the essay has less, then it's not strong." Laurel had been taught this rule both in high school and in her first college English class; no wonder, then, that she accepted its validity.

As opposed to Laurel, *Martha* possesses a whole arsenal of plans and rules with which to approach a humanities writing assignment, and, considering her background in biology, I wonder how many of them were formed out of the assumptions and procedures endemic to the physical sciences.[14] Martha will not put pen to first draft until she has spent up to two days generating an outline of remarkable complexity. I saw one of these outlines and it looked more like a diagram of protein synthesis or DNA structure than the timeworn pattern offered in composition textbooks. I must admit I was intrigued by the aura of process (vs. the static appearance of essay outlines) such diagrams offer, but for Martha these "outlines" only led to self-defeat: the outline would become so complex that all of its elements could never be included in a short essay. In other words, her plan locked her into the first stage of the composing process. Martha would struggle with the conversion of her outline into prose only to scrap the whole venture when deadlines passed and a paper had to be rushed together.

Martha's "rage for order" extends beyond the outlining process. She also believes that elements of a story or poem must evince a fairly linear structure and thematic clarity, or—perhaps bringing us closer to the issue—that analysis of a story or poem must provide the linearity or clarity that seems to be absent in the text. Martha, therefore, will bend the logic of her analysis to reason ambiguity out of existence. When I asked her about a strained paragraph in her paper on Camus' "The Guest," she said, "I didn't want to admit that it [the story's conclusion] was just hanging. I tried to force it into meaning."

Martha uses another rule, one that is not only problematical in itself, but one that often clashes directly with the elaborate plan and obsessive rule above. She believes that humanities papers must scintillate with insight, must present an array of images, ideas, ironies gleaned from the literature under

---

[14]Jane, a student not discussed in this paper, was surprised to find out that a topic paragraph can be rewritten after a paper's conclusion to make that paragraph reflect what the essay truly contains. She had gotten so indoctrinated with Psychology's (her major) insistence that a hypothesis be formulated and then left untouched before an experiment begins that she thought revision of one's "major premise" was somehow illegal. She had formed a rule out of her exposure to social science methodology, and the rule was totally inappropriate for most writing situations.

examination. A problem arises, of course, when Martha tries to incorporate her myriad "neat little things," often inherently unrelated, into a tightly structured, carefully sequenced essay. Plans and rules that govern the construction of impressionistic, associational prose would be appropriate to Martha's desire, but her composing process is heavily constrained by the non-impressionistic and non-associational. Put another way, the plans and rules that govern her exploration of text are not at all synchronous with the plans and rules she uses to discuss her exploration. It is interesting to note here, however, that as recently as three years ago Martha was absorbed in creative writing and was publishing poetry in high school magazines. Given what we know about the complex associational, often non-neatly-sequential nature of the poet's creative process, we can infer that Martha was either free of the plans and rules discussed earlier or they were not as intense. One wonders, as well, if the exposure to three years of university physical science either established or intensified Martha's concern with structure. Whatever the case, she now is hamstrung by conflicting rules when composing papers for the humanities.

Mike's difficulties, too, are rooted in a distortion of the problem-solving process. When the time of the week for the assignment of writing topics draws near, Mike begins to prepare material, strategies, and plans that he believes will be appropriate. If the assignment matches his expectations, he has done a good job of analyzing the professor's intentions. If the assignment *doesn't* match his expectations, however, he cannot easily shift approaches. He feels trapped inside his original plans, cannot generate alternatives, and blocks. As the deadline draws near, he will write something, forcing the assignment to fit his conceptual procrustian bed. Since Mike is a smart man, he will offer a good deal of information, but only some of it ends up being appropriate to the assignment. This entire situation is made all the worse when the time between assignment of topic and generation of product is attenuated further, as in an essay examination. Mike believes (correctly) that one must have a plan, a strategy of some sort in order to solve a problem. He further believes, however, that such a plan, once formulated, becomes an exact structural and substantive blueprint that cannot be violated. The plan offers no alternatives, no "sub-routines." So, whereas Ruth's, Laurel's, and some of Martha's difficulties seem to be rule-specific ("always catch your audience," "write grammatically"), Mike's troubles are more global. He may have strategies that are appropriate for various writing situations (e.g., "for this kind of political science assignment write a compare/contrast essay"), but his entire approach to formulating plans and carrying them through to problem solution is too mechanical. It is probable that Mike's behavior is governed by an explicitly learned or inferred rule: "Always try to 'psych out' a professor." But in this case this rule initiates a problem-solving procedure that is clearly dysfunctional.

While Ruth and Laurel use rules that impede their writing process and Mike utilizes a problem-solving procedure that hamstrings him, *Sylvia* has trouble deciding which of the many rules she possesses to use. Her problem can be characterized as cognitive perplexity: some of her rules are inappropriate, others are functional; some mesh nicely with her own definitions of good writing, others don't. She has multiple rules to invoke, multiple paths to follow, and that very complexity of choice virtually paralyzes her. More so than with the previous four students, there is probably a strong emotional dimension to Sylvia's blocking, but the cognitive difficulties are clear and perhaps modifiable.

Sylvia, somewhat like Ruth and Laurel, puts tremendous weight on the crafting of her first paragraph. If it is good, she believes the rest of the essay will be good. Therefore, she will spend up to five hours on the initial paragraph: "I won't go on until I get that first paragraph down." Clearly, this rule—or the strength of it—blocks Sylvia's production. This is one problem. Another is that Sylvia has other equally potent rules that she sees as separate, uncomplementary injunctions: one achieves "flow" in one's writing through the use of adquate transitions; one achieves substance to one's writing through the use of evidence. Sylvia perceives both rules to be "true," but several times followed one to the exclusion of the other. Furthermore, as I talked to Sylvia, many other rules, guidelines, definitions were offered, but none with conviction. While she is committed to one rule about initial paragraphs, and that rule is dysfunctional, she seems very uncertain about the weight and hierarchy of the remaining rules in her cognitive repertoire.

"If It Won't Fit My Work, I'll Change It"—The Non-blockers

Dale, Ellen, Debbie, Susan, and Miles all write with the aid of rules. But their rules differ from blockers' rules in significant ways. If similar in content, they are expressed less absolutely—e.g., "*Try* to keep audience in mind." If dissimilar, they are still expressed less absolutely, more heuristically—e.g., "I can use as many ideas in my thesis paragraph as I need and then develop paragraphs for each idea." Our non-blockers do express some rules with firm assurance, but these tend to be simple injunctions that free up rather than restrict the composing process, e.g., "When stuck, write!" or "I'll write what I can." And finally, at least three of the students openly shun the very textbook rules that some blockers adhere to: e.g., "Rules like 'write only what you know about' just aren't true. I ignore those." These three, in effect, have formulated a further rule that expresses something like: "If a rule conflicts with what is sensible or with experience, reject it."

On the broader level of plans and strategies, these five students also differ from at least three of the five blockers in that they all possess problem-solving plans that are quite functional. Interestingly, on first exploration these plans seem to be too broad or fluid to be useful and, in some cases, can barely be expressed with any precision. Ellen, for example, admits that she has a general "outline in [her] head about how a topic paragraph should look" but could not describe much about its structure. Susan also has a general plan to follow, but, if stymied, will quickly attempt to conceptualize the assignment in different ways: "If my original idea won't work, then I need to proceed differently." Whether or not these plans operate in TOTE-fashion, I can't say. But they do operate with the operate-test fluidity of TOTEs.

True, our non-blockers have their religiously adhered-to rules: e.g., "When stuck, write," and plans, "I couldn't imagine writing without this pattern," but as noted above, these are few and functional. Otherwise, these non-blockers operate with fluid, easily modified, even easily discarded rules and plans (Ellen: "I can throw things out") that are sometimes expressed with a vagueness that could almost be interpreted as ignorance. There lies the irony. Students that offer the least precise rules and plans have the least trouble composing. Perhaps this very lack of precision characterizes the functional composing plan. But perhaps this lack of precision simply masks habitually enacted alternatives and sub-routines. This is clearly an area that needs the illumination of further research.

And then there is feedback. At least three of the five non-blockers are an Information-Processor's dream. They get to know their audience, ask professors and T.A.s specific questions about assignments, bring half-finished products in for evaluation, etc. Like Ruth, they realize the importance of audience, but unlike her, they have specific strategies for obtaining and utilizing feedback. And this penchant for testing writing plans against the needs of the audience can lead to modification of rules and plans. Listen to Debbie:

> In high school I was given a formula that stated that you must write a thesis paragraph with *only* three points in it, and then develop each of those points. When I hit college I was given longer assignments. That stuck me for a bit, but then I realized that I could use as many ideas in my thesis paragraph as I needed and then develop paragraphs for each one. I asked someone about this and then tried it. I didn't get any negative feedback, so I figured it was o.k.

Debbie's statement brings one last difference between our blockers and non-blockers into focus; it has been implied above, but needs specific formulation: the goals these people have, and the plans they generate to attain these goals, are quite mutable. Part of the mutability comes from the fluid way the goals and plans are conceived, and part of it arises from the effective impact of feedback on these goals and plans.

Analyzing Writer's Block

Algorithms Rather Than Heuristics

In most cases, the rules our blockers use are not "wrong" or "incorrect"—it is good practice, for example, to "grab your audience with a catchy opening" or "craft a solid first paragraph before going on." The problem is that these rules seem to be followed as though they were algorithms, absolute dicta, rather than the loose heuristics that they were intended to be. Either through instruction, or the power of the textbook, or the predilections of some of our blockers for absolutes, or all three, these useful rules of thumb have been transformed into near-algorithmic urgencies. The result, to paraphrase Karl Dunker, is that these rules do not allow a flexible penetration into the nature of the problem. It is this transformation of heuristic into algorithm that contributes to the writer's block of Ruth and Laurel.

Questionable Heuristics Made Algorithmic

Whereas "grab your audience" could be a useful heuristic, "always make three or more points in an essay" is a pretty questionable one. Any such rule, though probably taught to aid the writer who needs structure, ultimately transforms a highly fluid process like writing into a mechanical lockstep. As heuristics, such rules can be troublesome. As algorithms, they are simply incorrect.

Set

As with any problem-solving task, students approach writing assignments with a variety of orientations or sets. Some are functional, others are not. Martha and Jane (see footnote 14), coming out of the life sciences and social sciences respectively, bring certain methodological orientations with them—certain sets or "directions" that make composing for the humanities a difficult, sometimes confusing, task. In fact, this orientation may cause them to misperceive the task. Martha has formulated a planning strategy from her predisposition to see processes in terms of linear, interrelated steps in a system. Jane doesn't realize that she can revise the statement that "committed" her to the direction her essay has taken. Both of these students are stymied because of formative experiences associated with their majors—experiences, perhaps, that nicely reinforce our very strong tendency to organize experiences temporally.

The Plan That Is Not a Plan

If fluidity and multi-directionality are central to the nature of plans, then the plans that Mike formulates are not true plans at all but, rather, inflexible and static cognitive blueprints.[15] Put another way, Mike's "plans" represent a restricted "closed system" (vs. "open system") kind of thinking, where closed system thinking is defined as focusing on "a limited number of units or items, or members, and those properties of the members which are to be used are known to begin with and do not change as the thinking proceeds," and open system thinking is characterized by an "adventurous exploration of multiple alternatives with strategies that allow redirection once 'dead ends' are

---

[15]Cf. "A plan is flexible if the order of execution of its parts can be easily interchanged without affecting the feasibility of the plan . . . the flexible planner might tend to think of lists of things he had to do; the inflexible planner would have his time planned like a sequence of cause-effect relations. The former could rearrange his lists to suit his opportunities, but the latter would be unable to strike while the iron was hot and would generally require considerable 'lead-time' before he could incorporate any alternative sub-plans" (Miller, Galanter, and Pribram, p. 120).

encountered."[16] Composing calls for open, even adventurous thinking, not for constrained, no-exit cognition.

Feedback

The above difficulties are made all the more problematic by the fact that they seem resistant to or isolated from corrective feedback. One of the most striking things about Dale, Debbie, and Miles is the ease with which they seek out, interpret, and apply feedback on their rules, plans, and productions. They "operate" and then they "test," and the testing is not only against some internalized goal, but against the requirements of external audience as well.

Too Many Rules—"Conceptual Conflict"

According to D. E. Berlyne, one of the primary forces that motivate problem-solving behavior is a curiosity that arises from conceptual conflict—the convergence of incompatible beliefs or ideas. In *Structure and Direction in Thinking,* [17] Berlyne presents six major types of conceptual conflict, the second of which he terms "perplexity":

> This kind of conflict occurs when there are factors inclining the subject toward each of a set of mutually exclusive beliefs. (p. 257)

If one substitutes "rules" for "beliefs" in the above definition, perplexity becomes a useful notion here. Because perplexity is unpleasant, people are motivated to reduce it by problem-solving behavior that can result in "disequalization":

> Degree of conflict will be reduced if either the number of competing . . . [rules] or their nearness to equality of strength is reduced. (p. 259)

But "disequalization" is not automatic. As I have suggested, Martha and Sylvia hold to rules that conflict, but their perplexity does *not* lead to curiosity and resultant problem-solving behavior. Their perplexity, contra Berlyne, leads to immobilization. Thus "disequalization" will have to be effected from without. The importance of each of, particularly, Sylvia's rules needs an evaluation that will aid her in rejecting some rules and balancing and sequencing others.

A Note On Treatment

Rather than get embroiled in a blocker's misery, the teacher or tutor might interview the student in order to build a writing history and profile: How much and what kind of writing was done in high school? What is the student's major? What kind of writing does it require? How does the student compose? Are there rough drafts or outlines available? By what rules does the student operate? How would he or she define "good" writing? etc. This sort

---

[16]Frederic Bartlett, *Thinking* (New York: Basic Books, 1958), pp. 74-76.
[17]*Structure and Direction in Thinking* (New York: John Wiley, 1965), p. 255.

of interview reveals an incredible amount of information about individual composing processes. Furthermore, it often reveals the rigid rule or the inflexible plan that may lie at the base of the student's writing problem. That was precisely what happened with the five blockers. And with Ruth, Laurel, and Martha (and Jane) what was revealed made virtually immediate remedy possible. Dysfunctional rules are easily replaced with or counter-balanced by functional ones if there is no emotional reason to hold onto that which simply doesn't work. Furthermore, students can be trained to select, to "know which rules are appropriate for which problems."[18] Mike's difficulties, perhaps because plans are more complex and pervasive than rules, took longer to correct. But inflexible plans, too, can be remedied by pointing out their dysfunctional qualities and by assisting the student in developing appropriate and flexible alternatives. Operating this way, I was successful with Mike. Sylvia's story, however, did not end as smoothly. Though I had three forty-five minute contacts with her, I was not able to appreciably alter her behavior. Berlyne's theory bore results with Martha but not with Sylvia. Her rules were in conflict, and perhaps that conflict was not exclusively cognitive. Her case keeps analyses like these honest; it reminds us that the cognitive often melds with, and can be overpowered by, the affective. So while Ruth, Laurel, Martha, and Mike could profit from tutorials that explore the rules and plans in their writing behavior, students like Sylvia may need more extended, more affectively oriented counseling sessions that blend the instructional with the psychodynamic.

---

[18]Flower and Hayes, "Plans and the Cognitive Process of Writing," p. 26.

Understanding Composing

by Sondra Perl

> Any psychological process, whether the development of thought or voluntary behavior, is a process undergoing changes right before one's eyes.... Under certain conditions it becomes possible to trace this development.[1]
>
> –L. S. Vygotsky

> It's hard to begin this case study of myself as a writer because even as I'm searching for a beginning, a pattern of organization, I'm watching myself, trying to understand my behavior. As I sit here in silence, I can see lots of things happening that never made it onto my tapes. My mind leaps from the task at hand to what I need at the vegetable stand for tonight's soup to the threatening rain outside to ideas voiced in my writing group this morning, but in between "distractions" I hear myself trying out words I might use. It's as if the extraneous thoughts are a counterpoint to the more steady attention I'm giving to composing. This is all to point out that the process is more complex than I'm aware of, but I think my tapes reveal certain basic patterns that I tend to follow.
>
> –Anne
> New York City Teacher

Anne is a teacher of writing. In 1979, she was among a group of twenty teachers who were taking a course in research and basic writing at New York University.[2] One of the assignments in the course was for the teachers to tape their thoughts while composing aloud on the topic, "My Most Anxious Moment as a Writer." Everyone in the group was given the topic in the morning during class and told to compose later on that day in a place where they would be comfortable and relatively free from distractions. The result was a tape of composing aloud and a written product that formed the basis for class discussion over the next few days.

One of the purposes of this assignment was to provide teachers with an

---

Reprinted from *College Composition and Communication* (December 1980). Copyright 1980 by the National Council of Teachers of English. Reprinted with permission.

[1] L. S. Vygotsky, *Mind in Society,* trans. M. Cole, V. John-Steiner, S. Scribner, and E. Souberman (Cambridge, Mass: Harvard University Press, 1978), p. 61.

[2] This course was team-taught by myself and Gordon Pradl, Associate Professor of English Education at New York University.

opportunity to see their own composing processes at work. From the start of the course, we recognized that we were controlling the situation by assigning a topic and that we might be altering the process by asking writers to compose aloud. Nonetheless we viewed the task as a way of capturing some of the flow of composing and, as Anne later observed in her analysis of her tape, she was able to detect certain basic patterns. This observation, made not only by Anne, then leads me to ask "What basic patterns seem to occur during composing?" and "What does this type of research have to tell us about the nature of the composing process?"

Perhaps the most challenging part of the answer is the recognition of recursiveness in writing. In recent years, many researchers including myself have questioned the traditional notion that writing is a linear process with a strict plan-write-revise sequence.[3] In its stead, we have advocated the idea that writing is a recursive process, that throughout the process of writing, writers return to substrands of the overall process, or subroutines (short successions of steps that yield results on which the writer draws in taking the next set of steps); writers use these to keep the process moving forward. In other words, recursiveness in writing implies that there is a forward-moving action that exists by virtue of a backward-moving action. The questions that then need to be answered are, "To what do writers move back?" "What exactly is being repeated?" "What recurs?"

To answer these questions, it is important to look at what writers do while writing and what an analysis of their processes reveals. The descriptions that follow are based on my own observations of the composing processes of many types of writers including college students, graduate students, and English teachers like Anne.

Writing does appear to be recursive, yet the parts that recur seem to vary from writer to writer and from topic to topic. Furthermore, some recursive elements are easy to spot while others are not.

1) The most visible recurring feature or backward movement involves rereading little bits of discourse. Few writers I have seen write for long periods of time without returning briefly to what is already down on the page.

For some, like Anne, rereading occurs after every few phrases; for others, it occurs after every sentence; more frequently, it occurs after a "chunk" of information has been written. Thus, the unit that is reread is not necessarily a syntactic one, but rather a semantic one as defined by the writer.

2) The second recurring feature is some key word or item called up by the topic. Writers consistently return to their notion of the topic throughout the process of writing. Particularly when they are stuck, writers seem to use the topic or a key word in it as a way to get going again. Thus many times it is

---

[3] See Janet Emig, *The Composing Processes of Twelfth-Graders*, NCTE Research Report No. 13 (Urbana, Ill: National Council of Teachers of English, 1971); Linda Flower and J. R. Hayes, "The Cognition of Discovery," *CCC*, 31 (February, 1980), 21-32; Nancy Sommers, "The Need for Theory in Composition Research," *CCC*, 30 (February, 1979), 46-49.

possible to see writers "going back," rereading the topic they were given, changing it to suit what they have been writing or changing what they have written to suit their notion of the topic.

3) There is also a third backward movement in writing, one that is not so easy to document. It is not easy because the move, itself, cannot immediately be identified with words. In fact, the move is not to any words on the page nor to the topic but to feelings or non-verbalized perceptions that *surround* the words, or to what the words already present *evoke* in the writer. The move draws on sense experience, and it can be observed if one pays close attention to what happens when writers pause and seem to listen or otherwise react to what is inside of them. The move occurs inside the writer, to what is physically felt. The term used to describe this focus of writers' attention is *felt sense*. The term "felt sense" has been coined and described by Eugene Gendlin, a philosopher at the University of Chicago. In his words, felt sense is

> the soft underbelly of thought ... a kind of bodily awareness that ... can be used as a tool ... a bodily awareness that ... encompasses everything you feel and know about a given subject at a given time. ... It is felt in the body, yet it has meanings. It is body *and* mind before they are split apart.[4]

This felt sense is always there, within us. It is unifying, and yet, when we bring words to it, it can break apart, shift, unravel, and become something else. Gendlin has spent many years showing people how to work with their felt sense. Here I am making connections between what he has done and what I have seen happen as people write.

When writers are given a topic, the topic itself evokes a felt sense in them. This topic calls forth images, words, ideas, and vague fuzzy feelings that are anchored in the writer's body. What is elicited, then, is not solely the product of a mind but of a mind alive in a living, sensing body.

When writers pause, when they go back and repeat key words, what they seem to be doing is waiting, paying attention to what is still vague and unclear. They are looking to their felt experience, and waiting for an image, a word, or a phrase to emerge that captures the sense they embody.

Usually, when they make the decision to write, it is after they have a dawning awareness that something has clicked, that they have enough of a sense that if they begin with a few words heading in a certain direction, words will continue to come which will allow them to flesh out the sense they have.

The process of using what is sensed directly about a topic is a natural one. Many writers do it without any conscious awareness that that is what they are doing. For example, Anne repeats the words "anxious moments," using these key words as a way of allowing her sense of the topic to deepen. She asks

---

[4] Eugene Gendlin, *Focusing* (New York: Everest House, 1978), pp. 35, 165.

herself, "Why are exams so anxiety provoking?" and waits until she has enough of a sense within her that she can go in a certain direction. She does not yet have the words, only the sense that she is able to begin. Once she writes, she stops to see what is there. She maintains a highly recursive composing style throughout and she seems unable to go forward without first going back to see and to listen to what she has already created. In her own words, she says:

> My disjointed style of composing is very striking to me. I almost never move from the writing of one sentence directly to the next. After each sentence I pause to read what I've written, assess, sometimes edit and think about what will come next. I often have to read the several preceding sentences a few times as if to gain momentum to carry me to the next sentence. I seem to depend a lot on the sound of my words and . . . while I'm hanging in the middle of this uncompleted thought, I may also start editing a previous sentence or get an inspiration for something which I want to include later in the paper.

What tells Anne that she is ready to write? What is the feeling of "momentum" like for her? What is she hearing as she listens to the "sound" of her words? When she experiences "inspiration," how does she recognize it?

In the approach I am presenting, the ability to recognize what one needs to do or where one needs to go is informed by calling on felt sense. This is the internal criterion writers seem to use to guide them when they are planning, drafting, and revising.

The recursive move, then, that is hardest to document but is probably the most important to be aware of is the move to felt sense, to what is not yet *in words* but out of which images, words, and concepts emerge.

The continuing presence of this felt sense, waiting for us to discover it and see where it leads, raises a number of questions.

Is "felt sense" another term for what professional writers call their "inner voice" or their feeling of "inspiration"?

Do skilled writers call on their capacity to sense more readily than unskilled writers?

Rather than merely reducing the complex act of writing to a neat formulation, can the term "felt sense" point us to an area of our experience from which we can evolve even richer and more accurate descriptions of composing?

Can learning how to work with felt sense teach us about creativity and release us from stultifyingly repetitive patterns?

My observations lead me to answer "yes" to all four questions. There seems to be a basic step in the process of composing that skilled writers rely on even when they are unaware of it and that less skilled writers can be taught. This process seems to rely on very careful attention to one's inner reflections and is often accompanied with bodily sensations.

When it's working, this process allows us to say or write what we've never said before, to create something new and fresh, and occasionally it provides us with the experience of "newness" or "freshness," even when "old words" or images are used.

The basic process begins with paying attention. If we are given a topic, it begins with taking the topic in and attending to what it evokes in us. There is less "figuring out" an answer and more "waiting" to see what forms. Even without a predetermined topic, the process remains the same. We can ask ourselves, "What's on my mind?" or "Of all the things I know about, what would I most like to write about now?" and wait to see what comes. What we pay attention to is the part of our bodies where we experience ourselves directly. For many people, it's the area of their stomachs; for others, there is a more generalized response and they maintain a hovering attention to what they experience throughout their bodies.

Once a felt sense forms, we match words to it. As we begin to describe it, we get to see what is there for us. We get to see what we think, what we know. If we are writing about something that truly interests us, the felt sense deepens. We know that we are writing out of a "centered" place.

If the process is working, we begin to move along, sometimes quickly. Other times, we need to return to the beginning, to reread, to see if we captured what we meant to say. Sometimes after rereading we move on again, picking up speed. Other times by rereading we realize we've gone off the track, that what we've written doesn't quite "say it," and we need to reassess. Sometimes the words are wrong and we need to change them. Other times we need to go back to the topic, to call up the sense it initially evoked to see where and how our words led us astray. Sometimes in rereading we discover that the topic is "wrong," that the direction we discovered in writing is where we really want to go. It is important here to clarify that the terms "right" and "wrong" are not necessarily meant to refer to grammatical structures or to correctness.

What is "right" or "wrong" corresponds to our sense of our intention. We intend to write something, words come, and now we assess if those words adequately capture our intended meaning. Thus, the first question we ask ourselves is "Are these words right for me?" "Do they capture what I'm trying to say?" "If not, what's missing?"

Once we ask "what's missing?" we need once again to wait, to let a felt sense of what is missing form, and then to write out of that sense.

I have labeled this process of attending, of calling up a felt sense, and of writing out of that place, the process of *retrospective structuring*. It is retrospective in that it begins with what is already there, inchoately, and brings whatever is there forward by using language in structured form.

It seems as though a felt sense has within it many possible structures or forms. As we shape what we intend to say, we are further structuring our sense while correspondingly shaping our piece of writing.

It is also important to note that what is there implicitly, without words, is not equivalent to what finally emerges. In the process of writing, we begin with what is inchoate and end with something that is tangible. In order to do so, we both discover and construct what we mean. Yet the term "discovery" ought not lead us to think that meaning exists fully formed inside of us and that all we need do is dig deep enough to release it. In writing, meaning cannot be discovered the way we discover an object on an archeological dig. In writing, meaning is crafted and constructed. It involves us in a process of coming-into-being. Once we have worked at shaping, through language, what is there inchoately, we can look at what we have written to see if it adequately captures what we intended. Often at this moment discovery occurs. We see something new in our writing that comes upon us as a surprise. We see in our words a further structuring of the sense we began with and we recognize that in those words we have discovered something new about ourselves and our topic. Thus when we are successful at this process, we end up with a product that teaches us something, that clarifies what we know (or what we knew at one point only implicitly), and that lifts out or explicates or enlarges our experience. In this way, writing leads to discovery.

All the writers I have observed, skilled and unskilled alike, use the process of retrospective structuring while writing. Yet the degree to which they do so varies and seems, in fact, to depend upon the model of the writing process that they have internalized. Those who realize that writing can be a recursive process have an easier time with waiting, looking, and discovering. Those who subscribe to the linear model find themselves easily frustrated when what they write does not immediately correspond to what they planned or when what they produce leaves them with little sense of accomplishment. Since they have relied on a formulaic approach, they often produce writing that is formulaic as well, thereby cutting themselves off from the possibility of discovering something new.

Such a result seems linked to another feature of the composing process, to what I call *projective structuring,* or the ability to craft what one intends to say so that it is intelligible to others.

A number of concerns arise in regard to projective structuring; I will mention only a few that have been raised for me as I have watched different writers at work.

1) Although projective structuring is only one important part of the composing process, many writers act as if it is the whole process. These writers focus on what they think others want them to write rather than looking to see what it is they want to write. As a result, they often ignore their felt sense and they do not establish a living connection between themselves and their topic.

2) Many writers reduce projective structuring to a series of rules or criteria for evaluating finished discourse. These writers ask, "Is what I'm writing correct?" and "Does it conform to the rules I've been taught?" While these concerns are important, they often overshadow all others and lock the writer in the position of writing solely or primarily for the approval of readers.

Projective structuring, as I see it, involves much more than imagining a strict audience and maintaining a strict focus on correctness. It is true that to handle this part of the process well, writers need to know certain grammatical rules and evaluative criteria, but they also need to know how to call up a sense of their reader's needs and expectations.

For projective structuring to function fully, writers need to draw on their capacity to move away from their own words, to decenter from the page, and to project themselves into the role of the reader. In other words, projective structuring asks writers to attempt to become readers and to imagine what someone other than themselves will need before the writer's particular piece of writing can become intelligible and compelling. To do so, writers must have the experience of being readers. They cannot call up a felt sense of a reader unless they themselves have experienced what it means to be lost in a piece of writing or to be excited by it. When writers do not have such experiences, it is easy for them to accept that readers merely require correctness.

In closing, I would like to suggest that retrospective and projective structuring are two parts of the same basic process. Together they form the alternating mental postures writers assume as they move through the act of composing. The former relies on the ability to go inside, to attend to what is there, from that attending to place words upon a page, and then to assess if those words adequately capture one's meaning. The latter relies on the ability to assess how the words on that page will affect someone other than the writer, the reader. We rarely do one without the other entering in; in fact, again in these postures we can see the shuttling back-and-forth movements of the composing process, the move from sense to words and from words to sense, from inner experience to outer judgment and from judgment back to experience. As we move through this cycle, we are continually composing and recomposing our meanings and what we mean. And in doing so, we display some of the basic recursive patterns that writers who observe themselves closely seem to see in their own work. After observing the process for a long time we may, like Anne, conclude that at any given moment the process is more complex than anything we are aware of; yet such insights, I believe, are important. They show us the fallacy of reducing the composing process to a simple linear scheme and they leave us with the potential for creating even more powerful ways of understanding composing.

The Intelligent Eye and
the Thinking Hand

by Ann E. Berthoff

Everything we deal with in composition theory is fundamentally and unavoidably philosophical. I believe that it is only by being philosophical that rhetoric can "take charge of the criticism of its own assumptions." That was the way I. A. Richards put it in 1936 in *The Philosophy of Rhetoric*, a book that can help rinse our minds of the effects of the positivist assumptions which are everywhere to be found in current rhetorical theory and are everywhere the chief cause of all our woe. Let me offer a polemical summary. Positivism is a philosophy with a fundamentally associationist epistemology. The positivist notion of critical inquiry is a naive misconception of scientific method—what is sometimes called "scientism." Positivists believe that empirical tests yield true facts and that's that. They find inimical the idea that theory and practice should be kept together. Underlying all positivist methods and models is a notion of language as, alternately, a set of slots into which we cram or pour our meanings, or as a veil which must be torn asunder to reveal reality directly, without the distorting mediation of form. (If that last sounds mystical, it's because if you scratch a positivist, you'll find a mystic: neither can tolerate the concept of mediation.) I believe that we should reject this false philosophy, root and branch; in so doing it is important to realize that we are in excellent company.

Philosophical Allies

We can count as allies, among others, Susanne K. Langer, William James, C. S. Peirce, and I. A. Richards. Langer, in the first volume of *Mind: An Essay on Human Feeling* (the very title is important) explains how it is that psychologists have developed no sound theories of mind: when they have seen that to ask "What is mind?" leads to a futile search for metaphysical quiddities, instead of reconceiving the critical questions which would yield working concepts, they have worshipped the "Idols of the Laboratory"— Physicalism, Mathematization, Objectivity, Methodology, and Jargon. Any teacher who has been intimidated by the false philosophy of positivism should read Langer's critique every morning before breakfast. In resisting the positivists, we will have another ally in William James, a great psychologist by virtue of being a great philosopher. (Alfred North Whitehead listed him as one of the four greatest of all times because of his understanding of the importance of experience.) James, in his typically lively *Talks to Teachers*, warns his audience not to expect insight into the nature of such aspects of thought as attention, memory, habit, and interest to be forthcoming from what he calls the "brass instrument" psychologists, those who measured such phenomena as the fatigue your finger suffered as you tapped it over three hundred and fifty-eight times. The new brass instrument psychologists, like the old, are concerned with what can be plotted and quantified, and that does not include the things we want to know about—the composing process or the writer's mind or modes of learning and their relationship to kinds of writing.

Our most important ally in rejecting positivism is C. S. Peirce, the philosopher who first conceptualized the structure and function of the sign. The inventor of semiotics (including the term itself) had an amused contempt for psychologists, who were, in the main, ignorant of logic. He scorned the notion that the study of meaning was of a kind with the study of natural phenomena. In one of his calmer moments, he declared: "Every attempt to import into psychics the conceptions proper to physics has only led those who made it astray."[1] And, to conclude this short list of allies, there is I. A. Richards who memorably wrote in *Speculative Instruments*: "The Linguistic Scientist... does not yet have a conception of the language which would make it respectable. He thinks of it as a code and has not yet learned that it is an organ—the supreme organ of the mind's self-ordering growth."[2] Note the "yet": Richards always included it in even the gloomiest of his assessments of the state of rhetoric. Our field continues to suffer incursions from those who have no intention of conceiving language as "the supreme organ of the mind's self-ordering growth," and I am not yet sure that we should emulate his patience.

The reason for impatience is simply that we might very well lose the advantage which the novel effort to think about mind could give us. Unless we think philosophically about thinking, what's likely to happen with *mind* is what has already happened with *process*: it will be used and manipulated within the framework of positivist assumptions and thus will not help us develop a pedagogy appropriate to teaching the composing process. To be able to use *mind* as a speculative instrument—Richards' term for an idea you can think *with*—we will have to become authentic philosophers—and quick.

If we are to avail ourselves of that incomparable resource, the minds of our students, we will have to know what we're looking for, to have some philosophically sound idea of the power the mind promises. I believe that for teachers of composition, such a philosophy of mind is best thought of as a

---

[1] *The Collected Papers of Charles Sanders Peirce*, ed. Charles Hartshorne and Paul Weiss (Cambridge, Mass.: Harvard University Press, 1931-58), 1. 255.
[2] *Speculative Instruments* (New York: Harcourt, 1955), 9.

theory of imagination. If we can reclaim imagination as the forming power of mind, we will have the theoretical wherewithal for teaching composition as a mode of thinking and a way of learning.

Reclaiming the Imagination

Reclaiming the imagination is necessary because the positivists have consigned it to something called "the affective domain," in contradistinction to "the cognitive domain." You can see the false philosophy at work there, importing conceptions appropriate to neurology and biochemistry into psychics: certainly, there are areas and domains in the brain, but to use the term *domain* about modes of mental operation is to create the same kind of confusion as when the word *code* is used to designate both linguistic operation and brain function. The false philosophy cannot account for imagination as a way of knowing or a means of making meaning because it understands imagination as ancillary or subordinate, not as fundamental and primordial. Coleridge here, as in so many other instances, is our best guide in developing a philosophy of rhetoric, defining the imagination as "the living power and prime agent of all human perception." Perception works by forming—finding forms, creating forms, interpreting forms. Rudolf Arnheim, in his superb book *Visual Thinking*, lists the operations involved in perception: "active exploration, selection, grasping of essentials, simplification, abstraction, analysis and synthesis, completion, correction, comparison, problem solving, as well as combining, separating, putting in context."[3] (Doesn't that sound like an excellent course in writing?)

To think of perception as *visual thinking* helps make the case for observation in the composition classroom, not for the sake of manufacturing spurious "specifics" and vivid detail about nothing much, but because perception is the mind in action. Thinking begins with perception; the point is nicely caught in the title of R. L. Gregory's book on perception: *The Intelligent Eye*. The "dialectical notebook" I've described in *Forming/Thinking/Writing*,[4] one in which students record observations and observe their observations, affords students the experience of mastery, because it exercises powers we do not have to teach: the natural power of forming in *per*ception and the natural power of *con*ception, concept formation, which in so many ways is modeled on the activities of the "intelligent eye." Observation of observation becomes the model of thinking about thinking, of "interpreting our interpretations," of "arranging of techniques for arranging." The consciousness represented in such circular formulations is not *self* consciousness but an awareness of the dynamic relationship of the *what* and the *how*; of the reflexive character of language; of the dialectic of forming. The consciousness of consciousness which is encouraged by looking and looking again is at the heart of any critical method.

---

[3] Visual Thinking (Berkeley: University of California Press, 1969), 13.
[4] *Forming/Thinking/Writing: The Composing Imagination* (Montclair, N.J.: Boynton/Cook, 1978), 13ff.

Once we give some thought to imagination, "the shaping power and prime agent of all human perception," we can see how it is that visualizing, making meaning by means of mental images, is the paradigm of all acts of mind: *imagining* is forming par excellence and it is therefore the emblem of the mind's power. Students who learn to look and look again, to observe and to observe their observations, are discovering powers they have not always known are related in any way to the business of writing. If we trust "the intelligent eye," we can teach our students to find in perception an ever-present model of the composing process; they will thereby be reclaiming their own imaginations.

Shaping is as important an emblem as visualizing of that forming which is the work of the active mind. The artist at work—especially the sculptor—is surely the very image of imagination as the creation of form, though artists often prefer to speak of their creative activity as a matter of finding form: Michelangelo famously spoke of liberating the form in the stone. The popular doctrine of art as, simply, the "expression" of "emotion" leaves out of account forming, shaping, and thus cannot contribute to a theory of imagination. As an antidote, let me quote a passage from the autobiography of Barbara Hepworth, the British sculptor: "My left hand is my thinking hand. The right is only a motor hand. This holds the hammer. The left hand, the thinking hand, must be relaxed, sensitive. The rhythms of thought pass through the fingers and grip of this hand into the stone." I like the echo in Susanne Langer's title, *Mind: An Essay on Human Feeling*, of Barbara Hepworth's phrases, "my thinking hand" and "rhythms of thought," and I leave it to you to consider the implications of the fact that neither the philosopher nor the artist considers it paradoxical to speak of thinking and feeling as a single activity of forming. (And I leave it to you to consider that both are women.)

Forming as Modes of Abstraction

That single activity of forming can be carried out in two modes, and no theory of imagination can be sound which does not recognize them both. What we call them is a matter of some interest since our pedagogy will be guided, sometimes surreptitiously, by what we take as the implications of the terms. I have been arguing that the positivist differentiation of cognitive and affective is wrongheaded and misleading: indeed, it is the root cause of the widespread failure to get from so-called personal writing to so-called expository writing, from informal to formal composition—even from so-called "pre-writing" to writing. This false differentiation creates an abyss which rhetoricians then spend their time trying to bridge by roping together topics and places and modes of discourse, by one or another methodological breeches buoy. A theory of imagination can help us solve the problem of the abyss by removing the problem: there is no abyss if composing is conceived of as forming and forming as proceeding by means of abstraction. I will conclude by suggesting how we can differentiate two modes of abstraction, but let me note briefly why it is that current rhetorical theory manifests no understanding of forming as abstraction.

That fact must be correlated, I have often thought, with the fact that though it's defunct elsewhere, General Semantics is alive and kicking in the midst of any assembly of rhetoricians. For General Semantics, abstraction is the opposite of reality: Cow^1, Cow^2, Cow^3, are real, but *cow* or *cows* are not real; they are words and they are "abstract." Now, General Semanticists have never understood that Laura, Linda, Louise—all cows of my acquaintance—are also abstract. The smellable, kickable, lovable, milkable cow is, of course, *there*: it is recalcitrant, in Kenneth Burke's sense of that term[5] and the dairy farmer's; it is part of the triadicity of the sign relationship, in Peirce's terms.[6] But this actual cow, this cow as *event*, as Whitehead would say, is known to us in the form provided by the intelligent eye—and the intelligent ear and the intelligent nose. That form—that percept—is a primordial abstraction. Abstraction is not the opposite of reality but our means of making meaning of reality in perception and in all that we do with symbolic forms.

Forming is a single activity of abstraction: once we have the genus, we can then develop the definition dialectically by recognizing the two kinds of abstraction. There is the *discursive* mode which proceeds by means of successive generalization and the *nondiscursive* or *presentational* mode which proceeds by means of "direct, intensive insight." These are Langer's terms; they derive from Cassirer and they are, I think, both flexible and trustworthy. The discursive mode is familiar because it is what rhetoric chiefly describes: generalization is at the heart of all discourse and of course it is central to concept formation. But it is not the only mode of abstraction: we do not dream or perceive or create works of art by generalizing. One of the chief reasons that composition theory is stymied is the dependence on a brass instrument manufactured by General Semantics, the Ladder of Abstraction. Rhetoricians continually use it to explain how we climb from the positive earth to the dangerous ether of concept. But it's that metaphoric ladder itself that's dangerous. We could rename it The Ladder of Degrees of Generality to avoid the misleading notion that all abstraction proceeds by means of generalizing, but the ladder metaphor is inappropriate even to the generalizing central to concept formation, because, as Vygotsky points out, conceptualizing is "a movement of thought constantly alternating in two directions": only Buster Keaton could handle that ladder!

When we see a chair, we do not do so by a process of conscious generalizing; when the artist creates or finds the form by means of which feelings and thoughts are to be re-presented, he or she does so not by generalizing but by symbolizing insight, by *imagining*. In perception and in art, forming is primarily nondiscursive, but the point should be made explicitly that both modes of abstraction function in all acts of mind. We can save the term *imagination* to name only the nondiscursive, but having reclaimed it, I think there is much to be said for using it as a speculative

---

[5] Kenneth Burke, *Permanence and Change* (1935; rpt. New York: Bobbs-Merrill, 1965), 6.
[6] *Speculative Instruments*, 21.

instrument to focus on what it means to say that composing is a process of making meaning. The emblems I've discussed—"the intelligent eye" and "the thinking hand"—are images of imagination in the larger sense, that is, as the forming power of mind.

The Winds of Change:
Thomas Kuhn and the Revolution
in the Teaching of Writing

by Maxine Hairston

In 1963, the University of Chicago Press published a book titled *The Structure of Scientific Revolutions*, written by Thomas Kuhn, a University of California professor of the history of science. In the book Kuhn hypothesizes about the process by which major changes come about in scientific fields, and conjectures that they probably do not evolve gradually from patient and orderly inquiry by established investigators in the field. Rather, he suggests, revolutions in science come about as the result of breakdowns in intellectual systems, breakdowns that occur when old methods won't solve new problems. He calls the change in theory that underlies this kind of revolution a *paradigm shift.* I believe we are currently at the point of such a paradigm shift in the teaching of writing, and that it has been brought about by a variety of developments that have taken place in the last 25 years.

Briefly, Kuhn's thesis in *The Structure of Scientific Revolutions* is this.

When a scientific field is going through a stable period, most of the practitioners in the discipline hold a common body of beliefs and assumptions; they agree on the problems that need to be solved, the rules that govern research, and on the standards by which performance is to be measured. They share a conceptual model that Kuhn calls a paradigm, and that paradigm governs activity in their profession. Students who enter the discipline prepare for membership in its intellectual community by studying that paradigm.

But paradigms are not necessarily immutable. When several people working in a field begin to encounter anomalies or phenomena that cannot be explained by the established model, the paradigm begins to show signs of instability. For a while, those who subscribe to the paradigm try to ignore the contradictions and inconsistencies that they find, or they make improvised, *ad hoc* changes to cope with immediate crises. Eventually, however, when enough anomalies accumulate to make a substantial number of scientists in the field question whether the traditional paradigm can solve many of the serious problems that face them, a few innovative thinkers will devise a new model. And if enough scientists become convinced that the new paradigm works better than the old one, they will accept it as the new norm.

This replacement of one conceptual model by another one is Kuhn's *paradigm shift*. He cites as classic examples the astronomers' substitution of the Copernican model of the solar system for the Ptolemaic model and the development of Newtonian physics. Such shifts are usually disorderly and often controversial, and the period in which they occur is apt to be marked by insecurity and conflict within the discipline.

Kuhn believes that because these shifts are so disruptive, they will occur only when the number of unsolved problems in a discipline reaches crisis proportions and some major figures in the field begin to focus on those unsolved problems. But even with mounting evidence that their conceptual model doesn't work, supporters of the traditional paradigm resist change because they have an intellectual and sometimes emotional investment in the accepted view. They particularly resist abandoning the conventional textbooks that set forth the precepts of their discipline in clear and unqualified terms. Those texts, as Richard Young points out in his essay, "Paradigms and Problems: Needed Research in Rhetorical Theory," are usually so similar that one way to discover the traditional paradigm of a field is to examine its textbooks.[1]

Finally, however, most of the resistance to the new paradigm will dissipate when its advocates can demonstrate that it will solve problems that the traditional paradigm could not solve. Most of the new generation of scholars working in the field will adopt the new model, and the older practitioners will gradually come around to it. Those who cling to the old paradigm lose their influence in the field because the leaders in the profession simply ignore their work. When that happens, the paradigm shift is complete, and the theory that was revolutionary becomes conventional.

This summary of Kuhn's book is sketchy and too simple, but I think it accurately reflects the key points in his theory. When he developed the theory, he considered only the so-called hard sciences, particularly chemistry, astronomy, and physics. He did not claim or even suggest that his model for scientific revolution could or should apply to social sciences or the humanities, where research is not done in laboratories and usually does not involve measurements or formulas. Nevertheless, I believe that composition theorists and writing teachers can learn from Thomas Kuhn if they see his theory of scientific revolutions as an analogy that can illuminate developments that are taking place in our profession. Those developments, the most prominent of which is the move to a process-centered theory of teaching writing, indicate that our profession is probably in the first stages of a paradigm shift.

---

[1] Richard Young, "Paradigms and Problems: Needed Research in Rhetorical Invention, *Research in Composing,* ed. Charles Cooper and Lee Odell (Urbana, Illinois: National Council of Teachers of English, 1978), p. 31.

The Current-Traditional Paradigm and Its Proponents

In order to understand the nature of that shift, we need to look at the principal features of the paradigm that has been the basis of composition teaching for several decades. In "Paradigms and Patterns" Richard Young describes it this way:

> The overt features . . . are obvious enough: the emphasis on the composed product rather than the composing process; the analysis of discourse into description, narration, exposition, and argument; the strong concern with usage . . . and with style; the preoccupation with the informal essay and research paper; and so on.[2]

Young adds that underlying the traditional paradigm is what he calls the "vitalist" attitude toward composing: that is, the assumption that no one can really teach anyone else how to write because writing is a mysterious creative activity that cannot be categorized or analyzed.

In an article in the Winter, 1980, *Freshman English News* James Berlin and Robert Inkster ascribe other features to the conventional paradigm. Basing their conclusions on an analysis of repeated patterns in four well-known and commercially successful rhetoric texts, they add that the traditional paradigm stresses expository writing to the virtual exclusion of all other forms, that it posits an unchanging reality which is independent of the writer and which all writers are expected to describe in the same way regardless of the rhetorical situation, that it neglects invention almost entirely, and that it makes style the most important element in writing.[3]

I would make three other points about the traditional paradigm. First, its adherents believe that competent writers know what they are going to say before they begin to write; thus their most important task when they are preparing to write is finding a form into which to organize their content. They also believe that the composing process is linear, that it proceeds system-atically from prewriting to writing to rewriting. Finally, they believe that teaching editing is teaching writing.

It is important to note that the traditional paradigm did not grow out of research or experimentation. It derives partly from the classical rhetorical model that organizes the production of discourse into invention, arrangement, and style, but mostly it seems to be based on some idealized and orderly vision of what literature scholars, whose professional focus is on the written product, seem to imagine is an efficient method of writing. It is a prescriptive and orderly view of the creative act, a view that defines the successful writer as one who can systematically produce a 500-word theme of five paragraphs, each with a topic sentence. Its proponents hold it *a priori;* they have not

---

[2] Young, p. 31.
[3] James A. Berlin and Robert P. Inkster, "Current-Traditional Rhetoric: Paradigm and Practice," *Freshman English News,* 8 (Winter, 1980), 1-4, 13-14.

tested it against the composing processes of actual writers.

At this point some of my readers may want to protest that I am belaboring a dead issue—that the admonition to "teach process, not product" is now conventional wisdom. I disagree. Although those in the vanguard of the profession have by and large adopted the process model for teaching composition and are now attentively watching the research on the composing process in order to extract some pedagogical principles from it, the overwhelming majority of college writing teachers in the United States are not professional writing teachers. They do not do research or publish on rhetoric or composition, and they do not know the scholarship in the field; they do not read the professional journals and they do not attend professional meetings such as the annual Conference on College Communication and Composition; they do not participate in faculty development workshops for writing teachers. They are trained as literary critics first and as teachers of literature second, yet out of necessity most of them are doing half or more of their teaching in composition. And they teach it by the traditional paradigm, just as they did when they were untrained teaching assistants ten or twenty or forty years ago. Often they use a newer edition of the same book they used as teaching assistants.

Out of necessity, apathy, and what I see as a benighted and patronizing view of the essential nature of composition courses, English department administrators encourage this unprofessional approach to the teaching of writing. In the first place, they may believe that they have so many writing classes to staff that they could not possibly hire well-qualified professionals to teach them; only a comparatively few such specialists exist. Second, most departmental chairpersons don't believe that an English instructor needs special qualifications to teach writing. As one of my colleagues says, our department wouldn't think of letting her teach Chaucer courses because she is not qualified; yet the chairman is delighted for her to teach advanced composition, for which she is far more unqualified. The assumption is that anyone with a Ph.D. in English is an expert writing teacher.

I think, however, that the people who do most to promote a static and unexamined approach to teaching writing are those who define writing courses as service courses and skills courses; that group probably includes most administrators and teachers of writing. Such a view, which denies that writing requires intellectual activity and ignores the importance of writing as a basic method of learning, takes away any incentive for the writing teacher to grow professionally. People who teach skills and provide services are traditionally less respected and rewarded than those who teach theory, and hiring hordes of adjuncts and temporary instructors and assigning them to composition courses reinforces this value system. Consequently there is no external pressure to find a better way to teach writing.

In spite of this often discouraging situation, many teachers who cling to the traditional paradigm work very hard at teaching writing. They devote far more time than they can professionally afford to working with their students, but because they haven't read Elbow or Bruffee they have no way of knowing that their students might benefit far more from small group meetings with each other than from the exhausting one-to-one conferences that the teachers hold. They both complain and brag about how much time they spend, meticulously marking each paper but because they haven't read Diederich or Irmscher they don't know that an hour spent meticulously marking every error in a paper is probably doing more harm than good. They are exhausting themselves trying to teach writing from an outmoded model, and they come to despise the job more and more because many of their students improve so little despite their time and effort.

But the writing teachers' frustration and disenchantment may be less important than the fact that if they teach from the traditional paradigm, they are frequently emphasizing techniques that the research has largely discredited. As Kuhn points out, the paradigm that a group of professionals accepts will govern the kinds of problems they decide to work on, and that very paradigm keeps them from recognizing important problems that cannot be discussed in the terminology of their model. Thus teachers who concentrate their efforts on teaching style, organization, and correctness are not likely to recognize that their students need work in invention. And if they stress that proofreading and editing are the chief skills one uses to revise a paper, they won't realize that their students have no concept of what it means to make substantive revisions in a paper. The traditional paradigm hides these problems.

Textbooks complicate the problem further. As Kuhn repeatedly points out, the standard texts in any discipline constitute a major block to a paradigm shift because they represent accepted authority. Many, though certainly not all, of the standard textbooks in rhetoric and composition for the past two decades have been product-centered books that focus on style, usage, and argumentation; Sheridan Baker's *The Practical Stylist* and Brooks and Warren's *Modern Rhetoric* are typical examples. When Donald Stewart made an analysis of rhetoric texts three years ago, he found that only seven out of the thirty-four he examined showed any awareness of current research in rhetoric. The others were, as he put it, "strictly current-traditional in their discussions of invention, arrangement, and style."[4] And textbooks change slowly. Publishers want to keep what sells, and they tend to direct the appeals of their books to what they believe the average composition teacher wants, not to what those in the vanguard of the profession would like to have.

Signs of Change

Nevertheless, changes are under way, and I see in the current state of our profession enough evidence of insecurity and instability to suggest that the traditional prescriptive and product-centered paradigm that underlies writing

---

[4] Donald Stewart, "Composition Textbooks and the Assault on Tradition," *College Composition and Communication,* 29 (May, 1978), 174.

instruction is beginning to crumble. I think that the forces contributing to its demise are both theoretical and concrete and come from both inside and outside of the profession. Changes in theory probably started, in the middle 1950's, from intellectual inquiry and speculation about language and language learning that was going on in several fields, notably linguistics, anthropology, and clinical and cognitive psychology. To identify and trace all these complex developments would go far beyond the scope of this article and beyond my current state of enlightenment. I can only touch on some of them here.

Probably one of the most important developments to affect writing theory was the publication of Noam Chomsky's *Syntatic Structures* in 1957. His theory of transformational grammar, with its insistent look at the rules by which language is generated, caused a new focus on the process by which language comes into being.* The publication of Francis Christensen's essays on the generative rhetoric of the sentence and the paragraph in the early 1960's also stimulated new interest in the processes by which writers produce texts. Certainly the tagmemicists also provoked a fresh look at the act of writing when they urged writers to generate ideas by thinking about subjects from a dynamic, three-faceted perspective. And when the humanistic psychologist Carl Rogers began to criticize behaviorist psychology just as Chomsky had criticized behaviorist theories of language, he probably hastened the shift away from product-response evaluation of writing.

A major event that encouraged the shift of attention to the process of writing was the famous Anglo-American Seminar on the Teaching of English, held at Dartmouth College in the summer of 1966. In the final report of this gathering of eminent educators from Britain and the United States, the participants deemphasized the formal teaching of grammar and usage in the classroom and emphasized having children engage directly in the writing process in a non-prescriptive atmosphere.

So the intellectual climate conducive to this change has been developing for more than two decades. Of course, if these shifts in theory and attitudes were the only forces that were putting pressure on the traditional approach to teaching writing, revolution in the profession would probably be long in coming. But other concrete and external forces have also been putting pressure on writing teachers. These teachers are plagued by embarrassing stories about college graduates who can't pass teacher competency tests, and by angry complaints about employees who can't write reports. And the professors agree. Their students come to them writing badly and they leave writing badly. Handbooks won't solve their problems, and having them revise papers does no good.

Worse, just at this time when they are most disheartened about teaching writing, large numbers of English professors are beginning to realize that most of them are going to be teaching a lot of writing to a lot of students

---

*I am indebted to my colleague Stephen Witte for bringing this development to my attention.

from now on. The prospect is grim, so grim that the English departments at Harvard and the University of Michigan have given up and turned the bulk of their composition teaching over to specialists outside the departments. But most professors can't do that, and instead they feel insecure and angry because they know they are teaching badly. In Kuhn's terminology, their methods have become anomalous; the system that they have always depended on no longer seems to work.

But why should the paradigm begin to break down just now? After all, as Richard Young points out, thousands of people have learned to write by the trial-and-error method of producing a text and having it criticized. Why shouldn't that slow, but often effective, method continue to work most of the time? Once more, I think, Kuhn has the answer. He says, "One need look no further than Copernicus and the calendar to discover that external conditions may help to transform a mere anomaly into a source of acute crisis."[5] I believe that the external conditions which have hastened the crisis in the teaching of writing are open admissions policies, the return to school of veterans and other groups of older students who are less docile and rule-bound than traditional freshmen, the national decline in conventional verbal skills, and the ever larger number of high school graduates going on to college as our society demands more and more credentials for economic citizenship. Any instructional system would come close to collapse under such a strain, and our system for teaching writing has been particularly vulnerable because it has been staffed largely by untrained teachers who have had little scholarly interest in this kind of teaching.

Following the pattern that Kuhn describes in his book, our first response to crisis has been to improvise *ad hoc* measures to try to patch the cracks and keep the system running. Among the first responses were the writing labs that sprang up about ten years ago to give first aid to students who seemed unable to function within the traditional paradigm. Those labs are still with us, but they're still giving only first aid and treating symptoms. They have not solved the problem. Another *ad hoc* remedy took the form of individualized instruction, but it has faded from the scene along with computer-assisted instruction. The first was too costly and too isolated, the second one proved too limited and impersonal. And the experiments with expressive writing also turned out to be *ad hoc* measures, although for a while they seemed to have enough strength to foreshadow a paradigm shift. Sentence combining, I predict, will prove to be another *ad hoc* measure that serves as only a temporary palliative for serious writing problems.

All these remedies have proved temporarily or partially useful; none, however, has answered the crucial question: what is the basic flaw in the traditional paradigm for teaching writing? Why doesn't it work?

---

[5] Thomas Kuhn, *The Structure of Scientific Revolutions,* 2nd. ed. (Chicago: University of Chicago Press, 1970), p. x.

The Transition Period

Someone who cares has to ask that question before the revolution can start because, as Kuhn points out, "novelty ordinarily emerges only for the man who, knowing *with precision* what he should expect, is able to recognize that something has gone wrong."[6] In the teaching of composition, the essential person who asked that question may not have been a man, but a woman, Mina Shaughnessy. In her book *Errors and Expectations,* Shaughnessy describes the educational experience that made her, a professor at a prestigious university, stop to ask. "What went wrong?"

In the spring of 1970, the City University of New York adopted an admissions policy that guaranteed to every city resident with a high school diploma a place in one of its eighteen tuition-free colleges, thereby opening its doors not only to a larger population of students than it had ever had before . . . but to a wider range of students than any college had probably ever admitted or thought of admitting to its campus. . . .

One of the first tasks these students faced when they arrived at college was to write a placement essay. . . . Judged by the results of these tests, the young men and women who were to be known as open admissions students fell into one of three groups: 1. Those who met the traditional requirements for college work, who appeared from their tests . . . to be able to begin at the traditional starting points; 2. those who had survived their secondary schooling . . . and whose writing reflected a flat competence; 3. {those} who had been left so far behind the others in their formal education that they appeared to have little chance of catching up, students whose difficulties with the written language seemed of a different order from those of other groups, as if they had come, you might say, from a different country.

. . . The third group contained true outsiders, . . . strangers in academia, unacquainted with the rules and rituals of college life, unprepared for the sorts of tasks their teachers were about to assign them. . . .

Not surprisingly, the essays these students wrote during their first weeks of class stunned the teachers who read them. Nothing, it seemed, short of a miracle was going to turn such students into writers. . . . To make matters worse, there were no studies nor guides, nor even suitable textbooks to turn to. Here were teachers trained to analyze the belletristic achievements of the ages marooned in basic writing classrooms with adult student writers who appeared by college standards to be illiterate.[7]

---

[6] Kuhn, p. 65.

[7] Mina Shaughnessy, *Errors and Expectations* (New York and London: Oxford University Press, 1977), pp. 1-3.

Relying on their previous experience with selectively-admitted students at the City University, Shaughnessy and her colleagues thought they knew what to expect from "college writers." The shock of facing a kind of writing that fit no familiar category, that met no traditional standards, forced Shaughnessy, at least, to recognize an anomaly. If these students had come through schools in which writing had been taught with standard textbooks and standard methods, then one had to conclude that the method and the textbooks did not work, at least not for a substantial and important group of students. The question was, "Why?"

To find the answer, Shaughnessy analyzed the placement essays of 4000 students and over a period of five years worked at trying to get at the roots of their problems and devise a way to overcome them. Eventually she became persuaded

> . . . that basic writers write the way they do, not because they are slow or non-verbal, indifferent to or incapable of academic excellence, but because they are beginners and must, like all beginners, learn by making mistakes . . . And the keys to their development as writers often lie in the very features of their writing that English teachers have been trained to brush aside with a marginal code letter or a scribbled injunction to "Proofread!" Such strategies ram at the doors of their incompetence while the keys that would open them lie in view. . . . The work {of teaching these students to write} must be informed by an understanding not only of what is missing or awry, but of *why this is so*.[8] (italics added)

Shaughnessy's insight is utterly simple and vitally important: we cannot teach students to write by looking only at what they have written. We must also understand *how* that product came into being, and *why* it assumed the form that it did. We have to try to understand what goes on during the internal act of writing and we have to intervene during the act of writing if we want to affect its outcome. We have to do the hard thing, examine the intangible process, rather than the easy thing, evaluate the tangible product.

Although Shaughnessy was not the first investigator to try to move behind students' written products and find out how those products came into being— Janet Emig and Charles Stallard had both done limited studies at about the same time as Shaughnessy, and James Britton and his colleagues in Great Britain were working on a very ambitious study of the development of writing abilities—she was the first to undertake a large-scale research project whose goal was to find practical ways to teach the new students of the seventies to write. Her example, her book, and her repeated calls for new research in composition have undoubtedly been important stimuli in spurring the profession's search for a new paradigm.

---

[8] Shaughnessy, p. 5.

Others in the profession have also given impetus to the search. In 1968 a journalist and professor named Donald Murray published a book called *A Writer Teaches Writing,* in which he suggests that if we want to teach students to write, we have to initiate them into the process that writers go through, not give them a set of rules. He insists that writers find their real topics only through the act of writing. In fact, Murray may have originated the admonition, "Teach Writing as Process, Not Product" in a 1972 article by that title.[9] A resurgence of interest in classical rhetoric in the seventies also sparked interest in a new approach to the teaching of writing. The books by rhetoricians Richard Weaver and Edward P. J. Corbett provided the theoretical foundations for the view that writing can not be separated from its context, that audience and intention should affect every stage of the creative process. When this premise became widely accepted at major universities—for example, the University of Iowa and the University of Texas—it inevitably put strains on the old product-centered paradigm.

Another major influence on the teaching of writing across the nation has come from California's Bay Area Writing Project, initiated in 1975. A cardinal principle of that project has been the revolutionary thesis that all writing teachers should write in order to understand the writing process first-hand. When teachers began to do so, the traditional textbook model for writing inevitably came into question. And as spin-offs of the Bay Area Writing Project have proliferated across the country, largely funded by grant money donated by agencies and foundations alarmed about the writing crisis, a growing number of teachers are changing to process-centered writing instruction.

The Emerging Paradigm

But the most promising indication that we are poised for a paradigm shift is that for the first time in the history of teaching writing we have specialists who are doing controlled and directed research on writers' composing processes. Sondra Perl of Herbert Lehman College of the City University of New York and Linda Flower and John Hayes of Carnegie-Mellon University are tape recording students' oral reports of the thoughts that come to them as they write and of the choices they make. They call their investigative strategy "protocol analysis," and they supplement it with interviews and questionnaires to put together composite pictures of the processes followed by working writers. Sharon Pianko of Rutgers University has done a study in which she matched groups of traditional and remedial writers, men and women writers, and 18-year-old and adult writers and compared their composing habits. Nancy Sommers of New York University has done a study comparing the revising practices of college freshmen and experienced professional writers, and Lester Faigley and Stephen Witte of the University of Texas now have a

---

[9] Donald Murray, "Teach Writing As Process, Not Product," in *Rhetoric and Composition,* ed. Richard L. Graves (Rochelle Park, New Jersey: Hayden Book Company, 1976), pp. 79-82.

federal grant to do a more comprehensive study on revising. (An article based on this study appeared in the December, 1981, issue of *CCC.*) Lee Odell of Rensselaer Polytechnic Institute and Dixie Goswami are currently involved in a federally-funded study of the practices of writers in business.

From these and other studies we are beginning to find out something about how people's minds work as they write, to chart the rhythm of their writing, to find out what constraints they are aware of as they write, and to see what physical behaviors are involved in writing and how they vary among different groups of writers. So far only a small amount of data has been collected, and the inferences we can draw from the studies are necessarily tentative. As Linda Flower puts it, because we are trying to chart and analyze an activity that goes on largely out of sight, the process is rather like trying to trace the path of a dolphin by catching glimpses of it when it leaps out of the water. We are seeing only a tiny part of the whole process, but from it we can infer much about what is going on beneath the surface.[10]

What are we finding out? One point that is becoming clear is that writing is an act of discovery for both skilled and unskilled writers; most writers have only a partial notion of what they want to say when they begin to write, and their ideas develop in the process of writing. They develop their topics intuitively, not methodically. Another truth is that usually the writing process is not linear, moving smoothly in one direction from start to finish. It is messy, recursive, convoluted, and uneven. Writers write, plan, revise, anticipate, and review throughout the writing process, moving back and forth among the different operations involved in writing without any apparent plan. No practicing writer will be surprised at these findings: nevertheless, they seriously contradict the traditional paradigm that has dominated writing textbooks for years.

But for me the most interesting data emerging from these studies are those that show us profound differences between the writing behaviors of skilled and unskilled writers and the behaviors of student and professional writers. Those differences involve the amount of time spent on writing, the amount of time preparing to write, the number of drafts written, the concern for audience, the number of changes made and the stages at which they are made, the frequency and length of pauses during writing, the way in which those pauses are used, the amount of time spent rereading and reformulating, and the kind and number of constraints that the writers are aware of as they work. This kind of information enables us to construct a tentative profile of the writing behaviors of effective writers; I have sketched such a profile in another paper, not yet published.

From all this activity in the field, the new paradigm for teaching writing is emerging. Its principal features are these:

---

[10]Linda Flower and John Hayes, "Identifying the Organization of the Writing Processes," *Cognitive Processes in Writing,* ed., Lee W. Gregg and Erwin R. Steinberg (Hillsdale, NJ: Lawrence Erlbaum Associates, 1980), pp. 9-10.

1. It focuses on the writing process; instructors intervene in students' writing during the process.
2. It teaches strategies for invention and discovery; instructors help students to generate content and discover purpose.
3. It is rhetorically based; audience, purpose, and occasion figure prominently in the assignment of writing tasks.
4. Instructors evaluate the written product by how well it fulfills the writer's intention and meets the audience's needs.
5. It views writing as a recursive rather than a linear process; pre-writing, writing, and revision are activities that overlap and intertwine.
6. It is holistic, viewing writing as an activity that involves the intuitive and non-rational as well as the rational faculties.
7. It emphasizes that writing is a way of learning and developing as well as a communication skill.
8. It includes a variety of writing modes, expressive as well as ex-pository.
9. It is informed by other disciplines, especially cognitive psychology and linguistics.
10. It views writing as a disciplined creative activity that can be analyzed and described; its practitioners believe that writing can be taught.
11. It is based on linguistic research and research into the composing process.
12. It stresses the principle that writing teachers should be people who write.

Portents for the Future

I believe that important events of the recent past are going to speed the revolution and help to establish this new paradigm in the nation's classrooms.

First, the University of Iowa's Writing Institute, which received a $680,000 grant from the National Endowment for the Humanities to train freshman composition directors, has this year completed its work and sent out forty administrators for writing programs who will almost certainly base those programs on the new model. They are bound to have a profound influence on their institutions.

Second, graduate programs in rhetoric are rapidly increasing across the country. The last count in the Spring, 1980, *Freshman English News* showed that fifty-three institutions have added graduate rhetoric courses since 1974, and that was not a complete list. Enrollment in these programs is climbing because students realize that English departments now offer more jobs in rhetoric and composition than in any other specialization. Most of these programs are going to produce young professionals who have been taught by scholars who know recent research and are committed to the new paradigm: Richard Young, Ross Winterowd, Joseph Comprone, James Kinneavy, Andrea

Lunsford, Elizabeth Cowan, Linda Flower, to name just a few. When these new graduates go into English departments where the traditional paradigm prevails, they are certain to start working for change.

Third, in many schools, even graduate assistants who are in traditional literary programs rather than rhetoric programs are getting their in-service training from the rhetoric and composition specialists in their departments. They are being trained in process-centered approaches to the teaching of composition, and when they enter the profession and begin teaching lower-division writing courses along with their literary specialities, they are most likely to follow the new paradigm. And, more and more, the methods courses for high-school teachers are also being taught by the rhetoric specialists; that change will have a profound effect on secondary school teaching.

Fourth, we now have process-based texts on the teaching of writing. Shaughnessy's *Errors and Expectations is* well known and widely used. It has been joined by Irmscher's *Teaching Expository Writing* and Neman's *Teaching Students to Write.* The authors of both these latter books incorporate research findings and recent developments in the profession into their philosophies of and methodologies for teaching writing.

Fifth, college composition textbooks are changing. Along with their traditional books, most publishers are now publishing at least one process-oriented, rhetorically-based writing text. Several are now on the market and more are forthcoming, most of them written by scholars and teachers who are leaders in the profession. Moreover, many major publishing houses now retain well-known composition specialists to advise them on manuscripts. The publishers sense change in the wind and realize that the new crop of well-informed and committed writing program directors who will be taking over are going to insist on up-to-date textbooks. The change will even reach into some high schools because one large company has hired one of the country's leading rhetoricians to supervise and edit their high school composition series. Many others will probably follow their example.

But no revolution brings the millenium nor a guarantee of salvation, and we must remember that the new paradigm is sketchy and leaves many problems about the teaching of writing unresolved. As Kuhn points out, new paradigms are apt to be crude, and they seldom possess all the capabilities of their predecessors. So it is important for us to preserve the best parts of earlier methods for teaching writing: the concern for style and the preservation of high standards for the written product. I believe we also need to continue giving students models of excellence to imitate.

Kuhn contends that "the transition between competing paradigms cannot be made a step at a time, forced by logic. . . . Like the gestalt switch, it must occur all at once (though not necessarily in an instant) or not at all."[11] He says, however, that, "if its supporters are competent, they will improve it {the paradigm}, explore its possibilities, and show what it would be like to belong

---

[11]Kuhn, p. 150.

to the community guided by it."[12] I see this last opportunity as the challenge to today's community of composition and rhetoric scholars: to refine the new paradigm for teaching composition so that it provides a rewarding, productive, and feasible way of teaching writing for the non-specialists who do most of the composition teaching in our colleges and universities.

---

[12]Kuhn, p. 159.

Decisions and Revisions: The Planning Strategies of a Publishing Writer

by Carol Berkenkotter

The clearest memory I have of Donald M. Murray is watching him writing at a long white wooden table in his study, which looks out on the New Hampshire woods. Beside his desk is a large framed poster of a small boy sitting on a bed staring at a huge dragon leaning over the railing glowering at him. The poster is captioned, "Donald imagined things." And so he did, as he addressed the problems writers face each time they confront a new assignment. During the summer of 1981, as I listened to him daily recording his thoughts aloud as he worked on two articles, a short story, and an editorial, I came to understand in what ways each writer's processes are unique and why it is important that we pay close attention to the setting in which the writer composes, the kind of task the writer confronts, and what the writer can tell us of his own processes. If we are to understand *how* writers revise, we must pay close attention to the context in which revision occurs.

Janet Emig, citing Eliot Mishler, has recently described the tendency of writing research toward "context stripping."[1] When researchers remove writers from their natural settings (the study, the classroom, the office, the dormitory room, the library) to examine their thinking processes in the laboratory, they create "a context of a powerful sort, often deeply affecting what is being observed and assessed."[2] Emig's essay points to the need to examine critically the effects of these practices.

The subject of the present study is not anonymous, as are most subjects, nor will he remain silent. I began the investigation with a critical eye regarding what he has said about revision, he with an equally critical attitude toward methods of research on cognitive processes. To some extent our original positions have been confirmed—yet I think each of us, researcher and writer, has been forced to question our assumptions and examine our dogmas. More important, this project stirs the dust a bit and suggests a new direction for research on composing processes.

Reprinted from *College Composition and Communication* (May 1983). Copyright 1983 by the National Council of Teachers of English. Reprinted with permission.

[1] Janet Emig, "Inquiry Paradigms and Writing," *College Composition and Communication,* 33 (February, 1982), p. 55.
[2] Emig, "Inquiry Paradigms and Writing," p. 67.

I met Mr. Murray at the Conference on College Composition and Communication meeting in Dallas, 1981. He appeared at the speaker's rostrum after my session and introduced himself, and we began to talk about the limitations of taking protocols in an experimental situation. On the spur of the moment I asked him if he would be willing to be the subject of a naturalistic study. He hesitated, took a deep breath, then said he was very interested in understanding his own composing processes, and would like to learn more. Out of that brief exchange a unique collaborative research venture was conceived.

To date there are no reported studies of writers composing in natural (as opposed to laboratory) settings that combine thinking-aloud protocols with the writers' own introspective accounts. Recently, researchers have been observing young children as they write in the classroom. In particular, we have seen the promising research of Donald Graves, Lucy Calkins, and Susan Sowers, who have worked intimately with children and their teachers in the Atkinson Schools Project.[3] By using video tapes and by actively working in the classroom as teachers and interviewers, these researchers were able to track the revising processes of individual children over a two year period. Studies such as these suggest that there may be other ways of looking at writers' composing processes than in conventional research settings.

There remains, however, the question: to what extent can a writer's subjective testimony be trusted? I have shared the common distrust of such accounts.[4] There is considerable cognitive activity that writers cannot report because they are unable to compose and monitor their processes simultaneously. Researchers have responded to this problem by taking retrospective accounts from writers immediately after they have composed,[5] or have studied writers' cognitive activity through the use of thinking-aloud protocols.[6] These protocols have been examined to locate the thoughts verbalized by the

---

[3] Donald Graves, "What Children Show Us About Revision," *Language Arts,* 56 (March, 1979), 312-319; Susan Sowers, "A Six Year Old's Writing Process: The First Half of the First Grade," *Language Arts,* 56 (October, 1979), 829-835; Lucy M. Calkins, "Children Learn the Writer's Craft," *Language Arts,* 57 (February, 1980), 207-213.

[4] Janet Emig, *The Composing Processes of Twelfth-Graders* (Urbana, IL: National Council of Teachers of English, 1971), pp. 8-11; Linda Flower and John R. Hayes, "A Cognitive Process Theory of Writing," *College Composition and Communication,* 32 (December, 1981), 368.

[5] See Janet Emig, *The Composing Processes of Twelfth-Graders,* p. 30; Sondra Perl, "Five Writers Writing: Case Studies of the Composing Processes of Unskilled College Writers," Diss. New York University, 1978, pp. 48, 387-391; "The Composing Processes of Unskilled College Writers," *Research in the Teaching of English,* 13 (December, 1979), 318; Nancy I. Sommers, "Revision Strategies of Student Writers and Experienced Adult Writers," paper delivered at the Annual Meeting of the Modern Language Association, New York, 28 December, 1978. A slightly revised version was published in *College Composition and Communication,* 32 (December, 1980), 378-388.

[6] See Linda Flower and John R. Hayes, "Identifying the Organization of Writing Processes," in *Cognitive Processes in Writing,* ed. Lee W. Gregg and Erwin R. Steinberg (Hillsdale, NJ: Lawrence Erlbaum Associates, 1981), p. 4; "The Cognition of Discovery: Defining a Rhetorical Problem," *College Composition and Communication,* 32 (February, 1980), 23; "The Pregnant Pause: An Inquiry into the Nature of Planning," *Research in the Teaching of English,* 19 (October, 1981), 233; "A Cognitive Process Theory of Writing," p. 368; Carol Berkenkotter, "Understanding a Writer's Awareness of Audience," *College Composition and Communication,* 32 (December, 1981), 389.

subjects while composing, rather than for the subjects' analysis of what they said. Typically, subjects were instructed to "say everything that comes to mind no matter how random or crazy it seems. Do not analyze your thoughts, just say them aloud." The effect of these procedures, however, has been to separate the dancer from the dance, the subject from the process. Introspective accounts made *in medias res* have not been possible thus far because no one has developed techniques that would allow a subject to write and comment on his or her processes between composing episodes. For this reason I had begun to entertain the idea of asking a professional writer to engage in a lengthy naturalistic study. When Donald Murray introduced himself, I knew I wanted him to be the subject.

Methodology

The objectives that I began with are modifications of those Sondra Perl identified in her study of five unskilled writers.[7] I wanted to learn more about the planning and revising strategies of a highly skilled and verbal writer, to discover how these strategies could be most usefully analyzed, and to determine how an understanding of this writer's processes would contribute to what we have already discovered about how skilled writers plan and revise.

The project took place in three stages. From June 15th until August 15th, 1981 (a period of 62 days), Mr. Murray turned on the tape recorder when he entered his study in the morning and left it running during the day wherever he happened to be working: in his car waiting in parking lots, his university office, restaurants, the doctor's office, etc. This kind of thinking-aloud protocol differs from those taken by Linda Flower and John R. Hayes since the subject's composing time is not limited to a single hour; in fact, during the period of time that Mr. Murray was recording his thoughts, I accumulated over one hundred and twenty hours of tape. The writer also submitted photocopies of all text, including notes and drafts made prior to the study. Thus I was able to study a history of each draft.

In the second stage, during a visit to my university, I gave the writer a task which specified audience, subject, and purpose. I asked him to think aloud on tape as he had previously, but this time for only one hour. Between the second and third stages, Mr. Murray and I maintained a dialogue on audiotapes which we mailed back and forth. On these tapes he compared his thoughts on his composing in his own environment over time to those on giving a one-hour protocol in a laboratory setting.

During the third stage of the study, I visited the writer at his home for two days. At this time I observed him thinking aloud as he performed a writing task which involved revising an article for a professional journal. After two sessions of thinking aloud on tape for two and one-half hours, Mr. Murray

---

[7] Perl, "Five Writers Writing: Case Studies of the Composing Processes of Unskilled College Writers," p. 1.

answered questions concerning the decisions he had made. Over the two-day period we taped an additional four hours of questions and answers regarding the writer's perceptions of his activities.

Another coder and I independently coded the transcripts of the protocols made in the naturalistic and laboratory settings. Using the same procedure I employed in my study of how writers considered their audience (i.e., first classifying and then counting all audience-related activities I could find in each protocol), my coder and I tallied all planning, revising, and editing activities, as well as global and local evaluations of text[8] that we agreed upon. I was particularly interested in Murray's editing activities. Having listened to the tapes I was aware that editing (i.e., reading the text aloud and making word- and sentence-level changes) sometimes led to major planning episodes, and I wanted to keep track of that sequence.

The study was not conducted without problems. The greatest of these arose from how the writer's particular work habits affected the gathering of the data and how he responded to making a one-hour protocol. Unlike most writers who hand draft or type, Mr. Murray spends much time making copious notes in a daybook, then dictates his drafts and partial drafts to his wife, who is an accomplished typist and partner in his work. Later, he reads aloud and edits the drafts. If he determines that copy-editing (i.e., making stylistic changes in the text) is insufficient, he returns to the daybook, makes further notes, and prepares for the next dictation. The revision of one of the articles he was working on went through eight drafts before he sent it off. Two days later he sent the editor an insert.

Murray's distinctive work habits meant that all of the cognitive activity occurring during the dictation that might ordinarily be captured in a protocol was lost since he processed information at a high speed. During these periods I could not keep track of the content of his thoughts, and became concerned instead with the problem of why he frequently would find himself unable to continue dictating and end the session. There turned out to be considerable value in following the breakdowns of these dictations. I was able to distinguish between those occasions when Murray's composing was, in Janet Emig's terms, "extensive," and when it was "reflexive,"[9] by comparing the relative ease with which he developed an article from well-rehearsed material presented at workshops with the slow evolution of a conceptual piece he had not rehearsed. According to Emig, "The extensive mode . . . focuses upon the writer's conveying a message or communication to another. . . . the style is assured, impersonal, and often reportorial." In contrast, reflexive composing ". . . focuses on the writer's thoughts and feelings. . . . the style is tentative,

---

[8] Evaluations of text were either global or local. An example of global evaluation is when the writer says, "There's a lack of fullness in the piece." When the writer was evaluating locally he would comment, ". . . and the ending seems weak."
[9] Emig, *The Composing Processes of Twelfth-Graders*, p. 4.

personal, and exploratory."[10] In the latter case the writer is generating, testing, and evaluating new ideas, rather than reformulating old ones. I could observe the differences between the two modes of composing Emig describes, given Murray's response to the task in which he was engaged. When the writer was thoroughly familiar with his subject, he dictated with great fluency and ease. However, when he was breaking new ground conceptually, his pace slowed and his voice became halting; often the drafts broke down, forcing him to return to his daybook before attempting to dictate again.[11]

A more critical problem arose during the giving of the one-hour protocol. At the time he came to my university, the writer had been working on tasks he had selected, talking into a tape recorder for two months in a familiar setting. Now he found himself in a strange room, with a specific writing task to perform in one short hour. This task was not simple; nor was it familiar. He was asked to "explain the concept of death to the ten- to twelve-year-old readers of *Jack and Jill* magazine." Under these circumstances, Murray clutched, producing two lines of text: *"Dear 11 year old. You're going to die. Sorry. Be seeing you. P. Muglump, Local Funeral Director."* Both the transcript and later retrospective testimony of the writer indicated that he did not have pets as a child and his memories of death were not of the kind that could be described to an audience of ten- to twelve-year-old children. He also had difficulty forming a picture of his audience, since he suspected the actual audience was grandparents in Florida who send their children subscriptions to *Jack and Jill.* Toward the end of the hour, he was able to imagine a reader when he remembered the daughter of a man he had met the previous evening. The protocol, however, is rich with his efforts to create rhetorical context—he plotted repeated scenarios in which he would be asked to write such an article. Nevertheless, it seems reasonable to conclude that Mr. Murray was constrained by what Lester Faigley and Stephen Witte call "situational variables":[12] the knowledge that he had only one hour in which to complete a draft, his lack of familiarity with the format of *Jack and Jill* (he had never

---

[10] *Ibid.* See also "Eye, Hand, and Brain," in *Research on Composing: Points of Departure,* ed. Charles R. Cooper and Lee Odell (Urbana, IL: National Council of Teachers of English), p. 70. Emig raises the question, "What if it is the case that classical and contemporary rhetorical terms such as . . . extensive and reflexive may represent centuries old understandings that the mind deals differentially with different speaking and writing tasks. To put the matter declaratively, if hypothetically, modes of discourse may represent measurably different profiles of brain activity."

[11] Janet Emig, observing her subject's writing processes, noted that "the *nature of the stimulus*" did not necessarily determine the response. Emig's students gave extensive responses to a reflexive task *(The Composing Processes of Twelfth-Graders,* pp. 30-31, 33). Similarly, Murray gave a reflexive response to an extensive task. Such a response is not unusual when we consider what the writer himself has observed: "The deeper we get into the writing process the more we may discover how affective concerns govern the cognitive, for writing is an intellectual activity carried on in an emotional environment, a precisely engineered sailboat trying to hold course in a vast and stormy Atlantic" ("Teaching the Other Self: The Writer's First Reader," *College Composition and Communication,* 33 {May, 1982}, p. 142). For a writer as deeply engaged in his work as Murray, drafting a conceptual piece was as personal and subjective as describing a closely felt experience.

[12] Lester Faigley and Stephen Witte, "Analyzing Revision," *College Composition and Communication,* 32 (December, 1981), 410-411.

seen the magazine), his doubts that an audience actually existed, and finally, the wash of unhappy memories that the task gave rise to. "So important are these variables," Faigley and Witte contend, "that writing skill might be defined as the ability to respond to them."[13]

One final problem is intrinsic to the case study approach. Although the tapes are rich in data regarding the affective conditions under which the writer composed (he was distracted by university problems, had to contend with numerous interruptions, encountered family difficulties that he had to resolve, not to mention experiencing his own anxiety about his writing), as Murray reported, the further away he was in time from what he had done, the less able he was to reconstruct decisions he had made.

Results

Planning and Revising

In this study I was primarily concerned with the writer's planning, revising, and editing activities. I had to develop a separate code category for the evaluation of text or content, since the writer frequently stopped to evaluate what he had written. Figure 1 indicates the percentage of coded activities devoted to planning, revising, and editing for three pieces of discourse.[14] These three pieces were among the projects Murray worked on over the two-month period when he was making the protocols.

The coded data (taken from the transcripts of the tapes he made during this time) showed that up to 45%, 56%, and 35% of the writer's activities were concerned with planning, 28%, 21%, and 18% with either global or local evaluation, 3.0%, 3.0%, and .0% with revising (a finding which surprised me greatly, and to which I shall return), and 24%, 20%, and 47% with editing.

Murray's planning activities were of two kinds: the first were the stating of "process goals"—mentioning procedures, that is, that he developed in order to write (e.g., "I'm going to make a list of titles and see where that gets me," or "I'm going to try a different lead.")[15] Frequently, these procedures (or "thinking plans" as they are also called)[16] led the writer to generate a series

---

[13]Faigley and Witte, p. 411.

[14]These three pieces of discourse were chosen because their results are representative of the writer's activities.

[15]Linda Flower and John R. Hayes describe "process goals" as "instructions and plans the writer gives herself for directing her own composing process." See "The Pregnant Pause: An Inquiry Into the Nature of Planning," p. 242. However, this definition is not always agreed upon by cognitive psychologists studying problem-solvers in other fields. On one hand, Allen Newell, Herbert A. Simon, and John R. Hayes distinguish between the goals and plans of a problem-solver, considering a goal as an end to be achieved and a plan as one kind of method for reaching that end. See John R. Hayes, *Cognitive Psychology* (Homewood, IL: The Dorsey Press, 1978), p. 192; Allen Newell and Herbert A. Simon, *Human Problem Solving* (Englewood Cliffs, NJ: Prentice-Hall, Inc., 1972), pp. 88-92, 428-29. On the other hand, George Miller, Eugene Galanter, and Karl H. Pribram use the term "plan" inclusively, suggesting that a plan is "any hierarchical process in the organism that can control the order in which a sequence of operations is to be performed." See *Plans and the Structure of Human Behavior* (New York: Holt, Rinehart, and Winston, Inc., 1960), p. 16.

	Journal of Basic Writing	College Composition and Communication	Editorial for Concord Monitor
Planning	45%	56%	35%
Evaluating	28%	21%	18%
Revising	3.0%	3.0%	.0%
Editing	24%	20%	47%

Figure 1. Percentage of Coded Activities Devoted to Planning, Evaluating, Revising, and Editing for Three Pieces of Discourse.

of sub-plans for carrying out the larger plan. The following excerpt is from the first draft of an article on revision that Murray was writing for *The Journal of Basic Writing*. He had been reading the manuscript aloud to himself and was nearly ready to dictate a second draft. Suddenly he stopped, took his daybook and began making copious notes for a list of examples he could use to make the point that the wise editor or teacher should at first ignore sentence level editing problems to deal with more substantive issues of revision (this excerpt as well as those which follow are taken from the transcript of the tape and the photocopied text of the daybook):

> Let me take another piece of paper here. Questions, ah . . . examples, and ah set up . . . situation . . . *frustration of writer. Cooks a five course dinner and gets response only to the table setting . . . or to the way the napkins are folded* or to the . . . *order of the forks.* All right. I can see from the material I have how that'll go. I'll weave in. Okay. *Distance in focus. Stand back. Read fast. Question writer.* Then *order doubles advocate. Then voice. Close in. Read aloud.* Okay, I got a number of different things I can see here that I'm getting to. I'm putting different order because that may be, try to emphasize this one. May want to put the techniques of editing and teaching first and the techniques of the writer second. So I got a one and a two to indicate that. {Italics identify words written down.}

In this instance we can see how a writing plan (taking a piece of paper and developing examples) leads to a number of sub-plans: "I'll weave in," "I'm putting in different order because that may be, try to emphasize this one," "May want to put the techniques of editing and teaching first and the

---

[16]Flower and Hayes use these terms interchangeably, as have I. "Thinking plans" are plans for text that precede drafting and occur during drafting. Thinking plans occur before the movements of a writer's hand. Because of the complexity of the composing process, it is difficult to separate thinking plans from "process goals." It is possible, however, to distinguish between *rhetorical goals* and *rhetorical plans.* Murray was setting a goal when he remarked, "The biggest thing is to . . . what I've got to get to satisfy the reader . . . is that point of what do we hear the other self saying and how does it help? He followed this goal with a plan to "Probe into the other self. What is the other self? How does it function?"

techniques of the writer second," etc.

A second kind of planning activity was the stating of rhetorical goals, i.e., planning how to reach an audience: "I'm making a note here, job not to explore the complexities of revision, but simply to show the reader how to do revision." Like many skilled writers, Murray had readers for his longer pieces. These readers were colleagues and friends whose judgment he trusted. Much of his planning activity as he revised his article for *College Composition and Communication* grew out of reading their responses to his initial draft and incorporating his summary of their comments directly onto the text. He then put away the text, and for the next several days made lists of titles, practiced leads, and made many outlines and diagrams in his daybook before dictating a draft. Through subsequent drafts he moved back and forth between the daybook and his edited dictations. He referred back to his readers' comments twice more between the first and last revised drafts, again summarizing their remarks in his notes in the daybook.

To say that Mr. Murray is an extensive planner does not really explain the nature or scope of his revisions. I had initially developed code categories for revising activities; however, my coder and I discovered that we were for the most part double-coding for revising and planning, a sign the two activities were virtually inseparable. When the writer saw that major revision (as opposed to copy-editing) was necessary, he collapsed planning and revising into an activity that is best described as *reconceiving*. To "reconceive" is to scan and rescan one's text from the perspective of an external reader and to continue re-drafting until all rhetorical, formal, and stylistic concerns have been resolved, or until the writer decides to let go of the text. This process, which Nancy Sommers has described as the resolution of the dissonance the writer senses between his intention and the developing text,[17] can be seen in the following episode. The writer had been editing what he thought was a final draft when he saw that more substantive changes were in order. The flurry of editing activity was replaced by reading aloud and scanning the text as the writer realized that his language was inadequate for expressing a goal which he began to formulate as he read:

> (reading from previous page)[18] *It was E. B. White who reminded us,* "Don't write about Man. Write about a man." O.K. I'm going to cut that paragraph there . . . I've already said it. *The conferences when the teacher listens to the student can be short. When the teacher listens to the student in conference . . . when the teacher listens to the student* . . . the conference is, well, *the conference can be short. The student learns to speak first of what is most important to the student at the point. To mention first what is most important . . . what most*

---

[17]Sommers, "Revision Strategies," pp. 385, 387. (See note 5, above.)
[18]The material italicized in the excerpts from these transcripts is text the subject is writing. The material italicized and underlined is text the subject is reading that has already been written.

concerns . . . the student about the draft or the process that produced it. The teacher listens . . . listens, reads the draft through the student's eyes then reads the draft, read or rereads . . . reads or . . . scans or re-scans the draft to confirm, adjust, or compromise the student's concerns. The range of student response includes the affective and the cognitive . . . It is the affective that usually controls the cognitive, and the affective responses usually have to be dealt with first . . . (continues reading down the page) *Once the feelings of inadequacy, overconfidence, despair or elation are dealt with, then the conference teacher will find the other self speaking in more cognitive terms. And usually these comments . . .* O.K. that would now get the monitor into, into the phrase. All right. Put this crisscross 'cause clearly that page is going to be retyped . . . I'll be dictating so that's just a note. (continues reading on next page) *Listening to students allows the teacher to discover if the student's concerns were appropriate to where the student is in the writing process. The student, for example, is often excessively interested in language at the beginning of the process. Fragmentary language is normal before there is a text.* Make a comment on the text. (writes *intervention*) Now on page ten scanning . . . my God, I don't . . . I don't think I want to make this too much a conference piece. I'm going to echo back to that . . . monitor and also to the things I've said on page two and three. O.K. Let's see what I can do . . . The biggest question that I have is how much detail needs to be on conferences. I don't think they're, I don't think I can afford too much. Maybe some stronger sense of the response that ah . . . students make, how the other self speaks. They've got to get a sense of the other self speaking.

The next draft was totally rewritten following the sentence in the draft: "When the teacher listens to the student, the conference can be short." The revision included previously unmentioned anecdotal reports of comments students had made in conferences, a discussion of the relevant implications of the research of Graves, Calkins, and Sowers, and a section on how the writing workshop can draw out the student's "other self" as other students model the idealized reader. This draft was nearly three pages longer than the preceding one. The only passage that remained was the final paragraph.

Granted that Mr. Murray's dictation frees him from the scribal constraints that most writers face, how can we account for such global (i.e., whole text) revision? One answer lies in the simple, yet elegant, principle formulated by Linda Flower and John R. Hayes.[19] In the act of composing, writers move back and forth between planning, translating (putting thoughts into words), and reviewing their work. And as they do, they frequently "discover" major rhetorical goals.[20] In the episode just cited we have seen the writer shifting

---

[19]Flower and Hayes, "A Cognitive Process Theory of Writing," 365-387.

gears from editing to planning to reconceiving as he recognized something missing from the text and identified a major rhetorical goal—that he had to make the concept of the other self still more concrete for his audience: "They've got to get a sense of the other self speaking." In this same episode we can also see the cognitive basis for alterations in the macrostructure, or "gist," of a text, alterations Faigley and Witte report having found in examining the revised drafts of advanced student and expert adult writers.[21]

Planning and Incubation

This discussion of planning would be incomplete without some attention to the role of incubation. Michael Polanyi describes incubation as "that persistence of heuristic tension through . . . periods of time in which problems are not consciously entertained."[22] Graham Wallas and Alex Osborn agree that incubation involves unconscious activity that takes place after periods of intensive preparation.[23]

Given the chance to observe a writer's processes over time, we can see incubation at work. The flashes of discovery that follow periods of incubation (even brief ones) are unexpected, powerful, and catalytic, as the following episode demonstrates. Mr. Murray was revising an article on revision for the *Journal of Basic Writing*. He had begun to review his work by editing copy, moving to more global issues as he evaluated the draft:

> The second paragraph may be . . . Seems to me I've got an awful lot of stuff before I get into it. (Counting paragraphs) 1, 2, 3, 4, 5, 6, 7, 8, 9, 10, ten paragraphs till I really get into the text. Maybe twelve or thirteen. I'm not going to try to hustle it too much. That might be all right.

The writer then reread the first two paragraphs, making small editorial changes and considering stylistic choices. At that point he broke off and noted on the text three questions, *"What is the principle? What are the acts? How can it be taught?"* He reminded himself to keep his audience in mind. "The first audience has got to be the journal, and therefore, teachers." He took a five-minute break and returned to report,

> But, that's when I realized . . . the word hierarchy ah, came to me and that's when I realized that in a sense I was making this too complicated for myself and simply what I have to do is show the reader . . .

[20]Berkenkotter, "Understanding a Writer's Awareness of Audience," pp. 392, 395.

[21]Faigley and Witte, pp. 406-410.

[22]Michael Polanyi, *Personal Knowledge: Toward a Post-Critical Philosophy* (Chicago: The University of Chicago Press, 1958), p. 122.

[23]Graham Wallas, *The Art of Thought* (New York: Jonathan Cape, 1926), pp. 85-88; Alex Osborn, *Applied Imagination: Principles and Procedures of Creative Problem-Solving,* 3rd rev. ed. (New York: Charles F. Scribner and Sons), pp. 314-325.

I'm making a note here . . . *Job not to explore complexities of revision, but simply to show the reader how to do revision.*

From a revision of his goals for his audience, Murray moved quickly into planning activity, noting on his text,

Hierarchy of problems. O.K. What I'm dealing with is a hierarchy of problems. *First, focus/content, second, order/structure, third, language/voice* . . . O.K. Now, let's see. I need to ah, need to put that word, hierarchy in here somewhere. Well, that may get into the second paragraph so put an arrow down there (draws arrow from hierarchy to second paragraph), then see what we can do about the title if we need to. Think of things like 'first problems first' (a miniplan which he immediately rejects). It won't make sense that title, unless you've read the piece. Ah well, come up with a new title.

Here we can observe the anatomy of a planning episode with a number of goals and sub-goals generated, considered, and consolidated at lightning speed: "O.K. What I'm dealing with is a hierarchy of problems." . . . "I need to ah, need to put that word, hierarchy in here somewhere." ". . . so put an arrow down there, then see what we can do about the title . . ." ". . . 'first problems first.' It won't make sense that title . . . Ah well, come up with a new title." We can also see the writer's process of discovery at work as he left his draft for a brief period and returned having identified a single meaning-laden word. This word gave Murray an inkling of the structure he wanted for the article—a listing of the problems writers face before they can accomplish clear, effective revision. In this case, a short period of incubation was followed by a period of intense and highly concentrated planning when Murray realized the direction he wanted the article to take.

Introspection

One of the most helpful sources in this project was the testimony of the writer as he paused between or during composing episodes. Instead of falling silent, he analyzed his processes, providing information I might have otherwise missed. The following segments from the protocols will demonstrate the kinds of insights subjects can give when not constrained by time. At the time of the first, Mr. Murray had completed the tenth list of titles he had made between June 26th and July 23rd while working on the revision of his article for *College Composition and Communication*. Frequently, these lists were made recursively, the writer flipping back in his daybook to previous lists he had composed:

I think I have to go back to titles. *Hearing the student's other self.* Hold my place and go back and see if I have any that hit me in the past. *Teaching the reader and the writer. Teaching the reader in the writer. Encouraging the internal dialogue.* I skipped something in my mind that I did not put down. *Make your students talk to themselves.*

Teaching the writer to read.

At this point he stopped to evaluate his process:

> All that I'm doing is compressing, ah, compressing is, ah, why I do a title . . . it compresses a draft for the whole thing. Title gives me a point of view, gets the tone, the difference between teaching and teach. A lot of time on that, that's all right.

The following morning the writer reported, "While I was shaving, I thought of another title. *Teaching the other self: the writer's first reader.* I started to think of it as soon as I got up." This became the final title for the article and led to the planning of a new lead.

Later that day, after he had dictated three pages of the fourth of eight drafts, he analyzed what he had accomplished:

> Well, I'm going to comment on what's happened here . . . this is a very complicated text. One of the things I'm considering, of course, is incorporating what I did in Dallas in here . . . ah, the text is breaking down in a constructive way, um, it's complex material and I'm having trouble with it . . . very much aware of pace of proportion; how much can you give to the reader in one part, and still keep them moving on to the next part. I have to give a little bit of head to teaching. . . . As a theatrical thing I am going to have to put some phrases in that indicate that I'm proposing or speculating, speculating as I revise this . . .

This last summation gave us important information on the writer's global and local evaluation of text as well as on his rhetorical and stylistic plans. It is unique because it shows Murray engaged in composing and introspecting at the same time. Generally speaking, subjects giving protocols are not asked to add the demands of introspection to the task of writing. But, in fact, as Murray demonstrated, writers *do* monitor and introspect about their writing simultaneously.

Summary

Some of the more provocative findings of this study concern the subprocesses of planning and revising that have not been observed in conventional protocols (such as those taken by Flower and Hayes) because of the time limitations under which they have been given. When coding the protocols, we noted that Mr. Murray developed intricate style goals:

> It worries me a little bit that the title is too imperative. When I first wrote, most of my articles were like this; they pound on the table, do this, do that. I want this to be a little more reflective.

He also evaluated his thinking plans (i.e., his procedures in planning): "Ah, reading through, ah, hmm . . . I'm just scanning it so I really can't read it. If I read it, it will be an entirely different thing."

Most important, the writer's protocols shed new light on the great and small decisions and revisions that form planning. These decisions and revisions form an elaborate network of steps as the writer moves back and forth between planning, drafting, editing, and reviewing.[24] This recursive process was demonstrated time after time as the writer worked on the two articles and the editorial, often discarding his drafts as he reconceived a major rhetorical goal, and returned to the daybook to plan again. Further, given his characteristic habit of working from daybook to dictation, then back to daybook, we were able to observe that Donald Murray composes at the reflexive and extensive poles described by Janet Emig. When working from material he had "rehearsed" in recent workshops, material with which he was thoroughly familiar, he was able to dictate virtually off the top of his head. At other times he was unable to continue dictating as he attempted to hold too much in suspension in short-term memory. On these occasions the writer returned to the daybook and spent considerable time planning before dictating another draft.

One final observation: although it may be impolitic for the researcher to contradict the writer, Mr. Murray's activity over the summer while he was thinking aloud suggests that he is wrong in his assertion that writers only consider their audiences when doing external revision, i.e., editing and polishing. To the contrary, his most substantive changes, what he calls "internal revision," occurred as he turned his thoughts toward his audience. According to Murray, internal revision includes

> everything writers do to discover and develop what they have to say, beginning with the reading of a completed first draft. They read to discover where their content, form, language, and voice have led them. They use language, structure, and information to find out what they have to say or hope to say. The audience is one person: the writer. (p 91)[25]

The writer, however, does not speak in a vacuum. Only when he begins to discern what his readers do not yet know can he shape his language, structure and information to fit the needs of those readers. It is also natural that a writer like Murray would not be aware of how significant a role his sense of audience played in his thoughts. After years of journalistic writing, his consideration of audience had become more automatic than deliberate. The value of thinking-aloud protocols is that they allow the researcher to eavesdrop at the workplace of the writer, catching the flow of thought that would remain otherwise unarticulated.

However, *how* the writer functions when working in the setting to which

---

[24]For a description of the development of a writer's goal structure, see Flower and Hayes, "A Cognitive Process Theory of Writing."

[25]Donald M. Murray, "Internal Revision A Process of Discovery," *Research on Composing: Points of Departure* (See note 10), p. 91.

he or she is accustomed differs considerably from how that writer will function in an unfamiliar setting, given an unfamiliar task, and constrained by a time period over which he or she has no control. For this reason, I sought to combine the methodology of protocol analysis with the techniques of naturalistic inquiry.

This project has been a first venture in what may be a new direction. Research on single subjects is new in our discipline; we need to bear in mind that each writer has his or her own idiosyncrasies. The researcher must make a trade-off, foregoing generalizability for the richness of the data and the qualitative insights to be gained from it. We need to replicate naturalistic studies of skilled and unskilled writers before we can begin to infer patterns that will allow us to understand the writing process in all of its complexity.

Writing and Knowing: Toward Redefining the Writing Process

by James A. Reither

> Who is this that darkeneth counsel
> by words without knowledge?
> Job 38:2

Composition Studies was transformed when theorists, researchers, and teachers of writing began trying to find out what actually happens when people write. Over the last decade or so, members of the discipline have striven primarily to discover and teach the special kinds of thinking, the processes, that occur during composing.[1] The goal has been to replace a prescriptive pedagogy (select a subject, formulate a thesis, outline, write, proofread) with a descriptive discipline whose members study and teach "process not product." Although the methodologies of process research have been challenged, its contributions to our understanding of composing have been applauded by theorists and practitioners alike. The consensus has generally been that process researchers have done a good job of answering the questions they have asked. Still, some are beginning to point to questions that, if they've been raised at all, have certainly not been answered.

Richard Larson, for example, has asked, "How does the impulse to write arise?" And, "How does the writer identify the elements needed for a solution [to a rhetorical problem], retrieve from memory or find in some other source(s) the items needed in the solution, and then test the trial solution to see whether it answers the problem?" (250-251).

Lee Odell, in a Four Cs paper entitled "Reading and Writing in the

Reprinted from *College English* (October 1985). Copyright 1985 by the National Council of Teachers of English. Reprinted with permission.

[1] Some well-known examples: Emig combined composing-aloud sessions, observation, and interviews to examine the composing processes of twelfth-grade writers. Perl used thinking-aloud protocols to uncover patterns or subroutines that occur and recur during composing. Flower and Hayes also tape and analyze thinking-aloud protocols, created by skilled and unskilled writers; their special concern has been to construct an accurate model of what happens as writers manage such subprocesses as planning, translating, and reviewing. Matsuhashi video-taped writers in the act of writing, paying special attention to planning and decision-making processes during pauses in composing. Sommers interviewed skilled and unskilled writers after they had revised pieces of writing, and then analyzed the pieces to determine the kinds of writer-concerns that motivated changes made from draft to draft. And, just as important, Murray has written to watch himself writing to learn what was happening as he wrote.

Workplace," observed that our questions about composing and inquiry processes have tended to stay "too close to the text." Odell's own research has led him to conclude that writing and inquiry are often (if not always) "socially collaborative" and that invention, discovery, and inquiry are closely tied to institutional relationships and strategies. Interpersonal and institutional contexts are, according to Odell, far more important than our literature has acknowledged, and he urges us to study more closely these contexts and strategies as necessary components of writing and inquiry processes.

Taking a different tack, Patricia Bizzell has divided composition theorists and researchers into two theoretical camps—those "interested in the structure of language-learning and thinking processes in their earliest state, prior to social influence"; and those "more interested in the social processes whereby language-learning and thinking capabilities are shaped and used in particular communities" (215). Bizzell laments the dominance of the "inner-directed" camp, arguing that Flower and Hayes, for example, pay too little attention to the role of knowledge in composing (229), and that "what looks like a cognitive difference [between unskilled and skilled writers often] turns out to have a large social component" (233). She thus argues that student writing difficulties often stem not from faulty or inefficient composing processes but, rather, from unfamiliarity with academic discourse conventions. "What is underdeveloped," she suggests, "is their knowledge of the ways experience is constituted and interpreted in the academic discourse community..." (230).

One result, as John Gage notes, is that the classical concept of *stasis* has all but vanished from the textbooks. The typical writing situation, according to Gage, is one in which reader and writer already share knowledge, "and it is the difference between what they know that motivates the need for communication—in both directions—and which therefore compels the act of writing" (2). Our practice, however, is to "send students in search of something to intend, . . . as if intention itself were subject to free choice. Students do not begin writing in order to fulfill an intention; rather, they are assumed to begin intentionless to search for something to want to say" (2).

What Larson, Odell, Bizzell, and Gage all point to is the tendency in composition studies to think of writing as a process which begins with an impulse to put words on paper; and the issues they raise should lead us to wonder if our thinking is not being severely limited by a concept of process that explains only the cognitive processes that occur as people write. Their questions and observations remind us that writing is not merely a process that occurs within contexts. That is, writing and what writers do during writing cannot be artificially separated from the social-rhetorical situations in which writing gets done, from the conditions that enable writers to do what they do, and from the motives writers have for doing what they do. Writing is not to context what a fried egg is to its pan.[2] Writing is, in fact, one of those processes which, in its use, *creates* and *constitutes* its own contexts.

---

[2] I owe the metaphor to my colleague Alan W. Mason (personal communication).

Assisted, however, by the notion that writing is itself a mode of learning and knowing, and by the popularity of such developments as the attacks on "Engfish" (with the concomitant emphasis on the values of expressive writing), process research—precisely because it has taught us so much—has bewitched and beguiled us into thinking of writing as a self-contained process that evolves essentially out of a relationship between writers and their emerging texts. That is, we conceptualize and teach writing on the "model of the individual writer shaping thought through language" (Bazerman, "Relationship" 657), as if the process began in the writer (perhaps with an experience of cognitive dissonance) and not in the writer's relationship to the world. In this truncated view, all writing—whether the writer is a seasoned veteran or a "placidly inexperienced nineteen-year-old" (Schor 72) begins naturally and properly with probing the contents of the memory and the mind to discover the information, ideas, and language that are the substance of writing. This model of what happens when people write does not include, at least not centrally, any substantive coming to know beyond that which occurs as writers probe their own present experience and knowledge. Composition studies does not seriously attend to the ways writers know what other people know or to the ways mutual knowing motivates writing—does not seriously attend, that is, to the knowing without which cognitive dissonance is impossible.

The upshot is that we proceed as if students come to us already widely-experienced, widely-read, well-informed beings who need only learn how to do the kinds of thinking that will enable them to probe their experience and knowledge to discover what Rohman calls the "writing ideas" (106) for their compositions. We teach them to look heuristically into their own hearts, experiences, long-term memories, information- and idea-banks to discover what they have to say on the assigned or chosen subject. In so doing, we send several obviously problematic messages. One, identified by Bizzell, is that "once students are capable of cognitively sophisticated thinking and writing, they are ready to tackle the problems of a particular writing situation" (217). Another is that composing can be learned and done outside of full participation in the knowledge/discourse communities that motivate writing. Another is that other kinds of learning which can and do impel and give substance to writing—those, for example, that result from deliberate, purposeful learning through observation, reading, research, inquiry—are not really part of writing.[3] Yet another is that those kinds of learning have already occurred sufficiently to impel and "authorize" writing. That is, writers do not need to know what they are talking about: they can learn what they are

---

[3] This reductive notion of writing allows one widely-adopted composition textbook, Cowan and Cowan's *Writing,* to advise students that in writing a research paper "you have to have a large number of skills—some writing skills, some nonwriting" (428). Students learning the shape and scope of the writing process from this textbook are advised that using the library, taking notes, incorporating notes into an essay, documenting sources, and using appropriate research paper forms are "nonwriting skills" (428). Inquiry outside the mind and memory of the writer, and the knowing required for conducting such inquiry, are not necessarily related and therefore readily separable from "writing."

talking about as they compose; they can write their way out of their ignorance.

We need to broaden our concept of what happens when people write. Writing is clearly a more multi-dimensioned process than current theory and practice would have us believe, and one that begins long before it is appropriate to commence working with strategies for invention. If we are going to teach our students to *need* to write, we will have to know much more than we do about the kinds of contexts that conduce—sometimes even force, certainly enable—the impulse to write. The "micro-theory" of process now current in composition studies needs to be expanded into a "macro-theory" encompassing activities, processes, and kinds of knowing that come into play long before the impulse to write is even possible.

To bring about that expansion, we need to press some new questions; and we need to know more than we now know, not only about cognitive processes during composing, but also about processes involved in coming to know generally. The focus of composition studies is presently on the first three of the five parts of classical rhetoric—on invention, arrangement, and style. It is time to look for ways to bring *stasis* back into the process and to learn more about its role in writing. We should use case studies, ethnographic studies, longitudinal studies, textual analysis, thinking-aloud protocol analysis, to answer such questions as these: What is the precise role in composing of substantive knowing—of concentrated participation in a knowledge/discourse community; of, simply, a fund of information on and ideas about the subject at hand? What, in this regard, is the precise relation between writing and reading? Where do we get our language for talking about things? What exactly *are* discourse conventions,[4] where do they come from, and how do we learn them? Are writers who know a great deal— who have engaged in direct and indirect sorts of inquiry within specific knowledge/discourse communities— likely to be better or different writers? Are writers who *know how* to find out likely to be better or different? What happens when people conduct inquiry and research? How *do* writers acquire the authority that impels writing? What *kinds* of knowing, and what kinds of knowing how, enable and assist writing?

Bizzell (238-239), Elaine Maimon, and Kenneth Bruffee ("Peer Tutoring") all argue that we must analyze and teach the conventions of academic discourse. It seems clear, however, that that's not enough. To do that is to continue to confine students to the "impoverished" "meanings carried by the conventional rules of language" (Cooper 108). Bruffee, citing Richard Rorty, notes that "In normal discourse . . . everyone agrees on the 'set of conventions about what counts as a relevant contribution, what counts as a question, what counts as having a good argument for that answer or a good criticism of it' " (8). He goes on to say, rightly, that "Not to have mastered the normal

---

[4] In this regard, see Bazerman, "What Written Knowledge Does." See also, on a different level, the two textbooks that have come out of the Beaver College writing-across-the-curriculum program: Maimon, et al., *Writing in the Arts and Sciences* and *Readings in the Arts and Sciences*.

discourse of a discipline, no matter how many 'facts' or data one may know, is not to be knowledgeable in that discipline" (9). But the obverse is equally true: What counts as a relevant contribution, question, answer, or criticism is determined not only by adherence to a set of discourse conventions, but also by such concerns as whether or not the contribution, question, answer, or criticism has already appeared in "the literature"—whether or not it is to the point, relevant, or timely. A writer addressing dead issues, posing questions already answered, or voicing irrelevant criticisms is judged ignorant and viewed as, at best, an initiate—not yet an insider, not yet a full member of the discipline. Rather more basically, what counts as relevant is a contribution in which the writer's version of "the facts of the matter" accords with the version held in general by the community addressed by the writing.

To belong to a discourse community is to belong to a knowledge community—an "inquiry community"; and the ways things are talked or written about are no more vital than the content of what's talked and written about. As Bruffee says, "Ordinary people write to inform and convince other people within the writer's own community..." (8). Because that's true, we must think not merely in terms of analysis and explanation; we must also think in terms of the other kinds of knowing required to belong to a community. We need to extend our understanding of the process of writing so that it will include not only experience- and memory-probing activities, but also inquiry strategies and techniques that will enable students to search beyond their own limited present experience and knowledge. We need to help students learn how to do the kinds of learning that will allow them, in their writing, to use what they *can* know, through effective inquiry, rather than suffer the limits of what they already know. We need to bring curiosity, the ability to conduct productive inquiry, and an obligation for substantive knowing into our model of the process of writing. To do that, we need to find ways to immerse writing students in academic knowledge/discourse communities so they can write from within those communities.

The writing-across-the-curriculum movement, when it's done well, seems to have a chance of doing that. So also does Bruffee's own collaborative learning, if it can be untied from the notion of peer tutoring. As matters now stand, however, neither of these adequately addresses the problem of teaching students how to come to know so they can write literally as "knowledgeable peers" (Bruffee, "Peer Tutoring" 6) in academic communities. Neither gives students opportunities to "indwell" (Polanyi) an actual academic knowledge/ discourse community, to learn, from the inside, its major questions, its governing assumptions, its language, its research methods, its evidential contexts, its forms, its discourse conventions, its major authors and its major texts—that is, its knowledge and its modes of knowing. Only this kind of immersion has a real chance of giving substance to their coming to know through composing.

The title of a course in which this immersion is to occur does not really matter. Neither does the name of the discipline or department in which the course is taught. It need not be a writing course. (In fact, obviously, this immersion need not occur in the context of a course at all. Most of us learned to do what we do on our own—perhaps in spite of the courses we took—and some students continue to do the same.) What does matter is that the course should be "organized as a collaborative investigation of a scholarly field rather than the delivery of a body of knowledge."[5]

As I have claimed above, discourse communities are also knowledge communities. The business of knowledge communities is inquiry—coming to know. In academia, inquiry necessarily begins with reading in the literature of a "scholarly field" (which may be almost anything: rhetoric or evolution, for instance; or deviant behavior, the literature of eighteenth-century England, the comedies of Shakespeare, Islamic religions, literacy, and so on). Because, in an essential way, the literature of a scholarly field *is* the scholarly field, reading in that literature is elemental to all other kinds and levels of investigation, including writing; and for all of us, but particularly for students, reading in the literature normally means library research. Furthermore, academic writing, reading, and inquiry are collaborative, social acts, social processes,[6] which not only result in, but also—and this is crucial—result *from,* social products: writing processes and written products are both elements of the *same social process.* Hence, academic writing, reading, and inquiry are inseparably linked; and all three are learned not by doing any one alone, but by doing them all at the same time. To "teach writing" is thus necessarily to ground writing in reading and inquiry.

In general terms, then, this immersion—this initiation—should image in important ways the "real world" of active, workaday academic inquirers. The course most effectively operates as a workshop[7] in which students read and write not merely for their teacher, but for themselves and for each other. In fact, students and teachers function best as co-investigators, with reading and writing being used collaboratively to conduct the inquiry. Organizing a course in this way allows an incredible range of reading activities—in everything from bibliographies to books; and a similar range of writing activities—from jotting down call numbers to writing formal articles of the sorts they are reading. What matters is that this should be language in use. In such a context, writing, reading, and inquiry are evaluated according to their

---

[5] Russell A. Hunt, my colleague at St. Thomas University, phrased it this way in a course description.

[6] Bizzell's article and Bruffee's "Peer Tutoring" (or his recontextualization of that article, "Collaborative Writing and the 'Conversation of Mankind,' ") are important here, not only for their discussions of the social grounding of writing, but also for their references to much of the important literature in this particular scholarly field. See (for example) the following theoretical works: Fleck, *Genesis and Development of a Scientific Fact;* Rorty, *Philosophy and the Mirror of Nature,* esp. Part III; Fish, *Is There a Text in This Class?;* and, most important, Kuhn, *The Structure of Scientific Revolutions.* Finally, for a sampling of various kinds of research in this area, see Bazerman's "What Written Knowledge Does"; the work of Odell and Goswami—for example, "Writing in a Nonacademic Setting"; and Myers, "Texts as Knowledge Claims."

[7] For a model of the kind of workshop this might be, see Knoblauch and Brannon. A major difference between their ideal workshop and mine is that I would embed the discourse community of the workshop in the socially-constructed knowing available in the record of the larger conversation going on in the literature of the scholarly field being investigated.

pragmatic utility: the important question is not "How good is it?" but, instead, "To what extent and how effectively does it contribute to and further the investigation?" The inquiry is made manageable in the same way all such inquiries are made manageable, not by "choosing" and "focusing" a topic, but by seeking answers to the questions which impel the investigation.

Out of this immersion in academic inquiry and out of the ways they see themselves and others (both their immediate peers and those who have authored the literature of the field) using reading and writing to conduct the inquiry, students can construct appropriate models. That is, they can see effective and ineffective writing, reading, and inquiry conventions, strategies, and behaviors at work— not just as those conventions and behaviors can be inferred by reading in the literature, but also as they are evolved and used by their teachers and *each other.* Student and teacher roles in the workshop evolve out of their own participation in the investigation: reading and writing; exchanging and using each others' information, ideas, notes, annotations, sources; defining goals and making plans; applying "truth-seeking procedures" (Bach and Harnish 43); bringing to bear topic and world knowledge to conduct what Bereiter and Scardamalia call "reflective inquiry" (5-6).

At the core of composition studies is the virtually unchallenged conviction that what we have to study and what we have to teach is "process not product." By process, however, we presently mean something that encourages in our students the notion that through writing they can, like Plato's Gorgias, "answer any question that is put to [them]" (20). Because we routinely put our students in arhetorical situations in which they can only write out of ignorance, they have little choice but to "hunt more after words than matter" (Bacon 29), and we stand open to the charge that we advocate "mere rhetoric" over writing informed by a profound relationship between writers and their worlds. It is time to redefine the writing process so that substantive social knowing is given due prominence in both our thinking and our teaching.

Works Cited

Bach, K., and R. M. Harnish. *Linguistic Communication and Speech Acts.* Cambridge: MIT P, 1979.

Bacon, Francis. *The Advancement of Learning.* Oxford: Oxford UP, 1951.

Bazerman, Charles. "A Relationship between Reading and Writing: The Conversational Model." *College English* **41** (1980): 656-661.

_____. "What Written Knowledge Does: Three Examples of Academic Discourse." *Philosophy of the Social Sciences* 11 (1981): 361-387.

Bereiter, Carl, and Marlene Scardamalia. "Levels of Inquiry in Writing Research." *Research on Writing: Principles and Methods.* Eds. Peter Mosenthal, Lynne Tamor, and Sean A. Walmsley. New York: Longman, 1983. 3-25.

Bizzell, Patricia. "Cognition, Convention, and Certainty: What We Need to Know about Writing." *PRE/TEXT* 3 (1982): 213-243.

Bruffee, Kenneth A. "Collaborative Writing and the 'Conversation of Mankind.'" *College English* 46 (1984): 635-652.

_____. "Peer Tutoring and the 'Conversation of Mankind.'" *Writing Centers: Theory and Administration.* Ed. Gary A. Olson. Urbana: NCTE, 1984. 3-15.

Cooper, Marilyn M. "Context as Vehicle: Implicatures in Writing." *What Writers Know: The Language, Process, and Structure of Written Discourse.* Ed. Martin Nystrand. New York: Academic, 1982. 105-128.

Cowan, Gregory, and Elizabeth Cowan. *Writing.* New York: Wiley, 1980.

Emig, Janet. *The Composing Processes of Twelfth Graders.* Urbana: NCTE, 1971.

Fish, Stanley. *Is There a Text in This Class?: The Authority of Interpretive Communities.* Cambridge: Harvard UP, 1980.

Fleck, Ludwik. *Genesis and Development of a Scientific Fact.* 1935. Chicago: U of Chicago P, 1979.

Flower, Linda, and John R. Hayes. "A Cognitive Process Theory of Writing." *College Composition and Communication* 32 (1981): 365-387.

Gage, John. "Towards an Epistemology of Composition." *Journal of Advanced Composition* 2 (1981): 1-9.

Knoblauch, C. H., and Lil Brannon. "Modern Rhetoric in the Classroom: Making Meaning Matter." *Rhetorical Traditions and the Teaching of Writing.* Upper Montclair, NJ: Boynton/Cook, 1984. 98-117.

Kuhn, Thomas. *The Structure of Scientific Revolutions.* 2nd ed., enlarged. Chicago: U of Chicago P. 1970.

Larson, Richard L. "The Writer's Mind: Recent Research and Unanswered Questions." *The Writer's Mind: Writing as a Mode of Thinking.* Ed. Janice M. Hays, et al. Urbana: NCTE, 1983. 239-251.

Maimon, Elaine P. "Maps and Genres: Exploring Connections in the Arts and Sciences." *Composition and Literature: Bridging the Gap.* Ed. Winifred Bryan Horner. Chicago: U of Chicago P, 1983. 110-125.

Maimon, Elaine P., et al. *Readings in the Arts and Sciences.* Boston: Little, 1984.

_____. *Writing in the Arts and Sciences.* Cambridge, MA: Winthrop, 1981.

Matsuhashi, Ann. "Pausing and Planning: The Tempo of Written Discourse Production." *Research in the Teaching of English* 15 (1981): 113-134.

Murray, Donald M. "Write Before Writing." *College Composition and Communication* 29 (1978): 375-381.

_____. "Writing as Process: How Writing Finds Its Own Meaning." *Eight Approaches to Teaching Composition.* Ed. Timothy R. Donovan and Ben W. McClelland. Urbana: NCTE, 1980. 3-20.

Myers, Greg. "Texts as Knowledge Claims: The Social Construction of Two Biology Articles." *Social Studies of Science.* Forthcoming.

Odell, Lee. "Reading and Writing in the Workplace." Conference on College Composition and Communication. New York City, 31 March 1984.

Odell, Lee, and Dixie Goswami. "Writing in a Nonacademic Setting." *New Directions in Composition Research.* Ed. Richard Beach and Lillian S. Bridwell. New York: Guilford, 1984. 233-258.

Perl, Sondra. "Understanding Composing." *College Composition and Communication* 31 (1980): 363-369.

Plato. *Gorgias.* Trans. Walter Hamilton. Harmondsworth: Penguin, 1971.

Polanyi, Michael. *Personal Knowledge: Towards a Post-Critical Philosophy.* Chicago: U of Chicago P, 1962.

Rohman, D. Gordon. "Pre-writing: The Stage of Discovery in the Writing Process." *College Composition and Communication* 16 (1965): 106-112.

Rorty, Richard. *Philosophy and the Mirror of Nature.* Princeton: Princeton UP, 1979.

Schor, Sandra. "Style Through Control: The Pleasures of the Beginning Writer." *Linguistics, Stylistics, and the Teaching of Composition.* Ed. Donald McQuade. Akron, OH: L and S, 1979. 72-80.

Sommers, Nancy. "Revision Strategies of Student Writers and Experienced Adult Writers." *College Composition and Communication* 31 (1980): 378-388.

Competing Theories of Process:
A Critique and a Proposal

by Lester Faigley

The recognition of the study of writing as an important area of research within English in North America has also led to a questioning of its theoretical underpinnings. While the teaching of writing has achieved programmatic or departmental status at many colleges and universities, voices from outside and from within the ranks question whether a discipline devoted to the study of writing exists or if those who teach writing simply assume it exists because they share common problems and interests. The convenient landmark for disciplinary historians is the Richard Braddock, Richard Lloyd-Jones, and Lowell Schoer review of the field in 1963, a survey that found a legion of pedagogical studies of writing, most lacking any broad theoretical notion of writing abilities or even awareness of similar existing studies. Contemporary reviewers of writing research point out how much happened in the years that followed, but no development has been more influential than the emphasis on writing as a process. For the last few years, Richard Young's and Maxine Hairston's accounts of the process movement as a Kuhnian paradigm shift have served as justifications for disciplinary status. Even though the claim of a paradigm shift is now viewed by some as an overstatement, it is evident that many writing teachers in grade schools, high schools, and colleges have internalized process assumptions. In the most optimistic visions, writing teachers K-13 march happily under the process banner. Slogans such as "revising is good for you" are repeated in nearly every college writing textbook as well as in many secondary and elementary classrooms. Paradigm, pre-paradigm, or no paradigm, nearly everyone seems to agree that writing as a process is good and "current-traditional rhetoric" is bad. It would seem, therefore, that any disciplinary claims must be based on some shared definition of process.

The problem, of course, is that conceptions of writing as a process vary from theorist to theorist. Commentators on the process movement (e.g., Berlin, *Writing Instruction)* now assume at least two major perspectives on composing, an *expressive view* including the work of "authentic voice" proponents such as William Coles, Peter Elbow, Ken Macrorie, and Donald

Stewart, and a *cognitive view* including the research of those who analyze composing processes such as Linda Flower, Barry Kroll, and Andrea Lunsford. More recently, a third perspective on composing has emerged, one that contends processes of writing are social in character instead of originating within individual writers. Statements on composing from the third perspective, which I call the *social view,* have come from Patricia Bizzell, Kenneth Bruffee, Marilyn Cooper, Shirley Brice Heath, James Reither, and authors of several essays collected in *Writing in Nonacademic Settings* edited by Lee Odell and Dixie Goswami.

Before I contrast the assumptions of each of these three views on composing with the goal of identifying a disciplinary basis for the study of writing, I want to raise the underlying assumption that the study and teaching of writing *should* aspire to disciplinary status. In a radical critique of education in America, Stanley Aronowitz and Henry Giroux see the development of writing programs as part of a more general trend toward an atheoretical and skills-oriented curriculum that regards teachers as civil servants who dispense pre-packaged lessons. Here is Aronowitz and Giroux's assessment:

> We wish to suggest that schools, especially the colleges and universities, are now battlegrounds that may help to determine the shape of the future. The proliferation of composition programs at all levels of higher education may signal a new effort to extend the technicization process even further into the humanities. . . . The splitting of composition as a course from the study of literature, [sic] is of course a sign of its technicization and should be resisted both because it is an attack against critical thought and because it results in demoralization of teachers and their alienation from work. (52)

While I find their conclusions extreme, their critique provokes us to examine writing in relation to larger social and political issues. Unlike most other Marxist educational theorists, Aronowitz and Giroux do not present a pessimistic determinism nor do they deny human agency. They allow for the possibility that teachers and students can resist domination and think critically, thus leaving open the possibility for a historically aware theory and pedagogy of composing.

I will outline briefly the histories of each of the dominant theoretical views of composing, drawing on an earlier book by Giroux, *Theory and Resistance in Education,* for a critical review of the assumptions of each position.[1] In the concluding section of this essay, however, I reject Aronowitz and Giroux's dour assessment of the study of writing as a discipline. Each of the theoretical positions on composing has given teachers of writing a pedagogy for resisting a narrow definition of writing based largely on

---

[1] Giroux directly criticizes "romantic" and "cognitive developmental" traditions of teaching literacy in *Theory and Resistance in Education.* Bruce Herzberg has extended Giroux's critique to particular composition theorists.

"correct" grammar and usage. Finally, I argue that disciplinary claims for writing must be based on a conception of process broader than any of the three views.

The Expressive View

The beginnings of composing research in the mid-1960s hardly marked a revolution against the prevailing line of research; in fact, early studies of composing issues typically were isolated pedagogical experiments similar to those described by Braddock, Lloyd-Jones, and Schoer. One of these experiments was D. Gordon Rohman and Albert Wlecke's study of the effects of "pre-writing" on writing performance, first published in 1964. Rohman and Wlecke maintained that thinking was different from writing and antecedent to writing; therefore, teachers should stimulate students' thinking by having them write journals, construct analogies, and, in the spirit of the sixties, meditate before writing essays. Young cites the Rohman and Wlecke study as one that helped to overturn the current-traditional paradigm. What Young neglects to mention is that Rohman and Wlecke revived certain Romantic notions about composing and were instigators of a "neo-Romantic" view of process. Rohman defines "good writing" as

> that discovered combination of words which allows a person the integrity to dominate his subject with a pattern both fresh and original. "Bad writing," then, is an echo of someone else's combination which we have merely taken over for the occasion of our writing. . . . "Good writing" must be the discovery by a responsible person of his uniqueness within his subject. (107-08)

This definition of "good writing" includes the essential qualities of Romantic expressivism—integrity, spontaneity, and originality—the same qualities M. H. Abrams uses to define "expressive" poetry in *The Mirror and the Lamp*.

Each of these expressivist qualities has motivated a series of studies and theoretical statements on composing. We can see the influence of the first notion—integrity—in the transmission of Rohman and Wlecke's definitions of "good" and "bad" writing. In 1969 Donald Stewart argued that the unified aim for writing courses should be writing with integrity. He illustrated his argument with a student paper titled "Money Isn't as Valuable as It Seems" that contained a series of predictable generalities. Stewart criticized the student not for failing to support his generalizations but because he "doesn't believe what he is saying. Worse yet, it is possible that he doesn't even realize he doesn't believe it" (225).[2] The problem with using integrity as a measure

---

[2] Even more strident attacks on cliches and conventional writing assignments came from Ken Macrorie, who damned "themes" as papers "not meant to be read but corrected" (686), and from William Coles, who accused textbook authors of promoting "themewriting" by presenting writing "as a trick that can be played, a device that can be put into operation . . . just as one can be taught or learn to run an adding machine, or pour concrete" (134-42).

of value is obvious in retrospect. Not only is the writer of the paper Stewart reproduces bound by his culture, as Stewart argues, but so too are Stewart's criticisms. Stewart's charges of insincerity are based on the assumption that the student is parroting the anti-establishment idealism of the late sixties. Conversely, career-oriented students of today are so unlikely to write such a paper, that if one started an essay with the same sentences as Stewart's example ("Having money is one of the least important items of life. Money only causes problems and heartaches among one's friends and self."), a teacher likely would assume that the student believed what she was saying, no matter how trite or predictable.

Because the sincerity of a text is finally impossible to assess, a second quality of Romantic expressivism—spontaneity—became important to the process movement primarily through Peter Elbow's *Writing without Teachers,* a book that was written for a broad audience, and that enjoyed great popular success. Elbow adopted Macrorie's method of free writing, but he presented the method as practical advice for writing spontaneously, not as a way of discovering "the truth." Elbow questioned Rohman and Wlecke's separation of thinking from writing, a model he maintained led to frustration. Instead, Elbow urged that we

> think of writing as an organic, developmental process in which you start writing at the very beginning—before you know your meaning at all—and encourage your words gradually to change and evolve. Only at the end will you know what you want to say or the words you want to say it with. (15)

Elbow chose the metaphor of organic growth to describe the operations of composing, the same metaphor Edward Young used to describe the vegetable concept of genius in 1759 and Coleridge borrowed from German philosophers to describe the workings of the imagination (see Abrams 198-225). Coleridge contrasted two kinds of form—one mechanical, when we impress upon any material a predetermined form, the other organic, when the material shapes itself from within. Coleridge also realized the plant metaphor implied a kind of organic determinism. (Tulip bulbs cannot grow into daffodils.) He avoided this consequence by insisting upon the free will of the artist, that the artist has foresight and the power of choice. In much the same way, Elbow qualifies his organic metaphor:

> It is true, of course, that an initial set of words does not, like a young live organism, contain within each cell a *plan* for the final mature stage and all the intervening stages that must be gone through. Perhaps, therefore, the final higher organization in words should only be called a borrowed reflection of a higher organization that is really in me or my mind. (23)

Elbow's point is one of the standards of Romantic theory: that "good" writing does not follow rules but reflects the processes of the creative imagination.

If writing is to unfold with organic spontaneity, then it ought to expose the writer's false starts and confused preliminary explorations of the topic. In other words, the writing should proceed obliquely as a "striving toward"—a mimetic of the writer's actual thought processes—and only hint at the goal of such striving. The resultant piece of writing would then seem fragmentary and unfinished, but would reveal what Coleridge calls a progressive method, a psychological rather than rhetorical organization, unifying its outwardly disparate parts. On the other hand, insofar as a piece of writing—no matter how expressive—is coherent, it must also be mimetic and rhetorical. At times Wordsworth and to a lesser extent Coleridge seem to argue that expressivism precludes all intentionality—as if such meditations as Wordsworth's "Tintern Abbey" and Coleridge's "This Lime-Tree Bower My Prison" weren't carefully *arranged* to seem spontaneous. Peter Elbow's solution to the dilemma of spontaneity comes in *Writing with Power,* where he discusses revision as the shaping of unformed material.

A third quality of Romantic expressivism—originality—could not be adapted directly to current theories of composing because the Romantic notion of originality is linked to the notion of natural genius, the difference between the poet who is born and the poet who is made. The concept of natural genius has been replaced in contemporary expressive theory with an emphasis on the innate potential of the unconscious mind. More limited statements of this position recommend teaching creative writing to stimulate originality.[3] Stronger statements come from those expressive theorists who apply the concept of "self-actualization" from psychoanalysis to writing. Rohman says teachers "must recognize and use, as the psychologists do in therapy, a person's desire to actualize himself" (108). The implication is that personal development aids writing development or that writing development can aid personal development, with the result that better psychologically integrated people become better writers. (Case histories of twentieth-century poets and novelists are seldom introduced in these discussions.) In an essay on meditation and writing James Moffett extends the self-actualization notion introduced by Rohman, saying "good therapy and composition aim at clear thinking, effective relating, and satisfying self-expression" (235).

Giroux, however, would see Moffett's essay as emblematic of what is wrong with the expressive view. Although Giroux grants that expressive theory came as a reaction against, to use his word, the "technicization" of education, he contends the result of the quest for "psychic redemption" and "personal growth" is a turning away from the relation of the individual to the social world, a world where "social practices situated in issues of class, gender, and race shape everyday experience" (219). For Giroux, the expressive view of composing ignores how writing works in the world, hides the social nature of language, and offers a false notion of a "private" self. Before I defend the expressive position against Giroux's attack, I will move on to the

---

[3] For example, Art Young advocates having students write poems, plays, and stories in writing-across-the-curriculum classes. During the 1920s and 1930s, there were numerous appeals to incorporate creative writing into the English curriculum; see, for example, Lou LaBrant.

cognitive view where Giroux's strongest criticisms center.

The Cognitive View

In addition to promoting expressive assumptions about composing, Rohman and Wlecke helped inspire research that led to the current cognitive view. Several researchers in the late sixties were encouraged by Rohman and Wlecke's mention of *heuristics* and their finding that students who were taught "pre-writing" activities wrote better essays. More important, Rohman and Wlecke's proposal of three linear stages in the writing process stimulated research in response. In 1964 Janet Emig first argued against a linear model of composing, and she redoubled her attack in her 1969 dissertation, later published as an NCTE research monograph. Emig was among the first writing researchers to act on calls for research on cognitive processes issued at the influential 1966 Dartmouth Seminar on English. She observed that high school writers, in contrast to standard textbook advice of the time, did not use outlines to compose and that composing "does not occur as a left-to-right, solid, uninterrupted activity with an even pace" (84). Instead, Emig described composing as "recursive," an adjective from mathematics that refers to a formula generating successive terms. While the term is technically misapplied, since writing processes do not operate this simply, the extent to which it is used by other researchers attests to Emig's influence. Another measure of Emig's influence is that denunciations of Rohman and Wlecke's *Pre-writing, Writing, Re-writing* model became a trope for introductions of later articles on composing.

In a recent consideration of Emig's monograph, Ralph Voss credits her with developing a "'science consciousness' in composition research" (279). Emig appropriated from psychology more than the case-study approach and think-aloud methodology. Her monograph is a mixture of social science and literary idioms, with one sentence talking about a "sense of closure," the next about "a moment in the process when one feels most godlike" (44). Emig's work was well received because writing researchers wanted to enter the mainstream of educational research. For example, Janice Lauer began a 1970 article directing writing researchers to psychologists' work in problem solving with the following sentence: "Freshman English will never reach the status of a respectable intellectual discipline unless both its theorizers and its practitioners break out of the ghetto" (396). Emig provided not only a new methodology but an agenda for subsequent research, raising issues such as pausing during composing, the role of rereading in revision, and the paucity of substantial revision in student writing. Her monograph led to numerous observational studies of writers' composing behavior during the next decade.[4]

The main ingredient Emig did not give researchers was a cognitive theory of composing. When writing researchers realized Chomsky's theory of transformational grammar could not explain composing abilities, they turned

---

[4] For a bibliographic review of cognitive studies of composing, see Faigley, Cherry, Jolliffe, and Skinner, chapters 1-5.

to two other sources of cognitive theory. The first was cognitive-developmental psychology, which James Britton and his colleagues applied to the developing sense of audience among young writers. Britton argued that children as speakers gain a sense of audience because the hearer is a reactive presence, but children as writers have more difficulty because the "other" is not present. Consequently, a child writing must imagine a generalized context for the particular text in all but the most immediate writing situations (such as an informal letter). Britton condemned most school writing assignments for failing to encourage children to imagine real writing situations (see *Development* 63-65). Other researchers probed the notion of developmental stages in writing. Barry Kroll adapted Jean Piaget's concept of *egocentrism*—the inability to take any perspective but one's own—to explain young children's lack of a sense of audience. He hypothesized, like Britton, that children's ability to *decenter*—to imagine another perspective—develops more slowly in writing than in speaking. Andrea Lunsford extended Piaget's stages of cognitive development to college basic writers, arguing that their tendency to lapse into personal narrative in writing situations that call for "abstract" discourse indicates they are arrested in an "egocentric stage."

The second source of cognitive theory came from American cognitive psychology, which has spawned several strands of research on composing. Many college writing teachers were introduced to a cognitive theory of composing through the work of Linda Flower and John R. Hayes. Flower and Hayes' main claims—that composing processes intermingle, that goals direct composing, and that experts compose differently from inexperienced writers—all have become commonplaces of the process movement. Less well understood by writing teachers, however, are the assumptions underlying Flower and Hayes' model, assumptions derived from a cognitive research tradition. Flower and Hayes acknowledge their debt to this tradition, especially to Allen Newell and Herbert A. Simon's *Human Problem Solving,* a classic work that helped define the aims and agenda for a cognitive science research program. Newell and Simon theorize that the key to understanding how people solve problems is in their "programmability"; in other words, how people use "a very simple information processing system" to account for their "problem solving in such tasks as chess, logic, and cryptarithmetic" (870). The idea that thinking and language can be represented by computers underlies much research in cognitive science in several camps, including artificial intelligence, computational linguistics, and cognitive psychology. Newell and Simon's historical overview of this movement credits Norbert Wiener's theory of *cybernetics* as the beginnings of contemporary cognitive science.[5] The basic principle of cybernetics is the *feedback loop,* in which the

---

[5] Wiener used the term *cybernetics*—derived from the Greek word for the pilot of a ship—as a metaphor for the functioning mind. He claimed as a precedent James Watt's use of the word *governor* to describe the mechanical regulator of a steam engine. Wiener's metaphor explained the mind as a control mechanism such as an automatic pilot of an airplane. For a historical overview of cybernetics and the beginnings of cognitive science, see Bell.

regulating mechanism receives information from the thing regulated and makes adjustments.

George A. Miller was among the first to introduce cybernetic theory as an alternative to the stimulus-response reflex arc as the basis of mental activity. In *Plans and the Structure of Behavior,* Miller, Eugene Galanter, and Karl Pribram describe human behavior as guided by plans that are constantly being evaluated as they are being carried out in a feedback loop. They theorize that the brain—like a computer—is divided into a *memory* and a *processing unit.* What Miller, Galanter, and Pribram do not attempt to theorize is where plans come from. To fill in this gap, Newell and Simon add to the feedback loop an entity they call the *task environment,* defined in terms of a goal coupled with a specific environment. Newell and Simon claim the resulting loop explains how people think.

If we look at the graphic representation of the Flower and Hayes model in the 1980 and 1981 versions, we can see how closely the overall design follows in the cognitive science tradition. The box labelled *Writing Processes* is analogous to the central processing unit of a computer. In the 1980 version, diagrams representing the subprocesses of composing *(planning, translating, and reviewing)* are presented as computer flowcharts. Like Newell and Simon's model of information processing, Flower and Hayes' model makes strong theoretical claims in assuming relatively simple cognitive operations produce enormously complex actions, and like Emig's monograph, the Flower and Hayes model helped promote a "science consciousness" among writing teachers. Even though cognitive researchers have warned that "novice writers cannot be turned into experts simply by tutoring them in the knowledge expert writers have" (Scardamalia 174), many writing teachers believed cognitive research could provide a "deep structure" theory of *the* composing process, which could in turn specify how writing should be taught. Furthermore, the Flower and Hayes model had other attractions. The place-ment of *translating* after *planning* was compatible with the sequence of invention, arrangement, and style in classical rhetoric. It also suited a popular conception that language comes after ideas are formed, a conception found in everyday metaphors that express ideas as objects placed in containers (e.g., "It's difficult to put my ideas into words").[6]

Giroux's response to the cognitive view of composing can be readily inferred. To begin, Giroux would be highly critical of any attempt to discover universal laws underlying writing. Writing for Giroux, like other acts of literacy, is not universal but social in nature and cannot be removed from culture. He would fault the cognitive view for collapsing cultural issues under the label "audience," which, defined unproblematically, is reduced to the status of a variable in an equation. He further would accuse the cognitive view of neglecting the content of writing and downplaying conflicts inherent

---

[6] Reddy discusses some of the consequences of the "conduit" metaphor for our understanding of lan-guage.

in acts of writing. As a consequence, pedagogies assuming a cognitive view tend to overlook differences in language use among students of different social classes, genders, and ethnic backgrounds.

At this point I'll let Giroux's bricks fly against my windows and use an article on revision I wrote with Steve Witte as a case in point. In this study Witte and I attempt to classify revision changes according to the extent they affect the content of the text. We apply a scheme for describing the structure of a text developed by the Dutch text linguist, Teun van Dijk. What seems obviously wrong with this article in hindsight is the degree to which we assign meaning to the text. Now even van Dijk admits there are as many macrostructures for a text as there are readers. Although our conclusions criticize the artificiality of the experiment and recognize that "revision cannot be separated from other aspects of composing," the intent of the study still suffers from what Giroux sees as a fundamental flaw of cognitivist research— the isolation of part from whole.

The Social View

The third perspective on composing I identified at the beginning of this essay—the social view—is less codified and less constituted at present than the expressive and cognitive views because it arises from several disciplinary traditions. Because of this diversity a comprehensive social view cannot be extrapolated from a collection of positions in the same way I have described the expressive and cognitive views of composing. Statements that propose a social view of writing range from those urging more attention to the immediate circumstances of how a text is composed to those denying the existence of an individual author. My effort to outline a social view will be on the basis of one central assumption: human language (including writing) can be understood only from the perspective of a society rather than a single individual. Thus taking a social view requires a great deal more than simply paying more attention to the context surrounding a discourse. It rejects the assumption that writing is the act of a private consciousness and that everything else—readers, subjects, and texts—is "out there" in the world. The focus of a social view of writing, therefore, is not on how the social situation influences the individual, but on how the individual is a constituent of a culture.

I will attempt to identify four lines of research that take a social view of writing, although I recognize that these positions overlap and that each draws on earlier work (e.g., Kenneth Burke). These four lines of research can be characterized by the traditions from which they emerge: poststructuralist theories of language, the sociology of science, ethnography, and Marxism.

In the last few years, writing researchers influenced by poststructuralist theories of language have brought notions of discourse communities to discussions of composing. Patricia Bizzell and David Bartholomae, for example, have found such ideas advantageous in examining the writing of college students. Those who believe that meaning resides in the text accuse any other position of solipsism and relativism, but concepts of discourse communities provide an alternative position, offering solutions to difficult problems in interpretative theory. Reading is neither an experience of extracting a fixed meaning from a text nor is it a matter of making words mean anything you want them to in *Alice in Wonderland* fashion. Ambiguity in texts is not the problem for humans that it is for computers—not so much because we are better at extracting meaning but because language is social practice; because, to paraphrase Bakhtin, words carry with them the places where they have been.

This view of language raises serious problems for cognitive-based research programs investigating adults' composing processes. For instance, Bizzell criticizes the separation of "Planning" and "Translating" in the Flower and Hayes model. Even though Flower and Hayes allow for language to generate language through rereading, Bizzell claims the separation of words from ideas distorts the nature of composing. Bizzell cites Vygotsky, whom many cognitive researchers lump together with Piaget, but whose understanding of language is very different from Piaget's. Vygotsky studied language development as a historical and cultural process, in which a child acquires not only the words of language but the intentions carried by those words and the situations implied by them.

From a social perspective, a major shortcoming in studies that contrast expert and novice writers lies not so much in the artificiality of the experimental situation, but in the assumption that expertise can be defined outside of a specific community of writers. Since individual expertise varies across communities, there can be no one definition of an expert writer. David Bartholomae explores the implications for the teaching of college writing. He argues that writing in college is difficult for inexperienced writers not because they are forced to make the transition from "writer-based" to "reader-based" prose but because they lack the privileged language of the academic community. Bartholomae's point is similar to Bizzell's: when students write in an academic discipline, they write in reference to texts that define the scholarly activities of interpreting and reporting in that discipline. Bartholomae alludes to Barthes' observation that a text on a particular topic always has "off-stage voices" for what has previously been written about that topic. Thus a social view of writing moves beyond the expressivist contention that the individual discovers the self through language and beyond the cognitivist position that an individual constructs reality through language. In a social view, any effort to write about the self or reality always comes in relation to previous texts.

A substantial body of research examining the social processes of writing in an academic discourse community now exists in the sociology of science. Most of this research has been done in Britain, but Americans Charles Bazerman and Greg Myers have made important contributions (see Myers' review article in the October, 1986, issue of *CE*). Research in scientific writing displays many of the theoretical and methodological differences mentioned at the beginning of this section, but this literature taken as a whole challenges the assumption that scientific texts contain autonomous presentations of facts; instead, the texts are "active social tools in the complex interactions of a research community" (Bazerman 3). In the more extreme version of this argument, which follows from Rorty and other pragmatists, science itself becomes a collection of literary forms. Writing about the basis of economics, Donald McCloskey calls statistics "figures of speech in numerical dress" (98). He goes on to say that "the scientific paper is, after all, a literary genre, with an actual author, an implied author, an implied reader, a history, and a form" (105). In contrast, current British research understands a dialectical relationship between external reality and the conventions of a community. A good introduction to this field is Nigel Gilbert and Michael Mulkay's 1984 book, *Opening Pandora's Box*.[7]

A third line of research taking a social view of composing develops from the tradition of ethnography. Ethnographic methodology in the 1970s and 1980s has been used to examine the immediate communities in which writers learn to write—the family and the classroom. These researchers have observed that for many children, the ways literacy is used at home and in the world around them matches poorly with the literacy expectations of the school.[8] The most important of these studies to date is Shirley Brice Heath's analysis of working-class and middle-class families in the Carolina Piedmont. Heath found that how children learn to use literacy originates from how families and communities are structured. Another line of research using ethnographic methodology investigates writing in the workplace, interpreting acts of writing and reading within the culture of the workplace (see Odell and Goswami for examples).

Finally, I include Marxist studies of literacy as a fourth social position on composing. The essential tenet of a Marxist position would be that any act of writing or of teaching writing must be understood within a structure of power related to modes of production. A Marxist critique of the other social positions would accuse each of failing to deal with key concepts such as class, power, and ideology.[9] Giroux finds discourse communities are often more concerned with ways of excluding new members than with ways of admitting them. He attacks non-Marxist ethnographies for sacrificing "theoretical depth for methodological refinement" (98). Indeed, much Marxist scholarship consists of faulting other theorists for their lack of political sophistication.

Toward a Synthesis

At the beginning of this essay I quoted Aronowitz and Giroux's conclusion that the spread of writing programs and, by implication, the process

---

[7] Gilbert and Mulkay provide a bibliography of social studies of scientific discourse on 194-95.

[8] Heath includes an annotated bibliography of school and community ethnographies in the end-notes of *Ways with Words.*

[9] Richard Ohmann's *English in America* remains the seminal Marxist analysis of American writing instruction.

movement itself are part of a general movement toward "atheoretical" and "skills-oriented" education in America. Now I would like to evaluate that claim. If process theory and pedagogy have up to now been unproblematically accepted, I see a danger that it could be unproblematically rejected. Process theory and pedagogy have given student writing a value and authority absent in current-traditional approaches. Each view of process has provided teachers with ways of resisting static methods of teaching writing—methods based on notions of abstract form and adherence to the "rules" of Standard English. Expressive theorists validate personal experience in school systems that often deny it. Cognitive theorists see language as a way of negotiating the world, which is the basis of James Berlin's dialogic redefinition of epistemic rhetoric *(Rhetoric and Reality)*. And social theorists such as Heath have found that children who are labelled remedial in traditional classrooms can learn literacy skills by studying the occurrences of writing in the familiar world around them (see *Ways with Words,* Chapter 9).

But equally instructive is the conclusion of Heath's book, where she describes how the curriculum she helped create was quickly swept away. It illustrates how social and historical forces shape the teaching of writing—relationships that, with few exceptions, are only now beginning to be critically investigated. If the process movement is to continue to influence the teaching of writing and to supply alternatives to current-traditional pedagogy, it must take a broader conception of writing, one that understands writing processes are historically dynamic—not psychic states, cognitive routines, or neutral social relationships. This historical awareness would allow us to reinterpret and integrate each of the theoretical perspectives I have outlined.

The expressive view presents one of two opposing influences in discourse—the unique character of particular acts of writing versus the conventions of language, genre, and social occasion that make that act understandable to others. The expressive view, therefore, leads us to one of the key paradoxes of literacy. When literacy began to be widespread in Northern Europe and its colonies during the eighteenth and nineteenth centuries, it reduced differences between language groups in those countries and brought an emphasis on standard usage. But at the same time linguistic differences were being reduced, individuals became capable of changing the social order by writing for a literate populace (witness the many revolutionary tracts published during the nineteenth century). Furthermore, modern notions of the individual came into being through the widespread publication of the many literary figures and philosophers associated with the Romantic movement and the later development of psychology as a discipline in the nineteenth century. Current technologies for electronic communications bring the potential for gaining access to large bodies of information from the home, yet at the same time these technologies bring increased potential for control through surveillance of communication and restriction of access. People, however, find ways to adapt technologies for their own interests. In organizations where computer technologies have become commonplace, people have taken advantage of opportunities for horizontal communication on topics of their choice through computer "bulletin boards," which function like radio call-in programs. For example, on ARPANET, the Department of Defense's computer network linking research facilities, military contractors, and universities, popular bulletin boards include ones for science fiction, movie reviews, and even a lively debate on arms control. How the possibilities for individual expression will be affected by major technological changes in progress should become one of the most important areas of research for those who study writing.

In a similar way, historical awareness would enhance a cognitive view of composing by demonstrating the historical origins of an individual writer's goals. The cognitive view has brought attention to how writers compose in the workplace. Many writing tasks on the job can be characterized as rhetorical "problems," but the problems themselves are not ones the writers devise. Writing processes take place as part of a structure of power. For instance, Lee Iacocca's autobiography reveals how writing conveys power in large organizations. Iacocca says he communicated good news in writing, but bad news orally. Surely Iacocca's goals and processes in writing are inseparable from what he does and where he works, which in turn must be considered in relation to other large corporations, and which finally should be considered within a history of capitalism.

Some social approaches to the study of discourse entail historical awareness, but a social view is not necessarily historical. The insight that the learning of literacy is a social activity within a specific community will not necessarily lead us to a desirable end. Raymond Williams observes that the term *community* has been used to refer to existing social relationships or possible alternative social relationships, but that it is always used positively, that there is no opposing term. Yet we know from the sad experiences of the twentieth century that consensus often brings oppression. How written texts become instruments of power in a community is evident in the history of colonial empires, where written documents served to implement colonial power. Some of the earliest recorded uses of writing in Mesopotamia and ancient Egypt were for collecting taxes and issuing laws in conquered territories. Written documents made possible the incident George Orwell describes in "The Hanging"—an essay frequently anthologized but rarely analyzed in writing classes for its political significance. Furthermore, in the effort to identify conventions that define communities of writers, commentators on writing processes from a social viewpoint have neglected the issue of what *cannot* be discussed in a particular community, exclusions Foucault has shown to be the exercise of power.

These questions are not mere matters of ivory-tower debate. The preoccupation with an underlying theory of the writing process has led us to neglect finding answers to the most obvious questions in college writing instruction today: why college writing courses are prevalent in the United States and rare in the rest of the world; why the emphasis on teaching writing occurring in the aftermath of the "literacy crisis" of the seventies has not abated; why the majority of college writing courses are taught by graduate students and other persons in nontenurable positions. Answers to such questions will come only when we look beyond who is writing to whom to the texts and social systems that stand in relation to that act of writing. If the teaching of writing is to reach disciplinary status, it will be achieved through recognition that writing processes are, as Stanley Fish says of linguistic knowledge, "contextual rather than abstract, local rather than general, dynamic rather than invariant" (438).

Works Cited

Abrams, M. H. *The Mirror and the Lamp.* New York: Oxford UP, 1953.

Aronowitz, Stanley, and Henry A. Giroux. *Education Under Siege.* South Hadley, MA: Bergin, 1985.

Bartholomae, David. "Inventing the University." *When A Writer Can't Write.* Ed. Mike Rose. New York: Guilford, 1985. 134-65.

Bazerman, Charles. "Physicists Reading Physics: Schema-Laden Purposes and Purpose-Laden Schema." *Written Communication* 2 (1985): 3-23.

Bell, Daniel. *The Social Sciences since the Second World War.* New Brunswick, NJ: Transaction, 1982.

Berlin, James. *Rhetoric and Reality: Writing in American Colleges, 1900-1975.* Carbondale: Southern Illinois UP, in press.

_____. *Writing Instruction in Nineteenth-Century American Colleges.* Carbondale: Southern Illinois UP, 1984.

Bizzell, Patricia. "Cognition, Convention, and Certainty: What We Need to Know about Writing." *PRE/ TEXT* 3 (1982): 213-43.

Braddock, Richard, Richard Lloyd-Jones, and Lowell Schoer. *Research in Written Composition.* Urbana: NCTE, 1963.

Britton, James, Tony Burgess, Nancy Martin, Alex McLeod, and Harold Rosen. *The Development of Writing Abilities* (11-18). London: Macmillan, 1975.

Bruffee, Kenneth A. "Collaborative Learning and the 'Conversion of Mankind.'" *College English* 46 (1984): 635-52.

Coleridge, Samuel Taylor. "On Method." *The Portable Coleridge.* Ed. I. A. Richards. New York: Viking, 1950. 339-86.

Coles, William, Jr. "Freshman Composition: The Circle of Unbelief." *College English* 31 (1969): 134-42.

Cooper, Marilyn M. "The Ecology of Writing." *College English* 48 (1986): 364-75.

Elbow, Peter. *Writing without Teachers.* New York: Oxford UP, 1973.

_____. *Writing with Power.* New York: Oxford UP, 1981.

Emig, Janet. *The Composing Processes of Twelfth Graders.* NCTE Research Report No. 13. Urbana: NCTE, 1971.

_____. "The Uses of the Unconscious in Composing." *College Composition and Communication* 16 (1964): 6-11.

Faigley, Lester, Roger D. Cherry, David A. Jolliffe, and Anna M. Skinner. *Assessing Writers' Knowledge and Processes of Composing.* Norwood, NJ: Ablex, 1985.

Faigley, Lester, and Stephen P. Witte. "Analyzing Revision." *College Composition and Communication* 32 (1981): 400-14.

Fish, Stanley. "Consequences." *Critical Inquiry* 11 (1985): 433-58.

Flower, Linda, and John R. Hayes. "A Cognitive Process Theory of Writing." *College Composition and Communication* 31 (1980): 365-87.

Foucault, Michel. *Power/Knowledge: Selected Interviews and Other Writings, 1972-1977.* Ed. Colin Gordon. New York: Pantheon, 1980.

Gilbert, G. Nigel, and Michael Mulkay. *Opening Pandora's Box: A Sociological Analysis of Scientists' Discourse.* Cambridge: Cambridge UP, 1984.

Giroux, Henry A. *Theory and Resistance in Education.* South Hadley, MA: Bergin, 1983.

Hairston, Maxine. "The Winds of Change: Thomas Kuhn and the Revolution in the Teaching of Writing." *College Composition and Communication* 33 (1982): 76-88.

Hayes, John R., and Linda Flower. "Identifying the Organization of Writing Processes." *Cognitive Processes in Writing: An Interdisciplinary Approach.* Ed. Lee Gregg and Erwin Steinberg. Hillsdale, NJ: Lawrence Erlbaum, 1980. 3-30.

Heath, Shirley Brice. *Ways with Words.* New York: Cambridge UP, 1983.

Herzberg, Bruce. "The Politics of Discourse Communities." Paper presented at the Conference on College Composition and Communication, New Orleans, March 1986.

Iacocca, Lee. *Iacocca: An Autobiography.* New York: Bantam, 1984.

Kroll, Barry M. "Cognitive Egocentrism and the Problem of Audience Awareness in Written Discourse." *Research in the Teaching of English* 12 (1978): 269-81.

LaBrant, Lou. "The Psychological Basis for Creative Writing." *English Journal* 25 (1936): 292-301.

Lauer, Janice. "Heuristics and Composition." *College Composition and Communication* 21 (1970): 396-404.

Lunsford, Andrea. "The Content of Basic Writers' Essays." *College Composition and Communication* 31 (1980): 278-90.

Macrorie, Ken. "To Be Read." *English Journal* 57 (1968): 686-92.

McCloskey, Donald N. "The Literary Character of Economics." *Daedalus* 113.3 (1984): 97-119.

Miller, George A., Eugene Galanter, and Karl Pribram. *Plans and the Structure of Behavior.* New York: Holt, 1962.

Moffett, James. "Writing, Inner Speech, and Meditation." *College English* 44 (1982): 231-44.

Myers, Greg. "Texts as Knowledge Claims: The Social Construction of Two Biologists' Articles." *Social Studies of Science* 15 (1985): 593-630.

———. "Writing Research and the Sociology of Scientific Knowledge: A Review of Three New Books." *College English* 48 (1986): 595-610.

Newell, Alan, and Herbert A. Simon. *Human Problem Solving.* Englewood Cliffs, NJ: Prentice-Hall, 1972.

Odell, Lee, and Dixie Goswami, eds. *Writing in Nonacademic Settings.* New York: Guilford, 1985.

Ohmann, Richard. *English in America: A Radical View of the Profession.* New York: Oxford UP, 1976.

Reddy, Michael J. "The Conduit Metaphor." *Metaphor and Thought.* Ed. Andrew Ortony. Cambridge: Cambridge UP, 1979. 284-324.

Reither, James A. "Writing and Knowing: Toward Redefining the Writing Process." *College English* 47 (1985): 620-28.

Rohman, D. Gordon, "Pre-Writing: The Stage of Discovery in the Writing Process." *College Composition and Communication* 16 (1965): 106-12.

Rohman, D. Gordon, and Alfred O. Wlecke. "Pre-Writing: The Construction and Application of Models for Concept Formation in Writing." U.S. Department of Health, Education, and Welfare Cooperative Research Project No. 2174. East Lansing: Michigan State U, 1964.

Scardamalia, Marlene, Carl Bereiter, and Hillel Goelman. "The Role of Production Factors in Writing Ability." *What Writers Know: The Language, Process, and Structure of Written Discourse.* Ed. Martin Nystrand. New York: Academic, 1982. 173-210.

Stewart, Donald. "Prose with Integrity: A Primary Objective." *College Composition and Communication* 20 (1969): 223-27.

Voss, Ralph. "Janet Emig's *The Composing Processes of Twelfth Graders:* A Reassessment." *College Composition and Communication* 34 (1983): 278-83.

Williams, Raymond. *Keywords: A Vocabulary of Culture and Society.* New York: Oxford, 1976.

Young, Art. "Considering Values: The Poetic Function of Language." *Language Connections.* Ed. Toby Fulwiler and Art Young. Urbana: NCTE, 1982. 77-97.

Young, Richard. "Paradigms and Problems: Needed Research in Rhetorical Invention." *Research on Composing: Points of Departure.* Ed. Charles R. Cooper and Lee Odell. Urbana: NCTE, 1978. 29-47.

Joseph Alkana, Andrew Cooper, Beth Daniell, Kristine Hansen, Greg Myers, Carolyn Miller, and Walter Reed made helpful comments on earlier drafts of this essay.

From Silence to Words:
Writing as Struggle

by Min-zhan Lu

> Imagine that you enter a parlor. You come late. When you arrive, others have long preceded you, and they are engaged in a heated discussion. . . . You listen for a while, until you decide that you have caught the tenor of the argument; then you put in your oar. Someone answers; you answer him; another comes to your defense; another aligns himself against you, to either the embarrassment or gratification of your opponent, depending upon the quality of your ally's assistance. However, the discussion is interminable. The hour grows late, you must depart. And you do depart, with the discussion still vigorously in progress.
>
> –Kenneth Burke, *The Philosophy of Literary Form*

> Men are not built in silence, but in word, in work, in action-reflection.
> –Paulo Freire, *Pedagogy of the Oppressed*

My mother withdrew into silence two months before she died. A few nights before she fell silent, she told me she regretted the way she had raised me and my sisters. I knew she was referring to the way we had been brought up in the midst of two conflicting worlds—the world of home, dominated by the ideology of the Western humanistic tradition, and the world of a society dominated by Mao Tse-tung's Marxism. My mother had devoted her life to our education, an education she knew had made us suffer political persecution during the Cultural Revolution. I wanted to find a way to convince her that, in spite of the persecution, I had benefited from the education she had worked so hard to give me. But I was silent. My understanding of my education was so dominated by memories of confusion and frustration that I was unable to reflect on what I could have gained from it.

   This paper is my attempt to fill up that silence with words, words I didn't have then, words that I have since come to by reflecting on my earlier experience as a student in China and on my recent experience as a composition teacher in the United States. For in spite of the frustration and confusion I experienced growing up caught between two conflicting worlds,

Reprinted from *College English* (April 1987). Copyright 1987 by the National Council of Teachers of English. Reprinted with permission.

the conflict ultimately helped me to grow as a reader and writer. Constantly having to switch back and forth between the discourse of home and that of school made me sensitive and self-conscious about the struggle I experienced every time I tried to read, write, or think in either discourse. Eventually, it led me to search for constructive uses for such struggle.

From early childhood, I had identified the differences between home and the outside world by the different languages I used in each. My parents had wanted my sisters and me to get the best education they could conceive of— Cambridge. They had hired a live-in tutor, a Scot, to make us bilingual. I learned to speak English with my parents, my tutor, and my sisters. I was allowed to speak Shanghai dialect only with the servants. When I was four (the year after the Communist Revolution of 1949), my parents sent me to a local private school where I learned to speak, read, and write in a new language—Standard Chinese, the official written language of New China.

In those days I moved from home to school, from English to Standard Chinese to Shanghai dialect, with no apparent friction. I spoke each language with those who spoke the language. All seemed quite "natural"—servants spoke only Shanghai dialect because they were servants; teachers spoke Standard Chinese because they were teachers; languages had different words because they were different languages. I thought of English as my family language, comparable to the many strange dialects I didn't speak but had often heard some of my classmates speak with their families. While I was happy to have a special family language, until second grade I didn't feel that my family language was any different than some of my classmates' family dialects.

My second grade homeroom teacher was a young graduate from a missionary school. When she found out I spoke English, she began to practice her English on me. One day she used English when asking me to run an errand for her. As I turned to close the door behind me, I noticed the puzzled faces of my classmates. I had the same sensation I had often experienced when some stranger in a crowd would turn on hearing me speak English. I was more intensely pleased on this occasion, however, because suddenly I felt that my family language had been singled out from the family languages of my classmates. Since we were not allowed to speak any dialect other than Standard Chinese in the classroom, having my teacher speak English to me in class made English an official language of the classroom. I began to take pride in my ability to speak it.

This incident confirmed in my mind what my parents had always told me about the importance of English to one's life. Time and again they had told me of how my paternal grandfather, who was well versed in classic Chinese, kept losing good-paying jobs because he couldn't speak English. My grandmother reminisced constantly about how she had slaved and saved to send my father to a first-rate missionary school. And we were made to understand that it was my father's fluent English that had opened the door to his success. Even though my family had always stressed the importance of English for my future, I used to complain bitterly about the extra English lessons we had to take after school. It was only after my homeroom teacher had "sanctified" English that I began to connect English with my education. I became a much more eager student in my tutorials.

What I learned from my tutorials seemed to enhance and reinforce what I was learning in my classroom. In those days each word had one meaning. One day I would be making a sentence at school: "The national flag of China is red." The next day I would recite at home, "My love is like a red, red rose." There seemed to be an agreement between the Chinese "red" and the English "red," and both corresponded to the patch of color printed next to the word. "Love" was my love for my mother at home and my love for my "motherland" at school; both "loves" meant how I felt about my mother. Having two loads of homework forced me to develop a quick memory for words and a sensitivity to form and style. What I learned in one language carried over to the other. I made sentences such as, "I saw a red, red rose among the green leaves," with both the English lyric and the classic Chinese lyric—red flower among green leaves—running through my mind, and I was praised by both teacher and tutor for being a good student.

Although my elementary schooling took place during the fifties, I was almost oblivious to the great political and social changes happening around me. Years later, I read in my history and political philosophy textbooks that the fifties were a time when "China was making a transition from a semi-feudal, semi-capitalist, and semi-colonial country into a socialist country," a period in which "the Proletarians were breaking into the educational territory dominated by Bourgeois Intellectuals." While people all over the country were being officially classified into Proletarians, Petty-bourgeois, National-bourgeois, Poor-peasants, and Intellectuals, and were trying to adjust to their new social identities, my parents were allowed to continue the upper middle-class life they had established before the 1949 Revolution because of my father's affiliation with British firms. I had always felt that my family was different from the families of my classmates, but I didn't perceive society's view of my family until the summer vacation before I entered high school.

First, my aunt was caught by her colleagues talking to her husband over the phone in English. Because of it, she was criticized and almost labeled a Rightist. (This was the year of the Anti-Rightist movement, a movement in which the Intellectuals became the target of the "socialist class-struggle.") I had heard others telling my mother that she was foolish to teach us English when Russian had replaced English as the "official" foreign language. I had also learned at school that the American and British Imperialists were the arch-enemies of New China. Yet I had made no connection between the arch-enemies and the English our family spoke. What happened to my aunt forced the connection on me. I began to see my parents' choice of a family language as an anti-Revolutionary act and was alarmed that I had participated in such an act. From then on, I took care not to use English outside home and to conceal my knowledge of English from my new classmates.

Certain words began to play important roles in my new life at the junior high. On the first day of school, we were handed forms to fill out with our parents' class, job, and income. Being one of the few people not employed by the government, my father had never been officially classified. Since he was a medical doctor, he told me to put him down as an Intellectual. My home-room teacher called me into the office a couple of days afterwards and told me that my father couldn't be an Intellectual if his income far exceeded that of a Capitalist. He also told me that since my father worked for Foreign Imperialists, my father should be classified as an Imperialist Lackey. The teacher looked nonplussed when I told him that my father couldn't be an Imperialist Lackey because he was a medical doctor. But I could tell from the way he took notes on my form that my father's job had put me in an un-favorable position in his eyes.

The Standard Chinese term "class" was not a new word for me. Since first grade, I had been taught sentences such as, "The Working class are the masters of New China." I had always known that it was good to be a worker, but until then, I had never felt threatened for not being one. That fall, "class" began to take on a new meaning for me. I noticed a group of Working-class students and teachers at school. I was made to understand that because of my class background, I was excluded from that group.

Another word that became important was "consciousness." One of the slogans posted in the school building read, "Turn our students into future Proletarians with socialist consciousness and education!" For several weeks we studied this slogan in our political philosophy course, a subject I had never had in elementary school. I still remember the definition of "socialist consciousness" that we were repeatedly tested on through the years: "Socialist consciousness is a person's political soul. It is the consciousness of the Proletarians represented by Marxist Mao Tse-tung thought. It takes expression in one's action, language, and lifestyle. It is the task of every Chinese student to grow up into a Proletarian with a socialist consciousness so that he can serve the people and the motherland." To make the abstract concept accessible to us, our teacher pointed out that the immediate task for students from Working-class families was to strengthen their socialist consciousnesses. For those of us who were from other class backgrounds, the task was to turn ourselves into Workers with socialist consciousnesses. The teacher never explained exactly how we were supposed to "turn" into Workers. Instead, we were given samples of the ritualistic annual plans we had to write at the beginning of each term. In these plans, we performed "self-criticism" on our consciousnesses and made vows to turn ourselves into Workers with socialist consciousnesses. The teacher's division between those who did and those who didn't have a socialist consciousness led me to reify the notion of "conscious-ness" into a thing one possesses. I equated this intangible "thing" with a concrete way of dressing, speaking, and writing. For instance, I never doubted that my political philosophy teacher had a socialist consciousness because she was from a steelworker's family (she announced this the first day of class) and was a Party member who wore grey cadre suits and talked like a philosophy textbook. I noticed other things about her. She had beautiful eyes and spoke Standard Chinese with such a pure accent that I thought she should be a film star. But I was embarrassed that I had noticed things that ought not to have been associated with her. I blamed my observation on my Bourgeois consciousness.

At the same time, the way reading and writing were taught through memorization and imitation also encouraged me to reduce concepts and ideas to simple definitions. In literature and political philosophy classes, we were taught a large number of quotations from Marx, Lenin, and Mao Tse-tung. Each concept that appeared in these quotations came with a definition. We were required to memorize the definitions of the words along with the quotations. Every time I memorized a definition, I felt I had learned a word: "The national red flag symbolizes the blood shed by Revolutionary ancestors for our socialist cause"; "New China rises like a red sun over the eastern horizon." As I memorized these sentences, I reduced their metaphors to dictionary meanings: "red" meant "Revolution" and "red sun" meant "New China" in the "language" of the Working class. I learned mechanically but eagerly. I soon became quite fluent in this new language.

As school began to define me as a political subject, my parents tried to build up my resistance to the "communist poisoning" by exposing me to the "great books"—novels by Charles Dickens, Nathaniel Hawthorne, Emily Bronte, Jane Austen, and writers from around the turn of the century. My parents implied that these writers represented how I, their child, should read and write. My parents replaced the word "Bourgeois" with the word "cultured." They reminded me that I was in school only to learn math and science. I needed to pass the other courses to stay in school, but I was not to let the "Red doctrines" corrupt my mind. Gone were the days when I could innocently write, "I saw the red, red rose among the green leaves," collapsing, as I did, English and Chinese cultural traditions. "Red" came to mean Revolution at school, "the Commies" at home, and adultery in *The Scarlet Letter.* Since I took these symbols and metaphors as meanings natural to people of the same class, I abandoned my earlier definitions of English and Standard Chinese as the language of home and the language of school. I now defined English as the language of the Bourgeois and Standard Chinese as the language of the Working class. I thought of the language of the Working class as someone else's language and the language of the Bourgeois as my language. But I also believed that, although the language of the Bourgeois was my real language, I could and would adopt the language of the Working class when I was at school. I began to put on and take off my Working class language in the same way I put on and took off my school clothes to avoid being criticized for wearing Bourgeois clothes.

In my literature classes, I learned the Working-class formula for reading. Each work in the textbook had a short "Author's Biography": "X X X, born in 19-- in the province of X X, is from a Worker's family. He joined the Revolution in 19--. He is a Revolutionary realist with a passionate love for the Party and Chinese Revolution. His work expresses the thoughts and emotions of the masses and sings praise to the prosperous socialist construction on all fronts of China." The teacher used the "Author's Biography" as a yardstick to measure the texts. We were taught to locate details in the texts that illustrated these summaries, such as words that expressed Workers' thoughts and emotions or events that illustrated the Workers' lives.

I learned a formula for Working-class writing in the composition classes. We were given sample essays and told to imitate them. The theme was always about how the collective taught the individual a lesson. I would write papers about labor-learning experiences or school-cleaning days, depending on the occasion of the collective activity closest to the assignment. To make each paper look different, I dressed it up with details about the date, the weather, the environment, or the appearance of the Master-worker who had taught me "the lesson." But as I became more and more fluent in the generic voice of the Working-class Student, I also became more and more self-conscious about the language we used at home.

For instance, in senior high we began to have English classes ("to study English for the Revolution," as the slogan on the cover of the textbook said), and I was given my first Chinese-English dictionary. There I discovered the English version of the term "class-struggle." (The Chinese characters for a school "class" and for a social "class" are different.) I had often used the English word "class" at home in sentences such as, "So and so has class," but I had not connected this sense of "class" with "class-struggle." Once the connection was made, I heard a second layer of meaning every time someone at home said a person had "class." The expression began to mean the person had the style and sophistication characteristic of the Bourgeoisie. The word lost its innocence. I was uneasy about hearing that second layer of meaning because I was sure my parents did not hear the word that way. I felt that therefore I should not be hearing it that way either. Hearing the second layer of meaning made me wonder if I was losing my English.

My suspicion deepened when I noticed myself unconsciously merging and switching between the "reading" of home and the "reading" of school. Once I had to write a report on *The Revolutionary Family,* a book about an illiterate woman's awakening and growth as a Revolutionary through the deaths of her husband and all her children for the cause of the Revolution. In one scene the woman deliberated over whether or not she should encourage her youngest son to join the Revolution. Her memory of her husband's death made her afraid to encourage her son. Yet she also remembered her earlier married life and the first time her husband tried to explain the meaning of the Revolution to her. These memories made her feel she should encourage her son to continue the cause his father had begun.

I was moved by this scene. "Moved" was a word my mother and sisters used a lot when we discussed books. Our favorite moments in novels were moments of what I would now call internal conflict, moments which we said "moved" us. I remember that we were "moved" by Jane Eyre when she was torn between her sense of ethics, which compelled her to leave the man she loved, and her impulse to stay with the only man who had ever loved her. We were also moved by Agnes in *David Copperfield* because of the way she restrained her love for David so that he could live happily with the woman he loved. My standard method of doing a book report was to model it on the review by the Publishing Bureau and to dress it up with detailed quotations from the book. The review of *The Revolutionary Family* emphasized the woman's Revolutionary spirit. I decided to use the scene that had moved me to illustrate this point. I wrote the report the night before it was due. When I had finished, I realized I couldn't possibly hand it in. Instead of illustrating her Revolutionary spirit, I had dwelled on her internal conflict, which could be seen as a moment of weak sentimentality that I should never have emphasized in a Revolutionary heroine. I wrote another report, taking care to illustrate the grandeur of her Revolutionary spirit by expanding on a quotation in which she decided that if the life of her son could change the lives of millions of sons, she should not begrudge his life for the cause of Revolution. I handed m my second version but kept the first in my desk.

I never showed it to anyone. I could never show it to people outside my family, because it had deviated so much from the reading enacted by the jacket review. Neither could I show it to my mother or sisters, because I was ashamed to have been so moved by such a "Revolutionary" book. My parents would have been shocked to learn that I could like such a book in the same way they liked Dickens. Writing this book report increased my fear that I was losing the command over both the "language of home" and the "language of school" that I had worked so hard to gain. I tried to remind myself that, if I could still tell when my reading or writing sounded incorrect, then I had retained my command over both languages. Yet I could no longer be confident of my command over either language because I had discovered that when I was not careful—or even when I was—my reading and writing often surprised me with its impurity. To prevent such impurity, I became very suspicious of my thoughts when I read or wrote. I was always asking myself why I was using this word, how I was using it, always afraid that I wasn't reading or writing correctly. What confused and frustrated me most was that I could not figure out why I was no longer able to read or write correctly without such painful deliberation.

I continued to read only because reading allowed me to keep my thoughts and confusion private. I hoped that somehow, if I watched myself carefully, I would figure out from the way I read whether I had really mastered the "languages." But writing became a dreadful chore. When I tried to keep a diary, I was so afraid that the voice of school might slip in that I could only list my daily activities. When I wrote for school, I worried that my Bourgeois sensibilities would betray me.

The more suspicious I became about the way I read and wrote, the more guilty I felt for losing the spontaneity with which I had learned to "use" these "languages." Writing the book report made me feel that my reading and writing in the "language" of either home or school could not be free of the interference of the other. But I was unable to acknowledge, grasp, or grapple with what I was experiencing, for both my parents and my teachers had suggested that, if I were a good student, such interference would and should not take place. I assumed that once I had "acquired" a discourse, I could simply switch it on and off every time I read and wrote as I would some electronic tool. Furthermore, I expected my readings and writings to come out in their correct forms whenever I switched the proper discourse on. I still regarded the discourse of home as natural and the discourse of school alien, but I never had doubted before that I could acquire both and switch them on and off according to the occasion.

When my experience in writing conflicted with what I thought should happen when I used each discourse, I rejected my experience because it contradicted what my parents and teachers had taught me. I shied away from writing to avoid what I assumed I should not experience. But trying to avoid what should not happen did not keep it from recurring whenever I had to write. Eventually my confusion and frustration over these recurring experiences compelled me to search for an explanation: how and why had I failed to learn what my parents and teachers had worked so hard to teach me?

I now think of the internal scene for my reading and writing about *The Revolutionary Family* as a heated discussion between myself, the voices of home, and those of school. The review on the back of the book, the sample student papers I came across in my composition classes, my philosophy teacher—these I heard as voices of one group. My parents and my home readings were the voices of an opposing group. But the conversation between these opposing voices in the internal scene of my writing was not as polite and respectful as the parlor scene Kenneth Burke has portrayed (see epigraph). Rather, these voices struggled to dominate the discussion, constantly incorporating, dismissing, or suppressing the arguments of each other, like the battles between the hegemonic and counter-hegemonic forces described in Raymond Williams' *Marxism and Literature* (108-14).

When I read *The Revolutionary Family* and wrote the first version of my report, I began with a quotation from the review. The voices of both home and school answered, clamoring to be heard. I tried to listen to one group and turn a deaf ear to the other. Both persisted. I negotiated my way through these conflicting voices, now agreeing with one, now agreeing with the other. I formed a reading out of my interaction with both. Yet I was afraid to have done so because both home and school had implied that I should speak in unison with only one of these groups and stand away from the discussion rather than participate in it.

My teachers and parents had persistently called my attention to the intensity of the discussion taking place on the external social scene. The story of my grandfather's failure and my father's success had from my early childhood made me aware of the conflict between Western and traditional Chinese cultures. My political education at school added another dimension to the conflict: the war of Marxist-Maoism against them both. Yet when my parents and teachers called my attention to the conflict, they stressed the anxiety of having to live through China's transformation from a semi-feudal, semi-capitalist, and semi-colonial society to a socialist one. Acquiring the discourse of the dominant group was, to them, a means of seeking alliance with that group and thus of surviving the whirlpool of cultural currents around them. As a result, they modeled their pedagogical practices on this utilitarian view of language. Being the eager student, I adopted this view of language as a tool for survival. It came to dominate my understanding of the discussion on the social and historical scene and to restrict my ability to participate in that discussion.

To begin with, the metaphor of language as a tool for survival led me to be passive in my use of discourse, to be a bystander in the discussion. In Burke's "parlor," everyone is involved in the discussion. As it goes on through history, what we call "communal discourses"—arguments specific to particular political, social, economic, ethnic, sexual, and family groups—form, re-form and transform. To use a discourse in such a scene is to participate in the argument and to contribute to the formation of the discourse. But when I was growing up, I could not take on the burden of such an active role in the discussion. For both home and school presented the existent conventions of the discourse each taught me as absolute laws for my action. They turned verbal action into a tool, a set of conventions produced and shaped prior to and outside of my own verbal acts. Because I saw language as a tool, I separated the process of producing the tool from the process of using it. The tool was made by someone else and was then acquired and used by me. How the others made it before I acquired it determined and guaranteed what it produced when I used it. I imagined that the more experienced and powerful members of the community were the ones responsible for making the tool. They were the ones who participated in the discussion and fought with opponents. When I used what they made, their labor and accomplishments would ensure the quality of my reading and writing. By using it, I could survive the heated discussion. When my immediate experience in writing the book report suggested that knowing the conventions of school did not guarantee the form and content of my report, when it suggested that I had to write the report with the work and responsibility I had assigned to those who wrote book reviews in the Publishing Bureau, I thought I had lost the tool I had earlier acquired.

Another reason I could not take up an active role in the argument was that my parents and teachers contrived to provide a scene free of conflict for practicing my various languages. It was as if their experience had made them aware of the conflict between their discourse and other discourses and of the struggle involved in reproducing the conventions of any discourse on a scene where more than one discourse exists. They seemed convinced that such conflict and struggle would overwhelm someone still learning the discourse. Home and school each contrived a purified space where only one discourse was spoken and heard. In their choice of textbooks, in the way they spoke, and in the way they required me to speak, each jealously silenced any voice that threatened to break the unison of the scene. The homogeneity of home and of school implied that only one discourse could and should be relevant in each place. It led me to believe I should leave behind, turn a deaf ear to, or forget the discourse of the other when I crossed the boundary dividing them. I expected myself to set down one discourse whenever I took up another just as I would take off or put on a particular set of clothes for school or home.

Despite my parents' and teachers' attempts to keep home and school discrete, the internal conflict between the two discourses continued whenever I read or wrote. Although I tried to suppress the voice of one discourse in the name of the other, having to speak aloud in the voice I had just silenced each time I crossed the boundary kept both voices active in my mind. Every "I think . . ." from the voice of home or school brought forth a "However . . ." or a "But . . ." from the voice of the opponents. To identify with the voice of home or school, I had to negotiate through the conflicting voices of both by restating, taking back, qualifying my thoughts. I was unconsciously doing so when I did my book report. But I could not use the interaction comfortably and constructively. Both my parents and my teachers had implied that my job was to prevent that interaction from happening. My sense of having failed to accomplish what they had taught silenced me.

To use the interaction between the discourses of home and school constructively, I would have to have seen reading or writing as a process in which I worked my way towards a stance through a dialectical process of identification and division. To identify with an ally, I would have to have grasped the distance between where he or she stood and where I was positioning myself. In taking a stance against an opponent, I would have to have grasped where my stance identified with the stance of my allies. Teetering along the "wavering line of pressure and counter-pressure" from both allies and opponents, I might have worked my way towards a stance of my own (Burke, *A Rhetoric of Motives* 23). Moreover, I would have to have understood that the voices in my mind, like the participants in the parlor scene, were in constant flux. As I came into contact with new and different groups of people or read different books, voices entered and left. Each time I read or wrote, the stance I negotiated out of these voices would always be at some distance from the stances I worked out in my previous and my later readings or writings.

I could not conceive such a form of action for myself because I saw reading and writing as an expression of an established stance. In delineating the conventions of a discourse, my parents and teachers had synthesized the stance they saw as typical for a representative member of the community. Burke calls this the stance of a "god" or the "prototype"; Williams calls it the "official" or "possible" stance of the community. Through the metaphor of the survival tool, my parents and teachers had led me to assume I could automatically reproduce the official stance of the discourse I used. Therefore, when I did my book report on *The Revolutionary Family,* I expected my knowledge of the official stance set by the book review to ensure the actual stance of my report. As it happened, I began by trying to take the official stance of the review. Other voices interrupted. I answered back. In the process, I worked out a stance approximate but not identical to the official stance I began with. Yet the experience of having to labor to realize my knowledge of the official stance or to prevent myself from wandering away from it frustrated and confused me. For even though I had been actually reading and writing in a Burkean scene, I was afraid to participate actively in the discussion. I assumed it was my role to survive by staying out of it.

Not long ago, my daughter told me that it bothered her to hear her friend "talk wrong." Having come to the United States from China with little English, my daughter has become sensitive to the way English, as spoken by her teachers, operates. As a result, she has amazed her teachers with her success in picking up the language and in adapting to life at school. Her concern to speak the English taught in the classroom "correctly" makes her uncomfortable when she hears people using "ain't" or double negatives, which her teacher considers "improper." I see in her the me that had eagerly learned and used the discourse of the Working class at school. Yet while I was torn between the two conflicting worlds of school and home, she moves with seeming ease from the conversations she hears over the dinner table to her teacher's words in the classroom. My husband and I are proud of the good work she does at school. We are glad she is spared the kinds of conflict between home and school I experienced at her age. Yet as we watch her becoming more and more fluent in the language of the classroom, we wonder if, by enabling her to "survive" school, her very fluency will silence her when the scene of her reading and writing expands beyond that of the composition classroom.

For when I listen to my daughter, to students, and to some composition teachers talking about the teaching and learning of writing, I am often alarmed by the degree to which the metaphor of a survival tool dominates their understanding of language as it once dominated my own. I am especially concerned with the way some composition classes focus on turning the classroom into a monological scene for the students' reading and writing. Most of our students live in a world similar to my daughter's, somewhere between the purified world of the classroom and the complex world of my adolescence. When composition classes encourage these students to ignore those voices that seem irrelevant to the purified world of the classroom, most students are often able to do so without much struggle. Some of them are so adept at doing it that the whole process has for them become automatic.

However, beyond the classroom and beyond the limited range of these students' immediate lives lies a much more complex and dynamic social and historical scene. To help these students become actors in such a scene, perhaps we need to call their attention to voices that may seem irrelevant to the discourse we teach rather than encourage them to shut them out. For example, we might intentionally complicate the classroom scene by bringing into it discourses that stand at varying distances from the one we teach. We might encourage students to explore ways of practicing the conventions of the discourse they are learning by negotiating through these conflicting voices. We could also encourage them to see themselves as responsible for forming or transforming as well as preserving the discourse they are learning.

As I think about what we might do to complicate the external and internal scenes of our students' writing, I hear my parents and teachers saying: "Not now. Keep them from the wrangle of the marketplace until they have acquired the discourse and are skilled at using it." And I answer: "Don't teach them to 'survive' the whirlpool of crosscurrents by avoiding it. Use the classroom to moderate the currents. Moderate the currents, but teach them from the beginning to struggle." When I think of the ways in which the teaching of reading and writing as classroom activities can frustrate the development of students, I am almost grateful for the overwhelming complexity of the circumstances in which I grew up. For it was this complexity that kept me from losing sight of the effort and choice involved in reading or writing with and through a discourse.

Works Cited

Burke, Kenneth. *The Philosophy of Literary Form: Studies in Symbolic Action.* 2nd ed. Baton Rouge: Louisiana State UP, 1967.
_____. *A Rhetoric of Motives.* Berkeley: U of California P, 1969.
Freire, Paulo. *Pedagogy of the Oppressed.* Trans. M. B. Ramos. New York: Continuum, 1970.
Williams, Raymond. *Marxism and Literature.* New York: Oxford UP, 1977.

Composing as a Woman

by Elizabeth A. Flynn

> It is not easy to think like a woman in a man's world, in the world of the professions; yet the capacity to do that is a strength which we can try to help our students develop. To think like a woman in a man's world means thinking critically, refusing to accept the givens, making connections between facts and ideas which men have left unconnected. It means remembering that every mind resides in a body; remaining accountable to the female bodies in which we live; constantly retesting given hypotheses against lived experience. It means a constant critique of language, for as Wittgenstein (no feminist) observed, "The limits of my language are the limits of my world." And it means that most difficult thing of all: listening and watching in art and literature, in the social sciences, in all the descriptions we are given of the world, for silences, the absences, the nameless, the unspoken, the encoded—for there we will find the true knowledge of women. And in breaking those silences, naming ourselves, uncovering the hidden, making ourselves present, we begin to define a reality which resonates to *us*, which affirms *our* being, which allows the woman teacher and the woman student alike to take ourselves, and each other, seriously: meaning, to begin taking charge of our lives.
>
> –Adrienne Rich, "Taking Women Students Seriously"

The emerging field of composition studies could be described as a feminization of our previous conceptions of how writers write and how writing should be taught.[1] In exploring the nature of the writing process, composition specialists expose the limitations of previous product-oriented approaches by demystifying the product and in so doing empowering developing writers and readers. Rather than enshrining the text in its final form, they demonstrate that the works produced by established authors are often the result of an extended, frequently enormously frustrating process and that creativity is an activity that results from experience and hard work rather

Reprinted from *College Composition and Communication* (December 1988). Copyright 1988 by the National Council of Teachers of English. Reprinted with permission.

[1] I received invaluable feedback on drafts of this essay from Carol Berkenkotter, Art Young, Marilyn Cooper, John Willinsky, Diane Shoos, John Flynn, Richard Gebhardt, and three anonymous *CCC* reviewers.

than a mysterious gift reserved for a select few. In a sense, composition specialists replace the figure of the authoritative father with an image of a nurturing mother. Powerfully present in the work of composition researchers and theorists is the ideal of a committed teacher concerned about the growth and maturity of her students who provides feedback on ungraded drafts, reads journals, and attempts to tease out meaning from the seeming incoherence of student language. The field's foremothers come to mind—Janet Emig, Mina Shaughnessy, Ann Berthoff, Win Horner, Maxine Hairston, Shirley Heath, Nancy Martin, Linda Flower, Andrea Lunsford, Sondra Perl, Nancy Sommers, Marion Crowhurst, Lisa Ede. I'll admit the term foremother seems inappropriate as some of these women are still in their thirties and forties—we are speaking here of a very young field. Still, invoking their names suggests that we are also dealing with a field that, from the beginning, has welcomed contributions from women—indeed, has been shaped by women.

The work of male composition researchers and theorists has also contributed significantly to the process of feminization described above. James Britton, for instance, reverses traditional hierarchies by privileging private expression over public transaction, process over product. In arguing that writing for the self is the matrix out of which all forms of writing develop, he valorizes an activity and a mode of expression that have previously been undervalued or invisible, much as feminist literary critics have argued that women's letters and diaries are legitimate literary forms and should be studied and taught alongside more traditional genres. His work has had an enormous impact on the way writing is taught on the elementary and high school levels and in the university, not only in English courses but throughout the curriculum. Writing-Across-the-Curriculum Programs aim to transform pedagogical practices in all disciplines, even those where patriarchal attitudes toward authority are most deeply rooted.

Feminist Studies and Composition Studies

Feminist inquiry and composition studies have much in common. After all, feminist researchers and scholars and composition specialists are usually in the same department and sometimes teach the same courses. Not surprisingly, there have been wonderful moments when feminists have expressed their commitment to the teaching of writing. Florence Howe's essay, "Identity and Expression: A Writing Course for Women," for example, published in *College English* in 1971, describes her use of journals in a writing course designed to empower women. Adrienne Rich's essay, "'When We Dead Awaken': Writing as Re-Vision," politicizes and expands our conception of revision, emphasizing that taking another look at the texts we have generated necessitates revising our cultural assumptions as well.

There have also been wonderful moments when composition specialists have recognized that the marginality of the field of composition studies is linked in important ways to the political marginality of its constituents, many of whom are women who teach part-time. Maxine Hairston, in "Breaking Our

Bonds and Reaffirming Our Connections," a slightly revised version of her Chair's address at the 1985 convention of the Conference on College Composition and Communication, draws an analogy between the plight of composition specialists and the plight of many women. For both, their worst problems begin at home and hence are immediate and daily. Both, too, often have complex psychological bonds to the people who frequently are their adversaries (273).

For the most part, though, the fields of feminist studies and composition studies have not engaged each other in a serious or systematic way. The major journals in the field of composition studies do not often include articles addressing feminist issues, and panels on feminism are infrequent at the Conference on College Composition and Communication.[2] As a result, the parallels between feminist studies and composition studies have not been delineated, and the feminist critique that has enriched such diverse fields as linguistics, reading, literary criticism, psychology, sociology, anthropology, religion, and science has had little impact on our models of the composing process or on our understanding of how written language abilities are acquired. We have not examined our research methods or research samples to see if they are androcentric. Nor have we attempted to determine just what it means to compose as a woman.

Feminist research and theory emphasize that males and females differ in their developmental processes and in their interactions with others. They emphasize, as well, that these differences are a result of an imbalance in the social order, of the dominance of men over women. They argue that men have chronicled our historical narratives and defined our fields of inquiry. Women's perspectives have been suppressed, silenced, marginalized, written out of what counts as authoritative knowledge. Difference is erased in a desire to universalize. Men become the standard against which women are judged.

---

[2] The 1988 Conference on College Composition and Communication was a notable exception. It had a record number of panels on feminist or gender-related issues and a number of sessions devoted to political concerns. I should add, too, that an exception to the generalization that feminist studies and composition studies have not confronted each other is Cynthia Caywood and Gillian Overing's very useful anthology, *Teaching Writing: Pedagogy, Gender, and Equity*. In their introduction to the book, Caywood and Overing note the striking parallels between writing theory and feminist theory. They conclude, "[T]he process model, insofar as it facilitates and legitimizes the fullest expression of the individual voice, is compatible with the feminist re-visioning of hierarchy, if not essential to it" (xiv). Pamela Annas, in her essay, "Silences: Feminist Language Research and the Teaching of Writing," describes a course she teaches at the University of Massachusetts at Boston, entitled "Writing as Women." In the course, she focuses on the question of silence—"what kinds of silence there are; the voices inside you that tell you to be quiet, the voices outside you that drown you out or politely dismiss what you say or do not understand you, the silence inside you that avoids saying anything important even to yourself, internal and external forms of censorship, and the stress that it produces" (3-4). Carol A. Stanger in "The Sexual Politics of the One-to-One Tutorial Approach and Collaborative Learning" argues that the one-to-one tutorial is essentially hierarchical and hence a male mode of teaching whereas collaborative learning is female and relational rather than hierarchical. She uses Gilligan's images of the ladder and the web to illustrate her point. Elisabeth Daeumer and Sandra Runzo suggest that the teaching of writing is comparable to the activity of mothering in that it is a form of "women's work." Mothers socialize young children to insure that they become acceptable citizens, and teachers' work, like the work of mothers, is usually devalued (45-46).

A feminist approach to composition studies would focus on questions of difference and dominance in written language. Do males and females compose differently? Do they acquire language in different ways? Do research methods and research samples in composition studies reflect a male bias? I do not intend to tackle all of these issues. My approach here is a relatively modest one. I will survey recent feminist research on gender differences in social and psychological development, and I will show how this research and theory may be used in examining student writing, thus suggesting directions that a feminist investigation of composition might take.

Gender Differences in Social and Psychological Development

Especially relevant to a feminist consideration of student writing are Nancy Chodorow's *The Reproduction of Mothering*, Carol Gilligan's *In a Different Voice*, and Mary Belenky, Blythe Clinchy, Nancy Goldberger, and Jill Tarule's *Women's Ways of Knowing*. All three books suggest that women and men have different conceptions of self and different modes of interaction with others as a result of their different experiences, especially their early relationship with their primary parent, their mother.

Chodorow's book, published in 1978, is an important examination of what she calls the "psychoanalysis and the sociology of gender," which in turn influenced Gilligan's *In a Different Voice* and Belenky et al.'s *Women's Ways of Knowing*. Chodorow tells us in her preface that her book originated when a feminist group she was affiliated with "wondered what it meant that women parented women." She argues that girls and boys develop different relational capacities and senses of self as a result of growing up in a family in which women mother. Because all children identify first with their mother, a girl's gender and gender role identification processes are continuous with her earliest identifications whereas a boy's are not. The boy gives up, in addition to his oedipal and preoedipal attachment to his mother, his primary identification with her. The more general identification processes for both males and females also follow this pattern. Chodorow says,

> Girls' identification processes, then, are more continuously embedded in and mediated by their ongoing relationship with their mother. They develop through and stress particularistic and affective relationships to others. A boy's identification processes are not likely to be so embedded in or mediated by a real affective relation to his father. At the same time, he tends to deny identification with and relationship to his mother and reject what he takes to be the feminine world; masculinity is defined as much negatively as positively. Masculine identification processes stress differentiation from others, the denial of affective relation, and categorical universalistic components of the masculine role. Feminine identification processes are relational, whereas masculine identification processes tend to deny relationship. (176)

Carol Gilligan's *In a Different Voice*, published in 1982, builds on

Chodorow's findings, focusing especially, though, on differences in the ways in which males and females speak about moral problems. According to Gilligan, women tend to define morality in terms of conflicting responsibilities rather than competing rights, requiring for their resolution a mode of thinking that is contextual and narrative rather than formal and abstract (19). Men, in contrast, equate morality and fairness and tie moral development to the understanding of rights and rules (19). Gilligan uses the metaphors of the web and the ladder to illustrate these distinctions. The web suggests interconnectedness as well as entrapment; the ladder suggests an achievement-orientation as well as individualistic and hierarchical thinking. Gilligan's study aims to correct the inadequacies of Lawrence Kohlberg's delineation of the stages of moral development. Kohlberg's study included only male subjects, and his categories reflect his decidedly male orientation. For him, the highest stages of moral development derive from a reflective understanding of human rights (19).

Belenky, Clinchy, Goldberger, and Tarule, in *Women's Ways of Knowing*, acknowledge their debt to Gilligan, though their main concern is intellectual rather than moral development. Like Gilligan, they recognize that male experience has served as the model in defining processes of intellectual maturation. The mental processes that are involved in considering the abstract and the impersonal have been labeled "thinking" and are attributed primarily to men, while those that deal with the personal and interpersonal fall under the rubric of "emotions" and are largely relegated to women. The particular study they chose to examine and revise is William Perry's *Forms of Intellectual and Ethical Development in the College Years* (1970). While Perry did include some women subjects in his study, only the interviews with men were used in illustrating and validating his scheme of intellectual and ethical development. When Perry assessed women's development on the basis of the categories he developed, the women were found to conform to the patterns he had observed in the male data. Thus, his work reveals what women have in common with men but was poorly designed to uncover those themes that might be more prominent among women. *Women's Ways of Knowing* focuses on "what else women might have to say about the development of their minds and on alternative routes that are sketchy or missing in Perry's version" (9).

Belenky et al. examined the transcripts of interviews with 135 women from a variety of backgrounds and of different ages and generated categories that are suited for describing the stages of women's intellectual development. They found that the quest for self and voice plays a central role in transformations of women's ways of knowing. Silent women have little awareness of their intellectual capacities. They live—selfless and voiceless—at the behest of those around them. External authorities know the truth and are all-powerful. At the positions of received knowledge and procedural knowledge, other voices and external truths prevail. Sense of self is embedded either in external definitions and roles or in identifications with institutions, disciplines, and methods. A sense of authority arises primarily through identification with the power of a group and its agreed-upon ways for knowing. Women at this stage of development have no sense of an authentic or unique voice, little awareness of a centered self. At the position of subjective knowledge, women turn away from others and any external authority. They have not yet acquired a public voice or public authority, though. Finally, women at the phase of constructed knowledge begin an effort to reclaim the self by attempting to integrate knowledge they feel intuitively with knowledge they have learned from others.

Student Writing

If women and men differ in their relational capacities and in their moral and intellectual development, we would expect to find manifestations of these differences in the student papers we encounter in our first-year composition courses. The student essays I will describe here are narrative descriptions of learning experiences produced in the first of a two-course sequence required of first-year students at Michigan Tech. I've selected the four because they invite commentary from the perspective of the material discussed above. The narratives of the female students are stories of interaction, of connection, or of frustrated connection. The narratives of the male students are stories of achievement, of separation, or of frustrated achievement.

Kim's essay describes a dreamlike experience in which she and her high school girlfriends connected with each other and with nature as a result of a balloon ride they decided to take one summer Sunday afternoon as a way of relieving boredom. From the start, Kim emphasizes communion and tranquility: "It was one of those Sunday afternoons when the sun shines brightly and a soft warm breeze blows gently. A perfect day for a long drive on a country road with my favorite friends." This mood is intensified as they ascend in the balloon: "Higher and higher we went, until the view was overpowering. What once was a warm breeze turned quickly into a cool crisp wind. A feeling of freedom and serenity overtook us as we drifted along slowly." The group felt as if they were "just suspended there on a string, with time non-existent." The experience made them contemplative, and as they drove quietly home, "each one of us collected our thoughts, and to this day we still reminisce about that Sunday afternoon." The experience solidified relationships and led to the formation of a close bond that was renewed every time the day was recollected.

The essay suggests what Chodorow calls relational identification processes. The members of the group are described as being in harmony with themselves and with the environment. There is no reference to competition or discord. The narrative also suggests a variation on what Belenky et al. call "connected knowing," a form of procedural knowledge that makes possible the most desirable form of knowing, constructed knowledge. Connected knowing is rooted in empathy for others and is intensely personal. Women who are connected knowers are able to detach themselves from the relationships and institutions to which they have been subordinated and begin to trust their own intuitions. The women in the narrative were connected doers rather than connected knowers. They went off on their own, left their families and teachers behind (it was summer vacation, after all), and gave themselves over to a powerful shared experience. The adventure was, for the most part, a silent one but did lead to satisfying talk.

Kathy also describes an adventure away from home, but hers was far less satisfying, no doubt because it involved considerably more risk. In her narrative she makes the point that "foreign countries can be frightening" by focusing on a situation in which she and three classmates, two females and a male, found themselves at a train station in Germany separated from the others because they had gotten off to get some refreshments and the train had left without them. She says,

> This left the four of us stranded in an unfamiliar station. Ed was the only person in our group that could speak German fluently, but he still didn't know what to do. Sue got hysterical and Laura tried to calm her down. I stood there stunned. We didn't know what to do.

What they did was turn to Ed, whom Kathy describes as "the smartest one in our group." He told them to get on a train that was on the same track as the original. Kathy realized, though, after talking to some passengers, that they were on the wrong train and urged her classmates to get off. She says,

> I almost panicked. When I convinced the other three we were on the wrong train we opened the doors. As we were getting off, one of the conductors started yelling at us in German. It didn't bother me too much because I couldn't understand what he was saying. One thing about trains in Europe is that they are always on schedule. I think we delayed that train about a minute or two.

In deciding which train to board after getting off the wrong one, they deferred to Ed's judgment once again, but this time they got on the right train. Kathy concludes, "When we got off the train everyone was waiting. It turned out we arrived thirty minutes later than our original train. I was very relieved to see everyone. It was a very frightening experience and I will never forget it."

In focusing on her fears of separation, Kathy reveals her strong need for connection, for affiliation. Her story, like Kim's, emphasizes the importance of relationships, though in a different way. She reveals that she had a strong need to feel part of a group and no desire to rebel, to prove her independence, to differentiate herself from others. This conception of self was a liability as well as a strength in the sense that she became overly dependent on the male authority figure in the group, whom she saw as smarter and more competent than herself. In Belenky et al.'s terms, Kathy acted as if other voices and external truths were more powerful than her own. She did finally speak and act, though, taking it on herself to find out if they were on the right train and ushering the others off when she discovered they were not. She was clearly moving toward the development of an authentic voice and a way of knowing that integrates intuition with authoritative knowledge. After all, she was the real hero of the incident.

The men's narratives stress individuation rather than connection. They are stories of individual achievement or frustrated achievement and conclude by emphasizing separation rather than integration or reintegration into a community. Jim wrote about his "Final Flight," the last cross-country flight required for his pilot's license. That day, everything seemed to go wrong. First, his flight plan had a mistake in it that took 1½ hours to correct. As a result, he left his hometown 2 hours behind schedule. Then the weather deteriorated, forcing him to fly as low as a person can safely fly, with the result that visibility was very poor. He landed safely at his first destination but flew past the second because he was enjoying the view too much. He says,

> Then I was off again south bound for Benton Harbor. On the way south along the coast of Lake Michigan the scenery was a beautiful sight. This relieved some of the pressures and made me look forward to the rest of the flight. It was really nice to see the ice flows break away from the shore. While enjoying the view of a power plant on the shore of Lake Michigan I discovered I had flown past the airport.

He finally landed and took off again, but shortly thereafter had to confront darkness, a result of his being behind schedule. He says,

> The sky turned totally black by the time I was half-way home. This meant flying in the dark which I had only done once before. Flying in the dark was also illegal for me to do at this time. One thing that made flying at night nice was that you could see lights that were over ninety miles away.

Jim does not emphasize his fear, despite the fact that his situation was more threatening than the one Kathy described, and his reference to his enjoyment of the scenery suggests that his anxiety was not paralyzing or debilitating. At times, his solitary flight was clearly as satisfying as Kim's communal one. When he focuses on the difficulties he encountered, he speaks only of his "problems" and "worries" and concludes that the day turned out to be "long and trying." He sums up his experience as follows: "That day I will long remember for both its significance in my goal in getting my pilot's license and all the problems or worries that it caused me during the long and problem-ridden flight." He emerges the somewhat shaken hero of his adventure; he has achieved his goal in the face of adversity. Significantly, he celebrates his return home by having a bite to eat at McDonald's by himself. His adventure does not end with a union or reunion with others.

Jim's story invites interpretation in the context of Chodorow's claims about male interactional patterns. Chodorow says that the male, in order to feel himself adequately masculine, must distinguish and differentiate himself from others. Jim's adventure was an entirely solitary one. It was also goal-directed—he wanted to obtain his pilot's license and, presumably, prove his competence to himself and others. His narrative calls into question, though, easy equations of abstract reasoning and impersonality with male modes of learning since Jim was clearly as capable as Kim of experiencing moments of exultation, of communion with nature.

Joe's narrative of achievement is actually a story of frustrated achievement, of conflicting attitudes toward an ethic of hard work and sacrifice to achieve a goal. When he was in high school, his father drove him twenty miles to swim practice and twenty miles home every Tuesday through Friday night between October and March so he could practice for the swim team. He hated this routine and hated the Saturday morning swim meets even more but continued because he thought his parents, especially his father, wanted him to. He says, "I guess it was all for them, the cold workouts, the evening practices, the weekend meets. I had to keep going for them even though I hated it." Once he realized he was going through his agony for his parents rather than for himself, though, he decided to quit and was surprised to find that his parents supported him. Ultimately, though, he regretted his decision. He says,

> As it turns out now, I wish I had stuck with it. I really had a chance to go somewhere with my talent. I see kids my age who stuck with something for a long time and I envy them for their determination. I wish I had met up to the challenge of sticking with my swimming, because I could have been very good if I would have had their determination.

Joe is motivated to pursue swimming because he thinks his father will be disappointed if he gives it up. His father's presumed hold on him is clearly tenuous, however, because once Joe realizes that he is doing it for him rather than for himself, he quits. Finally, though, it is his gender role identification, his socialization into a male role and a male value system, that allows him to look back on his decision with regret. In college, he has become a competitor, an achiever. He now sees value in the long and painful practices, in a singleminded determination to succeed. The narrative reminds us of Chodorow's point that masculine identification is predominantly a gender role identification rather than identification with a particular parent.

I am hardly claiming that the four narratives are neat illustrations of the feminist positions discussed above. For one thing, those positions are rich in contradiction and complexity and defy easy illustration. For another, the narratives themselves are as often characterized by inconsistency and contradiction as by a univocality of theme and tone. Kathy is at once dependent and assertive; Joe can't quite decide if he should have been rebellious or disciplined. Nor am I claiming that what I have found here are characteristic patterns of male and female student writing. I would need a considerably larger and more representative sample to make such a claim hold. I might note, though, that I had little difficulty identifying essays that revealed patterns of difference among the twenty-four papers I had to choose from, and I could easily have selected others. Sharon, for instance, described her class trip to Chicago, focusing especially on the relationship she and her classmates were able to establish with her advisor. Diane described "An

Unwanted Job" that she seemed unable to quit despite unpleasant working conditions. Mike, like Diane, was dissatisfied with his job, but he expressed his dissatisfaction and was fired. The frightening experience Russ described resulted from his failed attempt to give his car a tune-up; the radiator hose burst, and he found himself in the hospital recovering from third-degree burns. These are stories of relatedness or entanglement; of separation or frustrated achievement.

The description of the student essays is not meant to demonstrate the validity of feminist scholarship but to suggest, instead, that questions raised by feminist researchers and theorists do have a bearing on composition studies and should be pursued. We ought not assume that males and females use language in identical ways or represent the world in a similar fashion. And if their writing strategies and patterns of representation do differ, then ignoring those differences almost certainly means a suppression of women's separate ways of thinking and writing. Our models of the composing process are quite possibly better suited to describing men's ways of composing than to describing women's.[3]

Pedagogical Strategies

The classroom provides an opportunity for exploring questions about gender differences in language use. Students, I have found, are avid inquirers into their own language processes. An approach I have had success with is to make the question of gender difference in behavior and language use the subject to be investigated in class. In one honors section of first-year English, for instance, course reading included selections from Mary Anne Ferguson's *Images of Women in Literature*, Gilligan's *In a Different Voice*, Alice Walker's *Meridian*, and James Joyce's *A Portrait of the Artist as a Young Man*. Students were also required to keep a reading journal and to submit two formal papers. The first was a description of people they know in order to arrive at generalizations about gender differences in behavior, the second a comparison of some aspect of the Walker and Joyce novels in the light of our class discussions.

During class meetings we shared journal entries, discussed the assigned literature, and self-consciously explored our own reading, writing, and speaking behaviors. In one session, for instance, we shared retellings of Irwin Shaw's "The Girls in Their Summer Dresses," an especially appropriate story since it describes the interaction of a husband and wife as they attempt to

---

[3] It should be clear by now that my optimistic claim at the outset of the essay that the field of composition studies has feminized our conception of written communication needs qualification. I have already mentioned that the field has developed, for the most part, independent of feminist studies and as a result has not explored written communication in the context of women's special needs and problems. Also, feminist inquiry is beginning to reveal that work in cognate fields that have influenced the development of composition studies is androcentric. For an exploration of the androcentrism of theories of the reading process see Patrocinio P. Schweickart, "Reading Ourselves: Toward a Feminist Theory of Reading."

deal with the husband's apparently chronic habit of girl-watching. Most of the women were sympathetic to the female protagonist, and several males clearly identified strongly with the male protagonist.

The students reacted favorably to the course. They found Gilligan's book to be challenging, and they enjoyed the heated class discussions. The final journal entry of one of the strongest students in the class, Dorothy, suggests the nature of her development over the ten-week period:

> As this is sort of the wrap-up of what I've learned or how I feel about the class, I'll try to relate this entry to my first one on gender differences.
>
> I'm not so sure that men and women are so similar anymore, as I said in the first entry. The reactions in class especially make me think this. The men were so hostile toward Gilligan's book! I took no offense at it, but then again I'm not a man. I must've even overlooked the parts where she offended the men!
>
> Another thing really bothered me. One day after class, I heard two of the men talking in the hall about how you just have to be really careful about what you say in HU 101H about women, etc. Why do they have to be careful?! What did these two really want to say? That was pretty disturbing.
>
> However, I do still believe that MTU (or most any college actually) does bring out more similarities than differences. But the differences are still there—I know that.

Dorothy has begun to suspect that males and females read differently, and she has begun to suspect that they talk among themselves differently than they do in mixed company. The reading, writing, and discussing in the course have clearly alerted her to the possibility that gender affects the way in which readers, writers, and speakers use language.

This approach works especially well with honors students. I use somewhat different reading and writing assignments with non-honors students. In one class, for instance, I replaced the Gilligan book with an essay by Dale Spender on conversational patterns in high school classrooms. Students wrote a paper defending or refuting the Spender piece on the basis of their experiences in their own high schools. I have also devised ways of addressing feminist issues in composition courses in which the focus is not explicitly on gender differences. In a course designed to introduce students to fundamentals of research, for instance, students read Marge Piercy's *Woman on the Edge of Time* and did research on questions stimulated by it. They then shared their findings with the entire class in oral presentations. The approach led to wonderful papers on and discussions of the treatment of women in mental institutions, discrimination against minority women, and the ways in which technology can liberate women from oppressive roles.

I return now to my title and to the epigraph that introduces my essay. First, what does it mean to "compose as a woman"? Although the title invokes Jonathan Culler's "Reading as a Woman," a chapter in *On Deconstruction*, I do not mean to suggest by it that I am committed fully to Culler's deconstructive position. Culler maintains that "to read as a woman is to avoid reading as a man, to identify the specific defenses and distortions of male readings and provide correctives" (54). He concludes,

> For a woman to read as a woman is not to repeat an identity or an experience that is given but to play a role she constructs with reference to her identity as a woman, which is also a construct, so that the series can continue: a woman reading as a woman reading as a woman. The noncoincidence reveals an interval, a division within woman or within any reading subject and the "experience" of that subject. (64)

Culler is certainly correct that women often read as men and that they have to be encouraged to defend against this form of alienation. The strategy he suggests is almost entirely reactive, though. To read as a woman is to avoid reading as a man, to be alerted to the pitfalls of men's ways of reading.[4] Rich, too, warns of the dangers of immasculation, of identifying against oneself and learning to think like a man, and she, too, emphasizes the importance of critical activity on the part of the woman student—refusing to accept the givens of our culture, making connections between facts and ideas which men have left unconnected. She is well aware that thinking as a woman involves active construction, the recreation of one's identity. But she also sees value in recovering women's lived experience. In fact, she suggests that women maintain a critical posture in order to get in touch with that experience—to name it, to uncover that which is hidden, to make present that which has been absent. Her approach is active rather than reactive. Women's experience is not entirely a distorted version of male reality, it is not entirely elusive, and it is worthy of recuperation. We must alert our women students to the dangers of immasculation and provide them with a critical perspective. But we must also encourage them to become self-consciously aware of what their experience in the world has been and how this experience is related to the politics of gender. Then we must encourage our women students to write from the power of that experience.

---

[4] Elaine Showalter, in "Reading as a Woman: Jonathan Culler and the Deconstruction of Feminist Criticism," argues that "Culler's deconstructionist priorities lead him to overstate the essentialist dilemma of defining the *woman* reader, when in most cases what is intended and implied is a *feminist* reader" (126).

Works Cited

Annas, Pamela J. "Silences: Feminist Language Research and the Teaching of Writing." *Teaching Writing: Pedagogy, Gender, and Equity*. Ed. Cynthia L. Caywood and Gillian R. Overing. Albany: State U of New York P, 1987. 3-17.

Belenky, Mary Field, et al. *Women's Ways of Knowing: The Development of Self, Voice, and Mind*. New York: Basic Books, 1986.

Britton, James, et al. *The Development of Writing Abilities* (11-18). London: Macmillan Education, 1975.

Caywood, Cynthia L., and Gillian R. Overing. Introduction. *Teaching Writing: Pedagogy, Gender, and Equity*. Ed. Cynthia L. Caywood and Gillian R. Overing. Albany: State U of New York P, 1987. xi-xvi.

Chodorow, Nancy. *The Reproduction of Mothering: Psychoanalysis and the Sociology of Gender*. Berkeley: U of California P, 1978.

Culler, Jonathan. *On Deconstruction: Theory and Criticism after Structuralism*. Ithaca: Cornell UP, 1982.

Daeumer, Elisabeth, and Sandra Runzo. "Transforming the Composition Classroom." *Teaching Writing: Pedagogy, Gender, and Equity*. Ed. Cynthia L. Caywood and Gillian R. Overing. Albany: State U of New York P, 1987. 45-62.

Gilligan, Carol. *In a Different Voice: Psychological Theory and Women's Development*. Cambridge: Harvard UP, 1982.

Hairston, Maxine. "Breaking Our Bonds and Reaffirming Our Connections." *College Composition and Communication* 36 (October 1985): 272-82.

Howe, Florence. "Identity and Expression: A Writing Course for Women." *College English* 32 (May 1971): 863-71. Rpt. in Howe, *Myths of Coeducation: Selected Essays, 1964-1983*. Bloomington: Indiana UP, 1984. 28-37.

Kohlberg, Lawrence. "Moral Stages and Moralization: The Cognitive-Developmental Approach. *Moral Development and Behavior*. Ed. T. Lickona. New York: Holt, 1976. 31-53.

Perry, William G. *Forms of Intellectual and Ethical Development in the College Years*. New York: Holt, Rinehart & Winston, 1970.

Rich, Adrienne. "Taking Women Students Seriously." *On Lies, Secrets, and Silence: Selected Prose, 1966-1978*. New York: W. W. Norton, 1979. 237-45.

_____." 'When We Dead Awaken': Writing as Re-Vision." *On Lies, Secrets, and Silence: Selected Prose, 1966-1978*. New York: W. W. Norton, 1979. 33-49.

Schweickart, Patrocinio P. "Reading Ourselves Toward a Feminist Theory of Reading." *Gender and Reading: Essays on Readers, Texts, and Contexts*. Ed. Elizabeth A. Flynn and Patrocinio P. Schweickart. Baltimore: Johns Hopkins UP, 1986. 31-62.

Showalter, Elaine. "Reading as a Woman: Jonathan Culler and the Deconstruction of Feminist Criticism." *Men and Feminism*. Ed. Alice Jardine and Paul Smith. New York: Methuen, 1987. 123-27.

Stanger, Carol A. "The Sexual Politics of the One-to-One Tutorial Approach and Collaborative Learning." *Teaching Writing: Pedagogy, Gender, and Equity*. Ed. Cynthia L. Caywood and Gillian R. Overing. Albany: State U of New York P, 1987. 31-44.

Finding a Comfortable Identity

by William F. Irmscher

> To every thing there is a season . . .
> a time to mourn, and a time to dance.

I began to teach college composition in 1947 and have been involved with the discipline ever since. One actually doesn't need a forty-year perspective to know what composition teaching was then. Even though composition specialists often take a myopic view of progress, remnants of the attitudes and approaches of 1947 continue to be plentiful in 1987—in departmental policies, in the classroom, and especially in textbooks. In many colleges and universities, Freshman English still serves its traditional role: to get rid of the ill-prepared, not to help them become better writers.

Despite the perpetuation of ill-defined aims and ill-designed courses, remarkable changes have occurred in the past twenty-five years. Composition has established an identity of its own, not solely as a practitioner's art, but as a subject for scholarly study. The burgeoning membership of the Conference on College Composition and Communication testifies to wide professional interest. The organization has done more to advance composition studies than any other. *College Composition and Communication* and a variety of other periodicals provide outlets for publication. Because of newly established graduate programs, individuals are now able to specialize in rhetoric and composition studies. These people are even finding positions while their fellow-candidates in literature and criticism are not. New opportunities for study and development constantly emerge: writing projects, institutes, conferences, interdisciplinary ventures, explorations into technology, and studies of writing in nonacademic settings. All of these developments are cause for dancing.

Yet there is reason to have concern about the status of the composition profession and the future of those involved seriously in it. Those who received their Ph.D.'s five, six, or seven years ago and found themselves welcomed in the marketplace now face the harsh reality of tenure decisions and promotion. Increasing numbers of these people are being denied at institutions that predicate tenure and promotion on significant publication. Compared with other members of the English faculty, they know they are underpaid. Some are being shunted into administrative positions that may pay generously, but carry no job security or academic standing. This is a season for mourning.

These conditions need not be documented. We all recognize them. When Maxine Hairston addressed the annual convention of CCCC in 1985, tracing the same happy developments I have, she added the somber note that "we are fighting losing battles" in English departments and that "the time has come to break those bonds, not necessarily physically . . . but emotionally and intellectually" (273). She went on to say, "We have a sense of purpose and a camaraderie that energizes the profession. But I also see us stunted in our growth because we are not able to free ourselves from needing the approval of the literature people" (274). Her remarks were greeted by a cheering, standing ovation, indicating that many in the audience shared her views. It was a bold, therapeutic speech, both for her and for them. But Hairston looked more to causes outside than within. To a great extent, composition people have already freed themselves from the literature faculty. They don't think of themselves as second-rate intellects, even though they may often be treated like second-class citizens in the department. Yet if any group is undervalued or feels itself undervalued, it first needs to examine itself honestly, not take refuge in the ploy that others are to blame or that it hears a different drummer. If composition specialists have not yet acquired the academic respectability they seek, why not?

Part of the answer lies in the nature of research on composition. The direction of present research efforts may be traced to the publication of *Research in Written Composition* (1963) by Braddock, Lloyd-Jones, and Schoer, based on the work of an NCTE committee. That work led to the subsequent founding of *Research in the Teaching of English,* also an NCTE publication, with Richard Braddock serving as editor from its founding in 1967 until 1972. Richard Lloyd-Jones describes him as "a thorough empiricist" (163). Braddock, whose degree was in Education, was undoubtedly instrumental in shaping prescriptive, positivist standards for research in composition, encouraging a model that has prevailed in composition studies and has been fostered by the Research Foundation of the National Council of Teachers of English. Research in composition has become identified with one kind of research—controlled experimental studies producing statistical evidence. Janet Emig refers to this phenomenon as "conceptual synecdoche" ("Inquiry" 64). I have had Ph.D. candidates who wanted to specialize in composition think that they were obligated to undertake quantitative projects in order to write an acceptable dissertation. In Education, probably; in English, no.

When *Research in Written Composition* appeared, it was reviewed in *College English* by Jean Hagstrum. I remember Hagstrum's review about as vividly as any review I ever read, possibly because at the time I was annoyed that the book review editors picked an eighteenth-century scholar to review a book that was an assessment of empirical studies of the first two-thirds of this century, although it was a detailed treatment of only five studies. But I remember that review also because through the years I have found myself constantly reminded of it as I have read research studies, finally concluding in my own mind that Hagstrum was dead-center right from the beginning:

> These are undoubtedly the five best "scientific" studies ever conducted on written composition—virtually the cream of the cream. It is therefore extremely disheartening to have to say that (1) none of them strikes a layman [notice his identification of himself] as definitive or persuasive and (2) there is very little promise that, without rigorous antecedent thought, the "scientific" method applied to composition will yield better results in the future than it has in the past. (53)

Now, twenty-three years later, we have the sequel to the Braddock report, George Hillocks' *Research on Written Composition,* covering 1963-1982. Hagstrum's review can be reprinted with only the names, dates, and particulars changed. Hillocks' experience was not much different from Braddock's. Hillocks writes:

> In the present review of over 500 experimental studies, the most pervasive problem had to do with the control of variables. The major function of an experimental design is *control*—control over variables which might intervene to make a difference where none should be expected. (98)

A multitude of studies were excluded from his report because they did not "deal with a data set concerned with some aspect of written composition in a systematic way" (xvii).

As I read through the chapters of Hillocks' book, I am again and again reminded of another of Hagstrum's observations about one particular study in the Braddock report: "Reason and experience—those most indispensable tools of intellectual progress in any field are insulted and ultimately weakened when we run to the laboratory for proof of the obvious" (54). There, in one sentence, is the main reason most research on composition fails to gain respect. After one struggles through the prose and the statistics and the diagrams, one discovers that the investigator has complicated the familiar and obfuscated the obvious. To Braddock, Hillocks, and the tradition they represent, much of the research on composition lacks rigorous procedure. To others, not exclusively our literature compatriots, it lacks rigorous thought.

In their zeal to follow rigorous procedures, researchers frequently run counter to the act of composing or the act of teaching that they supposedly are studying. It is true that in recent years we have had a number of studies different from the frequency counts and comparison studies common in the Braddock era. But these more recent studies, especially of process, have not escaped the impelling force to be scientific by creating clinical, laboratory-like conditions to observe subjects, ignoring that they create a foreign environment and, in that controlled environment, set up obstacles to what might be natural or normal behavior of an individual in the act of composing.

Decontextualizing is the equivalent of distorting, because cause and effect relationships are perhaps the most difficult to establish. Hillocks admits that other variables do interfere and cannot necessarily be anticipated. It is practically a given that one cannot say positively what causes improvement in writing effectiveness or whether a particular teaching approach is responsible for change. The microanalysis of composing too often ignores the totality of the complex act. Donald Graves has set a precedent for studies that take a larger view. And researchers like Lee Odell, Dixie Goswami, and Lester Faigley are shifting the emphasis to the social setting, advocating ethnographic approaches, and producing results worthy of attention. But much research still ignores the complexity of composing.

In fairness to George Hillocks, let me add that his book is worth reading, not to denigrate it but to learn from it. It is an honest book. Hillocks does not hesitate to point out the limitations of some studies. On numerous occasions, he suggests that the data of a particular project could lead to alternative explanations. He is not reluctant to report general complaints about research and the problems of the researcher on composing or the teaching of composition. His own complaint is summarized in one of the concluding statements: "Without coordination, research may continue to be an atheoretical, hit-and-miss affair" (251). Of course, an effort has been made to move research in composing to scholarly maturity. That is Hillocks' purpose. He writes, "One hopes that the research effort in teaching composition will continue to expand. At the same time, one hopes that the quality of both experimental and case-study research will improve" (243).

I, too, hope that purposeful inquiry will continue, but I am not at all sure that the solution lies in refining the methods that have been used and repeatedly found wanting since 1963. I would propose that the solution lies in working toward a model of inquiry appropriate to our own discipline— composition as a part of English studies—consistent with its values, supporting and enlightening it. Up to this time, we have essentially imitated other disciplines, borrowed without fully considering the context and bounds of our own discipline. We have tried on garments that are ill-fitting. How do we remedy the situation that the zeal for verifiable data in the humanities has created?

We might begin, as Kenneth Burke does in "Terministic Screens," by "stressing the distinction between a 'scientific' and a 'dramatistic' approach to the nature of language" (44). Writing is dramatistic; it is symbolic action. It is performance. It is a rhetorical Act, inseparable from Actor, Scene, Agency, Attitude, and Purpose. The interaction of these components produces a rhetorical context, whether the writing represents a short story, a laboratory report, a business letter, or a treaty. The differences between these symbolic acts can be described, primarily in terms of their setting and purpose, but the differences can hardly be measured.

By all means, we should continue to borrow insights from other disciplines, but we need not adopt their methods. We can learn from Polanyi,

Vygotsky, Piaget, and others, but we cannot fully share the logic of their disciplines—the characteristic way a member of any discipline thinks. Janet Emig writes, "We view the universe differently, in part because in our paradigm we look to a different set of authorities." With this reasoning, she thinks we do not even share the view of "our colleagues in bellelettristic studies" ("Tacit Tradition" 11). I think we do, or at least we should. We share common ground in the English department with critics, textualists, historiographers, bibliographers, linguists, novelists, and poets, each of whom differs in approach, but all of whom represent the tradition of humane letters. What may be the basis of the present crisis is that composition specialists in English departments have deferred to the world view of English-Educationists.

We need to reassert the humanistic nature of our own discipline, which in this context means its concern for the individual as a human being, not as a quantity or specimen. We need to adopt procedures based on shared assumptions. If we accept the idea that the paradigm of a discipline represents the unspoken assumptions by which it functions, then we may find more implicit understanding about composition than explicit statement. What we do know is that scholars in the humanities characteristically distrust quantitative measures, even for linguistic or stylistic studies. Perhaps we need to voice more openly our fundamental assumptions. Certainly among them would be that introspection and imagination can prompt discovery and elicit truths as well as experiment and demonstration. And that language in all of its manifestations is our chief concern.

I would like to suggest a number of criteria and procedures for a model of scholarly inquiry, with the hope that those in composition now discontent with present models will be pleased to know that someone who has lived with the discipline for a full career finds these not only allowable but desirable.

Operating Assumptions

In studying the act of writing, investigators should:

- Recognize composing as an inside/outside process, the inner impulse and external constraints acting on one another as composing proceeds.
- Respect the individualistic, intuitive, creative nature of the act of writing, even for its most prosaic purposes.
- Represent subjects as people involved in writing for specific purposes.
- Consider the total act of composing in a natural environment that can be described in rich detail within the limits of the investigation.
- Disrupt as little as possible the natural setting of writing with cameras, tapes, and talk-aloud protocols.
- Use as many sources of information as will produce relevant data.
- Trust the voice of anecdotal evidence more than a staged performance of writing on videotape.

- Take pride in personal investigation, recognizing that it is necessarily limited, fallible, and selective.
- Acknowledge personal variables and idiosyncracies, always seeking in them patterns of behavior that have more general implications.
- Recognize that facts do not always speak for themselves, but need to be interpreted.
- Have confidence in one's own knowledge and perceptions, not as conclusive, but as a sensitive, sympathetic view of subjects and events.
- Seek possibilities rather than absolute certainties.
- Depend less on generalizations about all cases than on insights about particular cases in a selected discourse community.
- Use doubt as a springboard for unanticipated directions of investigation.

Methodology

In studying writing, investigators should:

- Prefer case-study and ethnographic inquiry to controlled group studies involving comparisons.
- Begin with a well-defined purpose and a limited number of crucial questions to be answered.
- Keep plans for research and writing as flexible as possible.
- Emphasize a close identification between observer and subject, yet reserve distance for purposes of disinterested analysis.
- Encourage introspection on the part of subjects, based on their confidence in the investigator.
- Note as accurately as possible what subjects do and say.
- Examine written texts to hypothesize about subjects' preconceptions, operating assumptions, and thinking processes.
- Resolve doubts by questioning the subjects.
- Use consistency as a criterion of reliability, not control.

Results

When reporting results, investigators should:

- Write as an insider to outsiders rather than as an insider to insiders.
- Describe and narrate in such a way that the subjects are revealed as living beings, not inanimate objects.
- Employ metaphor and analogy as means of explanation.
- Pursue analogues, particularly from other disciplines.

As I review these recommendations, here rather formally stated, it occurs to me that they represent the same kinds of inquiry and attitudes that an author might adopt in "researching" a novel, not less thorough than scholarly inquiry, not less demanding, not less true to experience. The task would be to present the fullness of experience—the experience of the project, the experience of the subject, the experience of the investigator. I can well imagine that an extended study could take the form of biography or narrative. We have a few precedents. Neither Elbow, Murray, nor E. B. White is reluctant to inject personal voice and experience. One of the most readable reports on pedagogy I know is William Coles's *The Plural I*. It reads like a short novel—or is it a dialogue? I get a clear notion what the instructor is like and how the students react. All of this is so vivid that I know I don't want to be like Coles. I don't want to use his approach, and I don't want to treat students as he does. But I *know* all of this because he has dramatized the situation. I don't ask how much is fictionalized. Is his presentation less reliable than factual reportage? I think not. And I see no reason why dissertations and scholarly articles need to be only barren factual statements.

Do we have to abandon the literary and critical values of our discipline in the name of scholarship? By denying these values, whom are we trying to please? Must we continue to be plagued by the scientific nemesis? By the specters of averages and standard deviations? If more students of composition began to reflect on the dramatistic nature of our discipline, I think we would find ourselves valued differently both by our colleagues in English departments and by the scholarly community at large. That, indeed, would be a season for dancing.

Works Cited

Braddock, Richard, Richard Lloyd-Jones, and Lowell Schoer. *Research in Written Composition.* Champaign: NCTE, 1963.

Burke, Kenneth. "Terministic Screens." *Language as Symbolic Action.* Berkeley: University of California Press, 1966. 44-62.

Coles, William E., Jr. *The Plural I.* New York: Holt, Rinehart and Winston, 1978.

Emig, Janet. "Inquiry Paradigms and Writing." *CCC* 33 (1982): 64-75.

____. "The Tacit Tradition: The Inevitability of a Multi-Disciplinary Approach to Writing Research" in *Reinventing the Rhetorical Tradition.* Eds. Aviva Freedman and Ian Pringle. Ottawa: Canadian Council of Teachers of English, 1980. 9-17.

Hagstrum, Jean H. Review of *Research in Written Composition. College English* 26 (1964): 53-56.

Hairston, Maxine. "Breaking Our Bonds and Reaffirming Our Connections." *CCC* 36 (1985): 272-282.

Hillocks, George, Jr. *Research on Written Composition.* Urbana: ERIC Clearinghouse on Reading and Communication Skills, 1986.

Lloyd-Jones, Richard. "Richard Braddock." *Traditions of Inquiry.* Ed. John Brereton. New York: Oxford University Press, 1985. 153-170.

Odell, Lee, and Dixie Goswami, eds. *Writing in Nonacademic Settings.* New York: Guilford, 1985.

Fun?

by Lex Runciman

On a rare quiet Friday morning last November, a morning initially marked only by creaking radiators and the occasional squeak of wet shoes on newly waxed linoleum, I pulled from the shelves the last two years' accumulation of *College English* and *College Composition and Communication* and began to browse. It was admittedly an impulsive act, but as I read, I realized part of what I was looking for: I was looking for some even oblique reference to writing and writing instruction as positive things, as activities yielding results other than difficulty, struggle, and frustration. Maybe it was the weather that day: dreary. Maybe it was some more significant if largely unconscious hunch that I'd forgotten something basic.

Looking for even vague encouragement or affirmation, I was distressed (doubly so that morning) to find so much support for difficulty and frustration. All teachers dealing with student writers know frustration. To write is to think, or to try to think. Cognitive psychology continues in its attempts to fully account for thinking, but we really don't know much about it. We don't know how to streamline it; we haven't discovered a vaccine for distraction. And though researchers in our own profession have made significant strides towards a grand unified theory of writing, this has yielded no sure-fire, good-for-all teaching methods. We are still challenged by the individual writers who show up in our classes. How, for example, does one apply the notion of discourse community to Alice, a woman whose face we recognize, someone who asks intelligent questions in class and attends regularly, yet hands in an essay or a report that we too quickly see is jumbled and embarrassingly anecdotal? How does one fruitfully bring notions of the social construction of all knowledge into a discussion with Jason, who complains that other members of his group are doing too little?

In a thoughtful and passionate essay on "things that go wrong in student-centered teaching," Mary Rose O'Reilley articulates much of this. She discusses student resistance and the myriad of problems confronting writing teachers. Her reference in this context is to none other than Joseph Conrad's *The Heart of Darkness:*

> *The Heart of Darkness* strikes me as an appropriate metaphor for the

> classroom in more ways than one. It's here we confront chaos and
> misrule, savage silence, chills, fever, and, at least in some places,
> where I've taught, failure of the airconditioning. (142)

Her essay is provocative and witty, full of weariness and exasperation and a
refusal to succumb.

That refusal was some consolation, but there were still many other articles
to browse through, and I found as I looked that my interest took on a larger
form. Feeling suddenly separate from what I do, feeling the stirrings of a
curiosity I assume anthropologists routinely feel, I found myself wondering
this: what have we determined as worth telling each other? What do we talk
about? What do we tell ourselves as true about writing and writing instruction?

Our journals constitute an astonishing swirl and eddy of topics, stances,
and assumptions, and viewed from the properly dreary angle, many of them
are depressing. We talk about our profession and the professional standards
we want to set for ourselves, and in doing so it is clear that we have had to
establish these standards as defensive measures. We have had to determine
and advocate appropriate working conditions (class size and the like)
precisely because we have so often been asked to work under inappropriate
conditions. We talk about the administration of various kinds of writing
programs, and we do so at least in part to combat the isolation in which we
work. We talk about the cultural forces that shape our classrooms and
ourselves, of what Terry Dean terms "the diversity within each of the cultures
that students bring with them" (36). And I don't think I'm alone in feeling
kinship with Dean's opening sentence: "Sometimes more than others, I sense
the cultural thin ice I walk on in my classrooms, and I reach out for more
knowledge than I could ever hope to acquire, just to hang on" (23).

And of course, part of what we talk about is writing itself; we try to
illuminate writing acts. Thus the same issue of *College English* that features
O'Reilley's essay also contains Muriel Harris's article titled "The Composing
Behaviors of One- and Multi-Draft Writers." Harris's article is one of several
which, whether in whole or in part, hinge on careful observation and
reporting:

> If we wish to draw a more inclusive picture of composing behavior
> for revision, we have to put together a description that accounts for
> differences in levels of ability and experience (from novice to expert),
> for differences in writing tasks, and also for differences in the as yet
> largely unexplored areas of composing process differences among
> writers. (177-78)

Given my initial short-tempered dreariness, I couldn't help but notice the
repetitions of *differences* (why not sameness, for once? why not consensus?)
and the commonplace phrase *unexplored areas*, a phrase which suddenly
reassumed some of its original awe and terror. Though I didn't want to admit
it, though I didn't want to listen, I heard a small, seemingly reasonable voice

asking simple questions: if writing is this complicated, why would anyone do it? If writing itself is so problematic, why then would anyone want to encourage it or teach it?

As I finished Harris's essay, I could see that it arrives at some startling and perhaps disquieting conclusions for those of us who routinely mandate revision. It turns out that some of these last-minute-write-it-all-now practitioners may not be as damnable as we may sometimes wish to paint them. Harris finds "one-drafters are efficient writers. . . . They are able to pace themselves and can probably perform comfortably in situations such as the workplace or in in-class writing where it is advantageous to produce first-draft final-draft pieces of discourse" (187). As she further describes these one-draft writers, she comments that "The interesting portion of a writing task, the struggle with text and sense of exploration, is largely completed when they [one-draft writers] commit themselves to paper (or computer screen). Because they are less likely to enjoy writing, the task of starting is more likely to be put off to the last minute and to become a stressful situation . . ."(187). As writers and writing teachers, we know a lot about stressful situations. But as I was reading that last bit, one word leapt out, and I want to surround it with lights; that word is *enjoy*.

We don't talk much about enjoyment, about the rewards of thinking and writing well. Maybe we do discuss such things within the informal confines of our classrooms, but we don't write articles about enjoyment nor do many textbooks mention it. For example, one of our best textbooks *(The St. Martin's Guide to Writing)* emphasizes writing is "hard work," that "sometimes the hardest part of writing is getting started," and that "for most writers frustration in the early period of drafting is natural"(4). To give Axelrod and Cooper their due, the introduction also goes on to mention "the great personal fulfillment and pride that writing often brings," and after quoting John Updike, James Michener, and Anne Sexton (among others), they work to further balance their negative emphasis by noting that "Many writers write in order to earn a living, but it is not true that they live lives of unrelenting torment. They struggle, but they also celebrate, and they find great satisfaction in the process of writing" (5).

If we take such textbook statements as in some way mirrors of our profession's working knowledge, then it's clear that most of us realize that at least some writers (the famously literary, at least) do find writing satisfying, even fun. But have we really acted on that knowledge?

We speak of writing as a process and by that we generally mean a series of problems to be solved. Linda Flower, John Hayes, and many others have worked and continue to work fruitfully in this regard, and in one sense that work has been tremendously positive: it has demystified writing activities. It has given students conscious and workable writing strategies, and whenever those strategies work, the result is (presumably) satisfaction. But it is this satisfaction—the second half of the equation—that I know I have often ignored or sometimes failed altogether to see.

The notion of writing as (at least in part) a problem-solving process has become almost ubiquitous, and it is the starting point for a wide variety of observations. Here, for example, is Charles Kostelnick's three ways in which writing process and design process paradigms have mirrored each other in their evolution. Both, says Kostelnick, have

- –Viewed creativity as a conscious, goal-directed activity in which problem definition plays a crucial role.
- –Shifted from applied to descriptive models, from devising practical methods to studying how writers and designers actually proceed.
- –Drawn on theories external to the discipline, (cognitive psychology, the philosophy of science) to redefine issues and to generate problem-solving models. (268)

Clearly, the word *problem* has become one of our buzz words; it's so familiar to us that in some ways we may not sense its effects. Consider this: in presuming that writing is difficult (and it is), in presuming that writing is at least in part a problem-solving activity, in "studying how writers . . . actually proceed," are we in danger of forgetting how writers actually feel as they proceed? Or in other words, have we focused so successfully on the difficulties and frustrations writers feel that we have neglected to mention (and reinforce) the rewards writers feel?

One trouble with pleasure (even that resulting from a demanding and rigorous mental activity) is that it's squishy, it's difficult to predict, and talking about it seems vaguely unprofessional. It seems frivolous. In his fascinating book *The Most Beautiful House in the World*, Witold Rybcznski speaks of the design process as "fun," but he is quick to note that "fun does not imply folly, or any lack of seriousness—quite the opposite" (39).

When we do acknowledge pleasure or satisfaction arising from the writing process, we tend to assign it to literary writers whom many of us still view as, by definition, loftier than we are, certainly loftier than our students. Literary types (I should note here that I write and publish poems) are a different breed. As Burton Hatlen (himself a poet) notes, "from the point of view of the scholar or critic, all 'writers' [poets and novelists] must seem at least a little mad" (792). Maybe the literary impulse somehow contains within it this strange, dependable joy and pleasure in writing—a pleasure and interest which, at least in my own case, crosses genre boundaries. But even as I say that, I don't really mean it. I don't really believe that writing is rewarding only for poets or creative writers, for I know that other essayists, theorists, article writers, researchers and, yes, technical writers *do* enjoy writing, finding it a satisfying and rewarding activity.

Yet as I read that November day I found little discussion of such rewards. Why don't we routinely discuss such things? Is it that we have too readily taken our notions of our profession and of our mission from a sense of ourselves as combatants? We're fighting the literacy wars. We're fighting the "Why Johnny and Annie Can't Write" war. We're fighting large class sizes and cultural inequalities. We're fighting the good grammar war. There seems no shortage of wars—good wars, important wars—that we have, sometime, somehow, signed on to fight. And certainly we must be affected by all those papers we have graded, many of them clearly the sights of struggle, of sad defeat, and at best modest success. But even in thinking of those successes, the struggles and misses can seem as numerous as Oregon raindrops in November; they tend to swallow up or submerge the outright victories.

On such days as that November Friday, I need some metaphoric caffeine, something to get the juices going again, something to remind me of why I write and why others write, something to remind me of what writing—all that effort—can give back. And reading along, I did find two brief mentions of writing and thinking, two writers suggesting that writing gives them some sort of substantial pleasure. Coincidentally (or not?), both references came from within students' statements. In an article discussing what Robert Brooke characterizes as "the paradox of control," Brooke begins by quoting two students identified only as Writer A and Writer B. Both respond to what Brooke routinely calls "the same writing problem":

> I'm having trouble with my writing. I'm stuck; I can't figure out what I've got to say, I'm frustrated. I'm a lousy writer. –Writer A

> I'm in the fun part of writing. At the moment, I don't know what I've got to say but I know if I just give myself time to wander around, to explore what I'm thinking, I'll end up with something insightful and powerful. Right now, I just have to let go and let my writing do its thing. –Writer B (405)

Brooke goes on to use these contrasting attitudes to show that, in fact, perhaps one trait of a good writer is that she doesn't worry too hard about being in control.

But what caught my eye here was the implied assertion that writing *is* fun, or at least that it can have a "fun part." The only other similar reference I could find comes from Joseph Harris's article titled "The Idea of Community in the Study of Writing." In that article, Harris quotes part of one of his student's end-of-term reflections: "As I look back over my writings for this course I see a growing acceptance of the freedom to write as I please, which is allowing me to almost enjoy writing (I can't believe it) . . . "(18). The quotation goes on, and Harris uses it to discuss students' initiations into new discourses, new communities. I think all of us have heard students say that they're finding writing enjoyable, and we know that it's typically said in a tone of surprise and disbelief. My response has usually been a self-indulgent one. I've usually smiled smugly as though to say, see, I told you so. But reading Harris's article and coming across that student comment, I found myself chilled at the thought—the possibility—that we've somehow persuaded most students that writing is and must be a negative, difficult, problematic, error-ridden, *and therefore* ultimately joyless activity.

Fun? Well, why not? What fun, to focus on an immediate example, is there in writing an essay such as this one? The question seems startling, liberating; it creates a rush of answers. The first pleasure is, oddly enough, simply that of tackling any large (it seems large at the outset anyway), inchoate response—in this case a direct response to reading two years of our journals. Some small part of the response appears almost immediately and sometimes with heartening clarity; even if that heartening clarity later gets cut or heavily revised, it at first *seems* clear, and at that point, the appearance is welcome and encouraging. Even if the first sentences seem awkward and unconnected, they *are* present; something begins to take some sort of shape. Blank paper (or an empty computer screen) begins to fill, and this is progress; this is worth affirming.

Why is this very first drafting pleasurable rather than scary or intimidating? Some of the reason must lie with trust in one's tools and in the process itself. In a word, experience. But some of it must lie in habits of mind, in how one has been encouraged or trained to view writing itself. If the inexperienced writer views *writing* as virtually synonymous with *problem*, then starting a new writing project may inevitably seem problematic. And if this inexperienced writer carries the added unfortunate baggage of a less-than-successful writing career to date, then distaste and fear and uncertainty seem unavoidable. The question is, can we modify this notion of writing as problem? Can we focus on the "solving" portion of the phrase "problem-solving?" Can we emphasize not just an awareness of the process's likely frustrations but also an appreciation of its equally likely satisfactions, its rewards?

Another pleasure, a recurring one though its frequency is unpredictable, lies in finding some accurate phrasing. This phrasing need not be particularly felicitous or pleasing to others; what makes it a source of pleasure is its accuracy. It fits, no, it accurately embodies some thought (however small) which had up until that moment not been verbalized. When it appears on screen or on the page, it clicks into place with a rightness which seems, even if only momentarily, unassailable. So eventually sentences begin to pile up, and sheer quantity becomes a source of private hopefulness, an indication that something is getting made; something is beginning to assume a separate physical presence. Eventually weariness sets in or distractions intervene, and that is enough writing for one sitting. But for me, and I trust for many others, the pattern of writing as fun has begun.

Looking at writing from this new perspective suggests how impatience remains as a formative factor in determining whether writing is rewarding or just frustrating. When writers lack adequate time to read or reread, when they realize only additional research will shed the required light, whenever they want to push the process faster than its own pace, whenever progress does not seem immediate, then impatience becomes a factor; and impatience leads directly to frustration. Yet even under these circumstances, writing pleasures do not disappear. And it is precisely under such circumstances that writers need to be doubly aware of the pleasures of a right phrasing or of even halting progress. This may sound like blithe optimism, but I see it as pragmatic and personally essential: Though pressed, frustrated, or tried, I stay with my own writing process because I habitually view that process as rewarding (for it is) and essentially positive. Curtailing or seriously abbreviating the process curtails or seriously abbreviates the opportunities for reward during writing; such abridgement of process also increases the likelihood that readers will misunderstand. Since I want those writing satisfactions (and accurate reader response is one of them), I work hard to try and guarantee them.

At the very least then, focusing on the rewards of the process becomes a way to balance the frustrations. For I think we have it right when we acknowledge writing is hard, often frustrating work (work not unlike our professional lives). But perhaps we have it only half right. Maybe we do need to professionally address the question of fun, of writing's satisfactions. Maybe we need to encourage student writers to discover and even savor the range of large and small rewards which attend their own writing and thinking. For at best, the activity of writing becomes self-rewarding though never effortless; it becomes, for some writers on some particularly good days, to borrow phrasing from Robert Frost, "the sweetest dream that labor knows" (17). We need—and I include myself in this "we"—to recognize such rewards as available to all writers, not just the great literary masters. Student writers need to recognize such feelings as their own, or at least as potentially their own. Maybe we can begin this process by rediscovering for ourselves the internal, even intrinsic, rewards of the single, marvelously complicated process we call writing and thinking—the rewards which (at least in part) led us to forsake careers in dentistry or plumbing.

Works Cited

Axelrod, Rise B., and Charles R. Cooper. *The St. Martin's Guide to Writing*. New York: St. Martin's, 1985.

Brooke, Robert. "Control in Writing: Flower, Derrida, and Images of the Writer." *College English* 51 (1989): 405-17.

Dean, Terry. "Multicultural Classrooms, Monocultural Teachers." *College Composition and Communication* 40 (1989): 23-37.

Frost, Robert. *The Poetry of Robert Frost*. Ed. Edward Connery Lathem. New York: Holt, 1969.

Harris, Joseph. "The Idea of Community in the Study of Writing." *College Composition and Communication* 40 (1989): 11-22.

Harris, Muriel. "Composing Behaviors of One- and Multi-Draft Writers." *College English* 51 (1989): 174-91.

Hatlen, Burton. "Michel Foucault and the Discourse[s] of English." *College English* 50 (1988): 786-801.

Kostelnick, Charles. "Process Paradigms in Design and Composition: Affinities and Directions." *College Composition and Communication* 40 (1989): 267-81.

O'Reilley, Mary Rose. " 'Exterminate . . . the Brutes'—And Other Things That Go Wrong in Student-Centered Teaching." *College English* 51 (1989): 142-46.

Rybczynski, Witold. *The Most Beautiful House in the World*. New York: Viking, 1989.

All Writing Is Autobiography

by Donald M. Murray

I publish in many forms—poetry, fiction, academic article, essay, newspaper column, newsletter, textbook, juvenile nonfiction and I have even been a ghost writer for corporate and government leaders—yet when I am at my writing desk I am the same person. As I look back, I suspect that no matter how I tuned the lyre, I played the same tune. All my writing—and yours—is autobiographical.

To explore this possibility, I want to share a poem that appeared in the March 1990 issue of *Poetry*.

At 64, Talking Without Words

The present comes clear when rubbed
with memory. I relive a childhood
of texture: oatmeal, the afternoon rug,
spears of lawn, winter finger tracing
frost on window glass, August nose
squenched against window screen. My history
of smell: bicycle oil, leather catcher's
mitt, the sweet sickening perfume of soldiers
long dead, ink fresh on the first edition.
Now I am most alone with others, companioned
by silence and the long road at my back,
mirrored by daughters. I mount the evening
stairs with mother's heavy, wearied
step, sigh my father's long complaint.
My beard grows to the sepia photograph
of a grandfather I never knew. I forget
if I turned at the bridge, but arrive
where I intended. My wife and I talk
without the bother of words. We know Lee
is 32 today. She did not stay twenty
but stands at each room's doorway. I place
my hand on the telephone. It rings.

What is autobiographical in this poem? I was 64 when I wrote it. The childhood memories were real once I remembered them by writing. I realized I was mirrored by daughters when the line arrived on the page. My other daughter would have been 32 on the day the poem was written. Haven't you all had the experience of reaching for the phone and hearing it ring?

There may even be the question of autobiographical language. We talk about our own language, allowing our students their own language. In going over this draft my spellcheck hiccupped at "squenched" and "companioned." As an academic I gulped; as a writer I said, "Well they are now."

Then Brock Dethier, one of the most perceptive of the test readers with whom I share drafts, pointed out the obvious—where all the most significant information is often hidden. He answered my question, "What is autobiographical in this poem?" by saying, "Your thinking style, your voice." Of course.

We are autobiographical in the way we write; my autobiography exists in the examples of writing I use in this piece and in the text I weave around them. I have my own peculiar way of looking at the world and my own way of using language to communicate what I see. My voice is the product of Scottish genes and a Yankee environment, of Baptist sermons and the newspaper city room, of all the language I have heard and spoken.

In writing this paper I have begun to understand, better than I ever have before, that all writing, in many different ways, is autobiographical, and that our autobiography grows from a few deep taproots that are set down into our past in childhood.

Willa Cather declared, "Most of the basic material a writer works with is acquired before the age of fifteen." Graham Greene gave the writer five more years, no more: "For writers it is always said that the first 20 years of life contain the whole of experience—the rest is observation."

Those of us who write have only a few topics. My poems, the novel I'm writing, and some of my newspaper columns keep returning to my family and my childhood, where I seek understanding and hope for a compassion that has not yet arrived. John Hawkes has said, "Fiction is an act of revenge." I hope not, but I can not yet deny the importance of that element in my writing. Revenge against family, revenge against the Army and war, revenge against school.

Another topic I return to is death and illness, religion and war, a great tangle of themes. During my childhood I began the day by going to see if my grandmother had made it through the night; I ended my day with, "Now I lay me down to sleep, I pray the Lord my soul to keep. If I should die before I wake, I pray the Lord my soul to take."

I learned to sing "Onward Christian Soldiers Marching as to War," and still remember my first dead German soldier and my shock as I read that his belt buckle proclaimed God was on *his* side. My pages reveal my obsession with war, with the death of our daughter, with that territory I explored in the hours between the bypass operation that did not work and the one that did.

Recently, Boynton/Cook/Heinemann published *Shoptalk*, a book I began in Junior High School that documents my almost lifelong fascination with how writing is made. I assume that many people in this audience are aware of my obsession with writing and my concern with teaching that began with my early discomfort in school that led to my dropping out and flunking out. My academic writing is clearly autobiographical.

Let's look now at a Freshman English sort of personal essay, what I like to call a reflective narrative. I consider such pieces of writing essays, but I suppose others think of them in a less inflated way as newspaper columns. I write a column, *Over Sixty*, for the *Boston Globe*, and the following one was published October 10th of 1989. It was based on an experience I had the previous August.

> Over sixty brings new freedoms, a deeper appreciation of life and the time to celebrate it, but it also brings, with increasing frequency, such terrible responsibilities as sitting with the dying.
>
> Recently it was my turn to sit with my brother-in-law as he slowly left us, the victim of a consuming cancer.
>
> When I was a little boy, I wanted—hungered—to be a grown-up. Well, now I am a grown-up. And when someone had to sit with the dying on a recent Saturday, I could not look over my shoulder. I was the one. My oldest daughter will take her turn. She is a grown-up as well, but those of us over sixty have our quota of grown-upness increase. Time and again we have to confront crisis: accident, sickness, death. There is no one else to turn to. It is our lonely duty.
>
> Obligation has tested and tempered us. No one always measures up all the time. We each do what we can do, what we must do. We learn not to judge if we are wise, for our judgments boomerang. They return. At top speed and on target.
>
> Most of us, sadly and necessarily, have learned to pace ourselves. We have seen friends and relatives destroyed by obligation, who have lost themselves in serving others. There is no end to duty for those who accept it.
>
> And we have seen others who diminish by shirking responsibility. When we call them for help the door is shut. We hear silence.
>
> We grow through the responsible acceptance of duty, obligation balanced by self-protection. We teeter along a high wire trying to avoid guilt or sanctimoniousness as we choose between duty and avoidance.
>
> And so my mind wanders as Harry sleeps, blessedly without pain for the moment, moving steadily toward a destination he seems no longer to fear.
>
> He would understand that as we mourn for him, we mourn for ourselves. Of course. We are learning from his dying how to live. We inevitably think of what he did that we can emulate and what we should try to avoid.
>
> And we learn, from his courage and his example, not to fear death. I remember how horrified I was years ago when a mother of a

friend of mine, in her late eighties, feeling poorly in the middle of the night, would get up, change into her best nightgown, the one saved for dying, and go back to sleep.

Now I understand. During my last heart attack I had a volcanic desire to live but no fear of dying. It was not at all like my earlier trips to the edge.

Harry continues my education. He did not want trouble while he lived and now he is dying the same way, causing no trouble, trying to smile when he wakes, trying to entertain me.

He needs the comfort of sleep and I leave the room, turning outside his door to see how quickly his eyes close. He wants nothing from us now. Not food, not drink, not, we think, much companionship. He accepts that his road is lonely and he does not even show much impatience at its length.

It is not a happy time, alone in the house with a dying man, but it is not a dreadful time either. I pat the cat who roams the house but will not go to the room where Harry lies; I read, write in my daybook, watch Harry, and take time to celebrate my living.

This house, strange to me, in an unfamiliar city, is filled with silence. No music, no TV, just the quiet in which I can hear his call. But he does not call. I cannot hear his light breathing. Every few minutes I go to the door to see if the covers still rise and fall.

He would understand as I turn from him to watch the tree branch brush the roof of the house next door, as I spend long moments appreciating the dance of shadows from the leaves on the roof, then the patterns of sunlight reflected up on the ceiling of the room where I sit, as I celebrate my remaining life.

Again I stand at the edge of the door watching, waiting, and take instructions from his dying. We should live the hours we have in our own way, appreciating their passing. And we should each die in our own way. I will remember his way, his acceptance, his not giving trouble, his lonely, quiet passing.

This is simple narrative with the facts all true, but it is really not that simple; few things are in writing or in life. The details are selective. A great deal of family history is left out. A great many details about the day, the illness, where it was taking place and why were left out. In fact, I wrote it in part for therapy, and it began as a note to myself several weeks after the experience to help me cut through a jungle of thoughts and emotions, to try to recover for myself what was happening that day. Later I saw that it might speak to others, give comfort or form to their own autobiographies. I did not write the whole truth of that day, although the facts in the piece are accurate; I wrote a limited truth seeking a limited understanding, what Robert Frost called "a momentary stay of confusion."

Yes, I confess it, I wrote, and write, for therapy. Writing autobiography is my way of making meaning of the life I have led and am leading and may lead.

Let's look at another autobiographical poem, one of my favorites, which, I suppose, means that it was one I especially needed to write for no autobiographical reason I can identify. It has not yet been published, although a great many of the best poetry editors in the country have failed in their obligation to Western culture by rejecting it.

Black Ice

On the first Saturday of winter, the boy
skated alone on Sailor's Home Pond, circling
from white ice to black, further each time
he rode the thin ice, rising, dipping, bending
the skin of the water until the crack raced
from shore to trick him but he heard, bent
his weight to the turn, make it back in time.

That winter he saw the fish frozen in ice,
its great unblinking eye examining him
each time he circled by. He dreamt that eye
all summer, wondered if Alex had seen
the fish eye before he rode the black ice,
did not hear the crack sneak out from shore,
imagined he learned to skate on water.

At night, after loving you, I fall back
to see that fish eye staring down, watch
Alex in shoe skates and knickers from below
as he skates overhead, circling faster, faster,
scissor legs carrying him from white ice
to black. His skates sing their cutting song,
etching larger, larger circles in my icy sky.

It is true that the boy, myself, skated on thin ice and that he skated at Sailor's Home Pond in Quincy, Massachusetts, although the thin ice may not have been on that pond. He did not, however, see a fish in the ice until he wrote the poem, although he was obsessed with the eyes of the fish, haddock and cod, that followed him when he went to Titus's fish store in Wollaston. Readers believe that Alex is my brother, although I was an only child. There was no Alex; no one I knew had drowned by falling through the ice until I received the poem; I did not, after loving, stare up to see him skating above me until after I wrote the poem. I do now. The poem that was for a few seconds imaginary has become autobiographical by being written.

Ledo Ivo, the Latin American writer, said, "I increasingly feel that my writing creates me. I am the invention of my own words" (*Lives on the Line*, Ed. Doris Meyer, U of California P). Don DeLillo explains, "Working at sentences and rhythms is probably the most satisfying thing I do as a writer. I think after a while a writer can begin to know himself through his language. He sees someone or something reflected back at him from these constructions.

Over the years it's possible for a writer to shape himself as a human being through the language he uses. I think written language, fiction, goes that deep. He not only sees himself but begins to make himself or remake himself" (*Anything Can Happen*, Ed. Tom LeClair and Larry McCaffery, U of Illinois P, 1988).

We become what we write. That is one of the great magics of writing. I am best known as a nonfiction writer, but I write fiction and poetry to free myself of small truths in the hope of achieving large ones. Here are the first pages from a novel I am writing.

Notebook in his lap, pen uncapped, Ian Fraser sat in the dark green Adirondack chair studying the New Hampshire scene that had so often comforted him as he put in his last years in his Washington office. The green meadow sloping unevenly over granite ledge to the lake and the point of land with its sentinel pine that marked the edge of his possession, and across the lake the hills rising into mountains touched with the reds, oranges, yellows that would flame into autumn this week or next. He was settled in at last and ready to begin the book he had so long delayed, but he could not write until he scanned this quiet scene with his infantryman's eyes for it still was, as were all his landscapes, a field of fire.

He had to know where to dig in, where the enemy would attack, what was at his back. He supposed it was what had attracted him to this old farmhouse, he could hold this position, he had a good field of fire. First he scanned the lake. Left to right, far edge to near, not one boat or canoe, nothing breaking the surface, no wind trail or wake. Now right to left to see what might be missed. Nothing.

The point of land, his furthest outpost. Scraggly pines, hulking ledge, ideal cover. He studied it close up, knew the pattern of shadows, where the ledge caught the light, where crevice was always dark. This is ridiculous, he thought, an old man whose wars are all over, but he could not stop the search for the enemies that had been there at the edge of other fields so long ago, so recent in memory.

The woods left, on the other side from sentinel point. Sweep his eyes at the woods a half a field away, open ground any enemy would have to cross. He made himself still; anyone watching would not know his eyes were on patrol. He could have hidden a platoon in these woods, tree and bush, ledge and rock wall, but there was no shadow that moved, no unexpected sound, no leaves that danced without wind.

And yet, Ian felt a presence as if he, the watcher, were being watched. He scanned the woods on the left again, moving from lake edge up. Nothing.

Now the woods on the right, he had cut back from the house when he bought it, saying he needed sun for vegetables. He needed open field. More hardwoods here, more openness, the road unseen beyond. It was where someone would come in. His flood lights targeted these woods, but it was not night. He examined these familiar woods, suddenly looking high in the old oak where a pileated woodpecker started his machine gun attack. Ian studied squirrel and crow, the pattern of light and dark, followed the trail of the quiet lake breeze that rose through the woods and was gone.

Now the field of fire itself, where a civilian would think no-one could hide. He smiled at the memory of a young paratrooper, himself, home on leave, telling Claire, who would become his first wife, to stand at the top of the field and spot him if she could as he crept up the slope, taking cover where there seemed no cover. She was patient with his soldiering—then. She knew her quarry and did not laugh as this lean young man crawled up the slope moving quickly from ledge to slight hollow to the cover of low bush blueberries that July in 1943.

He never knew if she saw him or not.

Do I have a green lawn that reaches down to a New Hampshire lake? No. Do I still see when I visit a new place, forty-six years after I have been in combat, a good field of fire? Yes. Did I have another wife than Minnie Mae? Yes. Was her name Claire? No. Did I play that silly game in the field when I was home on leave? Yes. Is the setting real? Let Herman Melville answer, "It is not down on any map: true places never are."

What is true, what is documentally autobiographical, in the novel will not be clear to me when I finish the last draft. I confess that at my age I am not sure about the source of most of my autobiography. I have written poems that describe what happened when I left the operating table, looked back and decided to return. My war stories are constructed of what I experienced, what I heard later, what the history books say, what I needed to believe to survive and recover—two radically different processes.

I dream every night and remember my dreams. Waking is often a release from a greater reality. I read and wear the lives of the characters I inhabit. I do not know where what I know comes from. Was it dreamt, read, overheard, imagined, experienced in life or at the writing desk? I have spun a web more coherent than experience.

But of course I've been talking about fiction, a liar's profession, so let us turn to the realistic world of nonfiction. That novel from which I have quoted is being written, more days than not, by a technique I call layering that I describe in the third edition of *Write to Learn*:

> One technique I've been using, especially in writing the novel, is to layer my writing. Once I did quite a bit of oil painting and my pictures were built up, layer after layer of paint until the scene was revealed to me and a viewer. I've been writing each chapter of the novel the same way, starting each day at the beginning of the chapter, reading and writing until the timer bings and my daily stint is finished. Each day I lay down a new layer of text and when I read it

the next day, the new layer reveals more possibility.

There is no one way the chapters develop. Each makes its own demands, struggles towards birth in its own way. Sometimes it starts with a sketch, other times the first writing feels complete (next day's reading usually shows it is not); sometimes I race ahead through the chapter, other times each paragraph is honed before I go on to the next one. I try to allow the text to tell me what it needs.

I start reading and when I see—or, more likely, hear—something that needs doing, I do it. One day I'll read through all the written text and move it forward from the last day's writing; another time I'll find myself working on dialogue; the next day I may begin to construct a new scene (the basic element of fiction); one time I'll stumble into a new discovery, later have to set it up or weave references to it through the text; I may build up background description, develop the conflict, make the reader see a character more clearly; I may present more documentation, evidence, or exposition, or hide it in a character's dialogue or action.

Well, that is academic writing, writing to instruct, textbook writing. It is clearly nonfiction, and to me it is clearly autobiography. And so, I might add, is the research and scholarship that instructs our profession. We make up our own history, our own legends, our own knowledge by writing our autobiography.

This has enormous implications for our students, or should have. In *Notebooks of the Mind* (U of New Mexico P, 1985), a seminal book for our discipline,   Vera John-Steiner documents the importance of obsession. "Creativity requires a *continuity of concern*, an intense awareness of one's active inner life combined with sensitivity to the external world." Again and again she documents the importance of allowing and even cultivating the obsessive interest of a student in a limited area of study. I read that as the importance of encouraging and supporting the exploration of the autobiographical themes of individual students—and the importance of allowing ourselves to explore the questions that itch our lives.

I do not think we should move away from personal or reflective narrative in composition courses, but closer to it; I do not think we should limit reflective narrative to a single genre; I do not think we should make sure our students write on many different subjects, but that they write and rewrite in pursuit of those few subjects which obsess them.

But then, of course, I am writing autobiographically, telling other people to do what is important to me.

And so all I can do is just rest my case on my own personal experience. I want to read my most recent poem in which the facts are all true. I had not seen as clearly before I wrote the poem the pattern of those facts, the way I—and a generation of children in the United States and Germany and Britain and Japan and China and Spain and France and Italy and Russia and so many other countries—was prepared for war. This piece of writing is factually true

but watch out as you hear it. Writing is subversive and something dangerous
may happen as you hear my autobiography.

A woman hearing this poem may write, in her mind, a poem of how she
was made into a docile helpmate by a society that had its own goals for her.
A black may write another autobiography as mine is heard but translated by
personal history. A person who has been mistreated in childhood, a person
who is a Jew, a person whose courage was tested at the urging of jeering
peers on a railroad bridge in Missouri, will all hear other poems, write other
poems in their minds as they hear mine.

Winthrop 1936, Seventh Grade

December and we comb our hair wet,
pocket our stocking caps and run,
uniformed in ice helmets,

to read frost etched windows:
castle, moat, battlements, knight,
lady, dragon, feel our sword

plunge in. At recess we fence
with icicles, hide coal in
snow balls, lie freezing

inside snow fort, make ice balls
to arc against the enemy: Hitler.
I lived in a town of Jews,

relatives hidden in silences,
letters returned, doors shut,
curtains drawn. Our soldier

lessons were not in books taught
by old women. In East Boston,
city of Mussolinis, we dance

combat, attack and retreat, sneak,
hide, escape, the companionship
of blood. No school, and side

staggered by icy wind we run
to the sea wall, wait
for the giant seventh wave

to draw back, curl mittens
round iron railing, brace
rubber boots, watch

the entire Atlantic rise
until there is no sky. Keep
mittens tight round iron rail,

prepare for the return of ocean,
that slow, even sucking back,
the next rising wave.

I suspect that when you read my poem, you wrote your own autobiography. That is the terrible, wonderful power of reading: the texts we
create in our own minds while we read—or just after we read—become part
of the life we believe we lived. Another thesis: all reading is autobiographical.

Between the Drafts

by Nancy Sommers

I cannot think of my childhood without hearing voices, deep, heavily-accented, instructive German voices.

I hear the voice of my father reading to me from *Struvelpater*, the German children's tale about a messy boy who refuses to cut his hair or his fingernails. Struvelpater's hair grows so long that birds nest in it, and his fingernails grow so long that his hands become useless. He fares better, though, than the other characters in the book who don't listen to their parents. Augustus, for instance, refuses to eat his soup for four days, becomes as thin as a thread, and on the fifth day he is dead. Fidgety Philip tilts his dinner chair like a rocking horse until his chair falls backwards; the hot food falls on top of him, and suffocates him under the weight of the table cloth. The worst story by far for me is that of Conrad, an incorrigible thumb-sucker, who couldn't stop sucking his thumb and whose mother warned him that a great, long, red-legged scissor-man would—and, yes, did—snip both his thumbs off.

As a child, I hated these horrid stories with their clear moral lessons, exhorting me to listen to my parents: do the right thing, they said; obey authority, or else catastrophic things—dissipation, suffocation, loss of thumbs—will follow. It never occurred to me as a child to wonder why my parents, who had escaped Nazi Germany in 1939, were so deferential to authority, so beholden to sanctioned sources of power. I guess it never occurred to them to reflect or to make any connections between generations of German children reading *Struvelpater*, being instructed from early childhood to honor and defer to the parental authority of the state, and the Nazis' easy rise to power.

When I hear my mother's voice, it is usually reading to me from some kind of guide book showing me how different *They*, the Americans, were from us, the German Jews of Terre Haute. My parents never left home without their passports; we had roots somewhere else. When we traveled westward every summer from our home in Indiana, our bible was the AAA tour guide, giving us the officially sanctioned version of America. We attempted to "see" America from the windows of our 1958 two-tone green Oldsmobile. We were literally the tourists from Terre Haute, those whom Walker Percy describes in "The Loss of the Creature," people who could never experience the Grand

Canyon because it had already been formulated for us by picture postcards, tourist folders, guide books, and the words *Grand Canyon*.

Percy suggests that tourists never see the progressive movement of depths, patterns, colors, and shadows of the Grand Canyon, but rather measure their satisfaction by the degree to which the canyon conforms to the expectations in their minds. My mother's AAA guide book directed us, told us what to see, how to see it, and how long it should take us to see it. We never stopped anywhere serendipitously, never lingered, never attempted to know a place.

As I look now at the black-and-white photographs of our trips, seeing myself in pony-tail and pedal pushers, I am struck by how many of the photos were taken against the car or, at least, with the car close enough to be included in the photograph. I am not sure we really saw the Grand Canyon or the Painted Desert or the Petrified Forest except from the security of a parking lot. We were travelling on a self-imposed visa that kept us close to our parked car; we lacked the freedom of our own authority and stuck close to each other and to the book itself.

My parents' belief that there was a right and a wrong way to do everything extended to the way they decided to teach us German. Wanting us to learn the correct way, not trusting their own native voices, they bought language-learning records with an officially sanctioned voice of an expert language teacher; never mind that they spoke fluent German.

It is 1959; I am 8 years old. We sit in the olive-drab living room with the drapes closed so the neighbors won't see in. What the neighbors would have seen strikes me now as a scene out of a *Saturday Night Live* skit about the Coneheads. The children and their parental-unit sitting in stiff, good-for-your-posture chairs that my brother and I call the electric chairs. Those chairs are at odd angles to each other so we all face the fireplace; we don't look at each other. I guess my parents never considered pulling the chairs around, facing each other, so we could just talk in German. My father's investment was in the best 1959 technology he could find; he was proud of the time and money he had spent, so that we could be instructed in the right way. I can still see him there in that room removing the record from its purple package, placing it on the hi-fi:

> Guten Tag.
> Wie geht es Dir?
> Wie geht es Werner/Helmut/Dieter?
> Werner ist heute krank.
> Oh, das tut mir Leid.
> Gute Besserung.

We are disconnected voices worrying over the health of Werner, Dieter, and Helmut, foreign characters, names, who have no place in our own family. We go on and on for an eternity with that dialogue until my brother passes gas, or commits some other unspeakable offense, something that sets my father's German sensibility on edge, and he finally says, "We will continue another time." He releases us back into another life, where we speak English, forgetting for yet another week about the health of Werner, Helmut, or Dieter.

I thought I had the issue of authority all settled in my mind when I was in college. My favorite T-shirt, the one I took the greatest pleasure in wearing, was one with the bold words *Question Authority* inscribed across my chest. It seemed that easy. As we said then, either you were part of the problem or you were part of the solution; either you deferred to authority or you resisted it by questioning. Twenty years later, it doesn't seem that simple. I am beginning to get a better sense of my legacy, beginning to see just how complicated and how far-reaching is this business of authority. It extends into my life and touches my student's lives, reminding me again and again of the delicate relationship between language and authority.

In 1989, 30 years after my German lessons at home, I'm having dinner with my daughters in an Italian restaurant. The waiter is flirting with 8-year-old Rachel, telling her she has the most beautiful name, that she is *una ragazza bellissima*. Intoxicated with this affectionate attention, she turns to me passionately and says, "Oh, Momma, Momma, can't we learn Italian?" I, too, for the moment am caught up in the brio of my daughter's passion. I say, "Yes, yes, we must learn Italian." We rush to our favorite bookstore where we find Italian language-learning tapes packaged in 30-, 60-, and 90-day lessons, and in our modesty buy the promise of fluent Italian in 30 lessons. Driving home together, we put the tape in our car tape player, and begin lesson number 1:

> Buon giorno.
> Come stai?
> Come stai Monica?

As we wind our way home, our Italian lessons quickly move beyond preliminaries. We stop worrying over the health of Monica, and suddenly we are in the midst of a dialogue about Signor Fellini who lives at 21 Broadway Street. We cannot follow the dialogue. Rachel, in great despair, betrayed by the promise of being a beautiful girl with a beautiful name speaking Italian in 30 lessons, begins to scream at me: "This isn't the way to learn a language. This isn't language at all. These are just words and sentences; this isn't about us; we don't live at 21 Broadway Street."

And I am back home in Indiana, hearing the disembodied voices of my family, teaching a language out of the context of life.

In 1987, I gave a talk at CCCC entitled "New Directions for Researching Revision." At the time, I liked the talk very much because it gave me an opportunity to illustrate how revision, once a subject as interesting to our profession as an autopsy, had received new body and soul, almost celebrity status, in our time. Yet as interesting as revision had become, it seemed to me that our pedagogies and research methods were resting on some shaky, unquestioned assumptions.

I had begun to see how students often sabotage their own best interests when they revise, searching for errors and assuming, like the eighteenth-century theory of words parodied in *Gulliver's Travels*, that words are a load of things to be carried around and exchanged. It seemed to me that despite all those multiple drafts, all the peer workshops that we were encouraging, we had left unexamined the most important fact of all: revision does not always guarantee improvement; successive drafts do not always lead to a clearer vision. You can't just change the words around and get the ideas right.

Here I am four years later, looking back on that abandoned talk, thinking of myself as a student writer, and seeing that successive drafts have not led me to a clearer vision. I have been under the influence of a voice other than my own.

I live by the lyrical dream of change, of being made anew, always believing that a new vision is possible. I have been gripped, probably obsessed, with the subject of revision since graduate school. I have spent hundreds of hours studying manuscripts, looking for clues in the drafts of professional and student writers, looking for the figure in the carpet. The pleasures of this kind of literary detective work, this literary voyeurism, are the peeps behind the scenes, the glimpses of the process revealed in all its nakedness, of what Edgar Allan Poe called "the elaborate and vacillating crudities of thought, the true purposes seized only at the last moment, the cautious selections and rejections, the painful erasures."

My decision to study revision was not an innocent choice. It is deeply satisfying to believe that we are not locked into our original statements, that we might start and stop, erase, use the delete key in life, and be saved from the roughness of our early drafts. Words can be retracted; souls can be reincarnated. Such beliefs have informed my study of revision, and yet, in my own writing, I have always treated revising as an academic subject, not a personal one. Every time I have written about revision, I have set out to argue a thesis, present my research, accumulate my footnotes. By treating revision as an academic subject, by suggesting that I could learn something only by studying the drafts of other experienced writers, I kept myself clean and distant from any kind of scrutiny. No Struvelpater was I; no birds could nest in my hair; I kept my thumbs intact. I have been the bloodless academic creating taxonomies, creating a hierarchy of student writers and experienced writers, and never asking myself how I was being displaced from my own work. I never asked, "What does my absence *signify*?"

In that unrevised talk from CCCC, I had let Wayne Booth replace my father. Here are my words:

> Revision presents a unique opportunity to study what writers know. By studying writers' revisions we can learn how writers locate themselves within a discourse tradition by developing a persona—a fictionalized self. Creating a persona involves placing the self in a textual community, seeing oneself within a discourse, and positing a self that shares or antagonizes the beliefs that a community of readers shares. As Wayne Booth has written, 'Every speaker makes a self with every word uttered. Even the most sincere statement implies a self

that is at best a radical selection from many possible roles. No one comes on in exactly the same way with parents, teachers, classmates, lovers, and IRS inspectors.'

What strikes me now, in this paragraph from my own talk, is that fictionalized self I invented, that anemic researcher, who set herself apart from her most passionate convictions. In that paragraph, I am a distant, imponderable, impersonal voice—inaccessible, humorless, and disguised like the packaged voice of Signor Fellini giving lessons as if absolutely nothing depends on my work. I speak in an inherited academic voice; it isn't mine.

I simply wasn't there for my own talk. Just as my father hid behind his language-learning records and my mother behind her guide books, I disguised myself behind the authority of "the researcher," attempting to bring in the weighty authority of Wayne Booth to justify my own statements, never gazing inward, never trusting my own authority as a writer.

Looking back on that talk, I know how deeply I was under the influence of a way of seeing: Foucault's "Discourse on Language," Barthes' *S/Z*, Scholes' *Textual Power*, and Bartholomae's "Inventing the University" had become my tourist guides. I was so much under their influence that I remember standing in a parking lot of a supermarket, holding two heavy bags of groceries, talking with a colleague who was telling me about his teaching. Without any reference, except to locate my own authority somewhere else, I felt compelled to suggest to him that he read Foucault. My daughter Alexandra, waiting impatiently for me, eating chocolate while pounding on the hood of the car with her new black patent-leather party shoes, spoke with her own authority. She reminded me that I, too, had bumped on cars, eaten Hershey Bars, worn party shoes without straps, never read Foucault, and knew, nevertheless, what to say on most occasions.

One of my colleagues put a telling cartoon on the wall of our Xerox room. It reads "Breakfast Theory: A morning methodology." The cartoon describes two new cereals: Foucault Flakes and Post-Modern Toasties. The slogan for Foucault Flakes reads: "It's French so it must be good for you. A breakfast commodity so complex that you need a theoretical apparatus to digest it. You don't want to eat it; you'll just want to read it. Breakfast as text." And Post-Modern Toasties: "More than just a cereal, it's a commentary on the nature of cereal-ness, cerealism, and the theory of cerealtivity. Free decoding ring inside."

I had swallowed the whole flake, undigested, as my morning methodology, but, alas, I never found the decoding ring. I was lost in the box. Or, to use the metaphor of revision, I was stuck in a way of seeing: reproducing the thoughts of others, using them as my guides, letting the post-structuralist vocabulary give authority to my text.

Successive drafts of my own talk did not lead to a clearer vision because it simply was not my vision. I, like so many of my students, was reproducing acceptable truths, imitating the gestures and rituals of the academy, not having confidence enough in my own ideas, nor trusting the native language I had learned. I had surrendered my own authority to someone else, to those other authorial voices.

Three years later, I am still wondering: Where does revision come from? Or, as I think about it now, what happens between the drafts? Something has to happen or else we are stuck doing mop and broom work, the janitorial work of polishing, cleaning, and fixing what is and always has been. What happens between drafts seems to be one of the great secrets of our profession.

Between drafts, I take lots of showers, hot showers, talking to myself as I watch the water play against the gestures of my hands. In the shower, I get lost in the steam. There I stand without my badges of authority. I begin an imagined conversation with my colleague, the one whom I told in the parking lot of the grocery store, "Oh, but you must read Foucault." I revise our conversation. This time I listen.

I understand why he showed so much disdain when I began to pay homage to Foucault. He had his own sources aplenty that nourished him. Yet he hadn't felt the need to speak through his sources or interject their names into our conversation. His teaching stories and experiences are his own; they give him the authority to speak.

As I get lost in the steam, I listen to his stories, and I begin to tell him mine. I tell him about my father not trusting his native voice to teach me German, about my mother not trusting her own eyes and reading to us from guide books, about my own claustrophobia in not being able to revise a talk about revision, about being drowned out by a chorus of authorial voices. And I surprise myself. I say, Yes, these stories of mine provide powerful evidence; they belong to me; I can use them to say what I must about revision.

I begin at last to have a conversation with all the voices I embody, and I wonder why so many issues are posed as either/or propositions. Either I suck my thumb *or* the great long-legged scissor-man will cut it off. Either I cook two chickens *or* my guests will go away hungry. Either I accept authority *or* I question it. Either I have babies and be in service of the species *or* I write books and be in service of the academy. Either I be personal *or* I be academic.

These either/or ways of seeing exclude life and real revision by pushing us to safe positions, to what is known. They are safe positions that exclude each other and don't allow for any ambiguity, uncertainty. Only when I suspend myself between either *and* or can I move away from conventional boundaries and begin to see shapes and shadows and contours—ambiguity, uncertainty, and discontinuity, moments when the seams of life just don't want to hold; days when I wake up to find, once again, that I don't have enough bread for the children's sandwiches or that there are no shoelaces for their gym shoes. My life is full of uncertainty; negotiating that uncertainty day to day gives me authority.

Maybe this is a woman's journey, maybe not. Maybe it is just my own, but the journey between home and work, between being personal and being authoritative, between the drafts of my life, is a journey of learning how to be both personal and authoritative, both scholarly *and* reflective. It is a journey that leads me to embrace the experiences of my life, and gives me the insight to transform these experiences into evidence. I begin to see discontinuous moments as sources of strength and knowledge. When my writing and my life actually come together, the safe positions of either/or will no longer pacify me, no longer contain me and hem me in.

In that unrevised talk, I had actually misused my sources. What they were saying to me, if I had listened, was pretty simple: don't follow us, don't reproduce what we have produced, don't live life from secondary sources like us, don't disappear. I hear Bob Scholes' and David Bartholomae's voices telling me to answer them, to speak back to them, to use them and make them anew. In a word, they say: revise me. The language lesson starts to make sense, finally: by confronting these authorial voices, I find the power to understand and gain access to my own ideas. Against all the voices I embody—the voices heard, read, whispered to me from off-stage—I must bring a voice of my own. I must enter the dialogue on my own authority, knowing that other voices have enabled mine, but no longer can I subordinate mine to theirs.

The voices I embody encourage me to show up as a writer and to bring the courage of my own authority into my classroom. I have also learned about the dangers of submission from observing the struggles of my own students. When they write about their lives, they write with confidence. As soon as they begin to turn their attention toward outside sources, they too lose confidence, defer to the voice of the academy, and write in the voice of Everystudent to an audience they think of as Everyteacher. They disguise themselves in the weighty, imponderable voice of acquired authority: "In today's society," for instance, or "Since the beginning of civilization mankind has . . . ." Or, as one student wrote about authority itself, "In attempting to investigate the origins of authority of the group, we must first decide exactly what we mean by authority."

In my workshops with teachers, the issue of authority, or deciding exactly what we mean by authority, always seems to be at the center of many heated conversations. Some colleagues are convinced that our writing programs should be about teaching academic writing. They see such programs as the welcome wagon of the academy, the Holiday Inn where students lodge as they take holy orders. Some colleagues fear that if we don't control what students learn, don't teach them to write as scholars write, we aren't doing our job and some great red-legged scissor-man will cut off our thumbs. Again it is one of those either/or propositions: either we teach students to write academic essays or we teach them to write personal essays—and then who knows what might happen? The world might become uncontrollable: Students might start writing about their grandmother's death in an essay for a sociology course. Or even worse, something more uncontrollable, they might just write essays and publish them in professional journals claiming the authority to tell stories about their families and their colleagues. The uncontrollable world of ambiguity and uncertainty opens up, my colleagues imagine, as soon as the academic embraces the personal.

But, of course, our students are not empty vessels waiting to be filled with authorial intent. Given the opportunity to speak their own authority as writers, given a turn in the conversation, students can claim their stories as primary source material and transform their experiences into evidence. They might, if given enough encouragement, be empowered not to serve the academy and accommodate it, not to write in the persona of Everystudent, but rather to write essays that will change the academy. When we create opportunities for something to happen between the drafts, when we create writing exercises that allow students to work with sources of their own that can complicate and enrich their primary sources, they will find new ways to write scholarly essays that are exploratory, thoughtful, and reflective.

I want my students to know what writers know—to know something no researchers could ever find out no matter how many times they pin my students to the table, no matter how many protocols they tape. I want my students to know how to bring their life and their writing together.

Sometimes when I cook a chicken and my children scuffle over the one wishbone, I wish I had listened to my grandmother and cooked two. Usually, the child who gets the short end of the wishbone dissolves into tears of frustration and failure. Interjecting my own authority as the earth mother from central casting, I try to make their life better by asking: On whose authority is it that the short end can't get her wish? Why can't both of you, the long and the short ends, get your wishes?

My children, on cue, as if they too were brought in from central casting, roll their eyes as children are supposed to do when their mothers attempt to impose a way of seeing. They won't let me control the situation by interpreting it for them. My interpretation serves my needs, temporarily, for sibling compromise and resolution. They don't buy my story because they know something about the sheer thrill of the pull that they are not going to let *me* deny *them*. They will have to revise my self-serving story about compromise, just as they will have to revise the other stories I tell them. Between the drafts, as they get outside my authority, they too will have to question, and begin to see for themselves their own complicated legacy, their own trail of authority.

It *is* in the thrill of the pull between someone else's authority and our own, between submission and independence that we must discover how to define ourselves. In the uncertainty of that struggle, we have a chance of finding the voice of our own authority. Finding it, we can speak convincingly . . . at long last.

The Writing Life

by Annie Dillard

When you write, you lay out a line of words. The line of words is a miner's pick, a woodcarver's gouge, a surgeon's probe. You wield it, and it digs a path you follow. Soon you find yourself deep in new territory. Is it a dead end, or have you located the real subject? You will know tomorrow, or this time next year.

You make the path boldly and follow it fearfully. You go where the path leads. At the end of the path, you find a box canyon. You hammer out reports, dispatch bulletins.

The writing has changed, in your hands, and in a twinkling, from an expression of your notions to an epistemological tool. The new place interests you because it is not clear. You attend. In your humility, you lay down the words carefully, watching all the angles. Now the earlier writing looks soft and careless. Process is nothing; erase your tracks. The path is not the work. I hope your tracks have grown over; I hope birds ate the crumbs; I hope you will toss it all and not look back.

The line of words is a hammer. You hammer against the walls of your house. You tap the walls, lightly, everywhere. After giving many years' attention to these things, you know what to listen for. Some of the walls are bearing walls; they have to stay, or everything will fall down. Other walls can go with impunity; you can hear the difference. Unfortunately, it is often a bearing wall that has to go. It cannot be helped. There is only one solution, which appalls you, but there it is. Knock it out. Duck.

Courage utterly opposes the bold hope that this is such fine stuff the work needs it, or the world. Courage, exhausted, stands on bare reality: this writing weakens the work. You must demolish the work and start over. You can save some of the sentences, like bricks. It will be a miracle if you can save some of the paragraphs, no matter how excellent in themselves or hard-won. You can waste a year worrying about it, or you can get it over with now. (Are you a woman, or a mouse?)

The part you must jettison is not only the best-written part; it is also, oddly, that part which was to have been the very point. It is the original key passage, the passage on which the rest was to hang, and from which you yourself drew the courage to begin. Henry James knew it well, and said it best. In his preface to *The Spoils of Poynton*, he pities the writer, in a comical pair of sentences that rises to a howl: "Which is the work in which he hasn't surrendered, under dire difficulty, the best thing he meant to have kept? In which indeed, before the dreadful *done*, doesn't he ask himself what has become of the thing all for the sweet sake of which it was to proceed to that extremity?"

So it is that a writer writes many books. In each book, he intended several urgent and vivid points, many of which he sacrificed as the book's form hardened. "The youth gets together his materials to build a bridge to the moon," Thoreau noted mournfully, "or perchance a palace or temple on the earth, and at length the middle-aged man concludes to build a wood-shed with them." The writer returns to these materials, these passionate subjects, as to unfinished business, for they are his life's work.

· · · · ·

The line of words fingers your own heart. It invades arteries, and enters the heart on a flood of breath; it presses the moving rims of thick valves; it palpates the dark muscle strong as horses, feeling for something, it knows not what. A queer picture beds in the muscle like a worm encysted—some film of feeling, some song forgotten, a scene in a dark bedroom, a corner of the woodlot, a terrible dining room, that exalting sidewalk; these fragments are heavy with meaning. The line of words peels them back, dissects them out. Will the bared tissue burn? Do you want to expose these scenes to the light? You may locate them and leave them, or poke the spot hard till the sore bleeds on your finger, and write with that blood. If the sore spot is not fatal, if it does not grow and block something, you can use its power for many years, until the heart resorbs it.

· · · · ·

The line of words feels for cracks in the firmament.

The line of words is heading out past Jupiter this morning. Traveling 150 kilometers a second, it makes no sound. The big yellow planet and its white moons spin. The line of words speeds past Jupiter and its cumbrous, dizzying orbit; it looks neither to the right nor to the left. It will be leaving the solar system soon, single-minded, rapt, rushing heaven like a soul. You are in Houston, Texas, watching the monitor. You saw a simulation: the line of words waited still, hushed, pointed with longing. The big yellow planet spun toward it like a pitched ball and passed beside it, low and outside. Jupiter was so large, the arc of its edge at the screen's bottom looked flat. The probe twined on; its wild path passed between white suns small as dots; these stars fell away on either side, like the lights on a tunnel's walls.

Now you watch symbols move on your monitor; you stare at the signals the probe sends back, transmits in your own tongue, numbers. Maybe later you can guess at what they mean—what they might mean about space at the edge of the solar system, or about your instruments. Right now, you are flying. Right now, your job is to hold your breath.

Writing For Your Life

by Deena Metzger

The Words That Are Ours By Right

The way we see a room, a landscape, our awareness of differences and resemblances, the emotions we feel, the ideas we have about ourselves—all of these are embedded in language and in our relationship to words. Some of this relationship is straightforward—we are shown a color and told it is red. But some of it is far more complex. In the course of our development, red begins to attract public and private meanings to itself.

Red flag, red-light district, red-blooded, Red Cross, red herring, red-bait, red-eye, red man, red-hot, red-faced—these are all variations on a theme that goes far beyond the simple association of color and word. To make these images, we must pass the words through our own consciousness and particularity. And in this act of trying to know something else in its specificity, our own particularity is likewise revealed.

Some people fear seeing or feeling anything about which there is no general agreement. For others, it is thrilling to be aware of innuendo, shading, complexity. For those who do not wish to step away from consensus, the creative is useless at best; at worst, it is dangerous. But for those who are intrigued by the multiplicity of reality and the unique possibilities of their own vision, the creative is the path they must pursue. It is the creative and the worlds it opens that we wish to consider here.

The Forbidden Inner World

For my tenth birthday, my father, who was a printer, surprised me with one hundred copies of a little book of my poems, which he called *My First Ten*. But by that time, the poet in me was already in hiding. What was supposed to be a gift actually mortified me. By the time I was ten, I was judging my poems and was certain they weren't good enough. I was embarrassed by wanting to write poetry. In addition, my father's intense pride in the book somehow subsumed my own efforts and amplified my sense of their limitations.

These feelings are not unique to children. Traveling to the inner realm, even though it is explicitly and absolutely ours, is often forbidden or constrained. Each of us knows the fear that if we speak our minds openly, we will be embarrassed or endangered. The reasons for this are obvious. About the inner world and its revelations there can be neither consensus nor prior definition. The inner world is always, by its nature, every moment, for one's entire life, new territory. And, therefore, the inner world is always outside the prescribed behaviors, outside constraints, rules, and regulations, outside traditional and legislated ways of seeing and behaving. Someone who lives in the inner world and abides by its rules is, almost by definition, an outsider.

And there we have it: the fundamental contradiction and challenge of creativity. If we practice it, if we enter the inner world, we find ourselves outside the perimeter of conventional society—outsiders feeling all the loneliness of that disconnection. And yet we are simultaneously as far as we can get from loneliness because we are, finally, with ourselves.

Furthermore, it doesn't take us long to realize that when we inhabit this inner realm, when we are with ourselves, we are participating in a vast underground world of common understanding and communality some of which may have been with us from the very beginning of time. What Carl Jung calls the collective unconscious—what I like to think of as the creative unconscious (in its communal aspect) or the imagination (in its personal aspect)—is the sea of internal and eternal values, images, cultural memories, and experiences that inform dreams and creative work while, just as often, challenging the prevailing modes of the state, the society, or the community in which one lives.

Another contradiction: while this world we are discussing can be contained within us, it is also vast, endless, and complex. It is the world of worlds. It is infinite. To enter it is to come to know something of it and to learn of the boundlessness of the self. To go within, therefore, is never a diminishment. To stay adamantly without is always a limitation, for the self, the inner world, the imagination, all open out into everything that has ever existed or can ever or may ever exist.

The inner world is for each one of us—novelist, diarist, or diplomat—in our equally ordinary and extraordinary lives the essential territory where everything that might be known resides until it can be called forth into the public arena. Credited or not, the images, inspirations, dreams, nightmares, intuitions, hunches, understandings that arise from the inner world are the *prima materia* from which everything, including ourselves, is constructed. To be willing to live within the imagination is to commit oneself to the gathering together of the pieces that might begin to form a self. To avoid this territory is to avoid the encounters that might validate, inform, or enhance one's experience.

Yet the truth of the matter is that just as the inner territory is proscribed, the self in modern times is also under assault. To go inside is considered solipsistic, narcissistic, small. The smaller intimate history of individuals or marginalized peoples and cultures is not extended the dignity and value accorded to the history of nation-states and canonized philosophic or religious movements. Autobiography, journal writing, and life history are considered lesser forms when compared with the grand sweep of novels, elegies, epics, and biographies of public people. Confessional writing is degraded by the very term used to describe this revelation of one's most intimate story, while objectivity, distance, detachment, and impartiality are valorized. Similarly, the professional writer is often applauded merely for commercial success, while the one who writes primarily for himself or herself is diminished, no matter what the content of the writing, the quality of the search, and the dedication of the effort. The public has prestige over the intimate, the domestic, the interior, yet both the professional writer and the most private journal keeper suffer the same terrors, engage in the same struggles, impose the same disciplines in their encounter with creativity.

Because the inner exploration is so essential to every creative life, we must challenge these attitudes and risk the exploration of these forbidden realms. For despite the prevailing judgments, it is clear that vitality, zest, the very life force itself lie inside and are not to be dismissed, that what is acceptable never has the range of what is still unknown and unexplored, and, finally, that it is the unique vision and exploration, our own subjectivity, that we all secretly seek and cherish.

And so, novice and expert alike, we journey into this territory of the imagination. Like any unexplored territory, it will, each time, turn out to be both strange and familiar. And we go into it, each time, as if we have never been there before and also as if we are coming home.

Let us go with respect and with the commitment that we will not exploit it, colonize it, or decimate it. That we will honor what it offers us, that we will use it in keeping with the principles of the territory, and that we will think of its treasures as gifts to us that we will pass on. In this way we will be able to transform inner exploration into public concern.

A Way of Writing

by William Stafford

A writer is not so much someone who has something to say as he is someone who has found a process that will bring about new things he would not have thought of if he had not started to say them. That is, he does not draw on a reservoir; instead, he engages in an activity that brings to him a whole succession of unforeseen stories, poems, essays, plays, laws, philosophies, religions, or—but wait!

Back in school, from the first when I began to try to write things, I felt this richness. One thing would lead to another; the world would give and give. Now, after twenty years or so of trying, I live by that certain richness, an idea hard to pin, difficult to say, and perhaps offensive to some. For there are strange implications in it.

One implication is the importance of just plain receptivity. When I write, I like to have an interval before me when I am not likely to be interrupted. For me, this means usually the early morning, before others are awake. I get pen and paper, take a glance out of the window (often it is dark out there), and wait. It is like fishing. But I do not wait very long, for there is always a nibble—and this is where receptivity comes in. To get started I will accept anything that occurs to me. Something always occurs, of course, to any of us. We can't keep from thinking. Maybe I have to settle for an immediate impression: it's cold, or hot, or dark, or bright, or in between! Or—well, the possibilities are endless. If I put down something, that thing will help the next thing come, and I'm off. If I let the process go on, things will occur to me that were not at all in my mind when I started. These things, odd or trivial as they may be, are somehow connected. And if I let them string out, surprising things will happen.

If I let them string out. . . . Along with initial receptivity, then, there is another readiness: I must be willing to fail. If I am to keep on writing, I cannot bother to insist on high standards. I must get into action and not let anything stop me, or even slow me much. By "standards" I do not mean "correctness"—spelling, punctuation, and so on. These details become mechanical for anyone who writes for a while. I am thinking about such matters as social significance, positive values, consistency, etc. I resolutely disregard these. Something better, greater, is happening! I am following a

Reprinted from *Field*, no. 2. Copyright Spring 1970. Used by permission.

process that leads so wildly and originally into new territory that no judgment can at the moment be made about values, significance, and so on. I am making something new, something that has not been judged before. Later others—and maybe I myself—will make judgments. Now, I am headlong to discover. Any distraction may harm the creating.

So, receptive, careless of failure, I spin out things on the page. And a wonderful freedom comes. If something occurs to me, it is all right to accept it. It has one justification: it occurs to me. No one else can guide me. I must follow my own weak, wandering, diffident impulses.

A strange bonus happens. At times, without my insisting on it, my writings become coherent; the successive elements that occur to me are clearly related. They lead by themselves to new connections. Sometimes the language, even the syllables that happen along, may start a trend. Sometimes the materials alert me to something waiting in my mind, ready for sustained attention. At such times, I allow myself to be eloquent, or intentional, or for great swoops (Treacherous! Not to be trusted!) reasonable. But I do not insist on any of that; for I know that back of my activity there will be the coherence of my self, and that indulgence of my impulses will bring recurrent patterns and meanings again.

This attitude toward the process of writing creatively suggests a problem for me, in terms of what others say. They talk about "skills" in writing. Without denying that I do have experience, wide reading, automatic orthodoxies and maneuvers of various kinds, I still must insist that I am often baffled about what "skill" has to do with the precious little area of confusion when I do not know what I am going to say and then I find out what I am going to say. That precious interval I am unable to bridge by skill. What can I witness about it? It remains mysterious, just as all of us must feel puzzled about how we are so inventive as to be able to talk along through complexities with our friends, not needing to plan what we are going to say, but never stalled for long in our confident forward progress. Skill? If so, it is the skill we all have, something we must have learned before the age of three or four.

A writer is one who has become accustomed to trusting that grace, or luck, or—skill.

Yet another attitude I find necessary: most of what I write, like most of what I say in casual conversation, will not amount to much. Even I will realize, and even at the time, that it is not negotiable. It will be like practice. In conversation I allow myself random remarks—in fact, as I recall, that is the way I learned to talk—so in writing I launch many expendable efforts. A result of this free way of writing is that I am not writing for others, mostly; they will not see the product at all unless the activity eventuates in something that later appears to be worthy. My guide is the self, and its adventuring in the language brings about communication.

This process-rather-than-substance view of writing invites a final, dual reflection:

1. Writers may not be special—sensitive or talented in any usual sense.

They are simply engaged in sustained use of a language skill we all have. Their "creations" come about through confident reliance on stray impulses that will, with trust, find occasional patterns that are satisfying.

2. But writing itself is one of the great, free human activities. There is scope for individuality, and elation, and discovery, in writing. For the person who follows with trust and forgiveness what occurs to him, the world remains always ready and deep, an inexhaustible environment, with the combined vividness of an actuality and flexibility of a dream. Working back and forth between experience and thought, writers have more than space and time can offer. They have the whole unexplored realm of human vision.

Everybody Is Talented, Original and Has Something Important to Say

by Brenda Ueland

I have been writing a long time and have learned some things, not only from my own long hard work, but from a writing class I had for three years. In this class were all kinds of people: prosperous and poor, stenographers, housewives, salesmen, cultivated people and little servant girls who had never been to high school, timid people and bold ones, slow and quick ones.

This is what I learned: that everybody is talented, original and has something important to say.

And it may comfort you to know that the only people you might suspect of *not* having talent are those who write very easily and glibly, and without inhibition or pain, skipping gaily through a novel in a week or so. These are the only ones who did not seem to improve much, to go forward. You cannot get much out of them. They give up working presently and drop out. But these, too, were talented underneath. I am sure of that. It is just that they did not break through the shell of easy glibness to what is true and alive underneath,—just as most people must break through a shell of timidity and strain.

Everybody Is Talented

EVERYBODY IS TALENTED because everybody who is human has something to express. Try *not* expressing anything for twenty-four hours and see what happens. You will nearly burst. You will want to write a long letter or draw a picture or sing, or make a dress or a garden. Religious men used to go into the wilderness and impose silence on themselves, but it was so that they would talk to God and nobody else. But they expressed something: that is to say they had thoughts welling up in them and the thoughts went out to someone, whether silently or aloud.

Writing or painting is putting these thoughts on paper. Music is singing them. That is all there is to it.

Everybody Is Original

EVERYBODY IS ORIGINAL, if he tells the truth, if he speaks from himself.

But it must be from his *true* self and not from the self he thinks he *should* be. Jennings at Johns Hopkins, who knows more about heredity and the genes and chromosomes than any man in the world, says that no individual is exactly like any other individual, that no two identical persons have ever existed. Consequently, if you speak or write from *yourself* you cannot help being original.

So remember these two things: you are talented and you are original. Be sure of that. I say this because self-trust is one of the very most important things in writing and I will tell why later.

This creative power and imagination is in everyone and so is the need to express it, i.e., to share it with others. But what happens to it?

It is very tender and sensitive, and it is usually drummed out of people early in life by criticism (so-called "helpful criticism" is often the worst kind), by teasing, jeering, rules, prissy teachers, critics, and all those unloving people who forget that the letter killeth and the spirit giveth life. Sometimes I think of life as a process where everybody is discouraging and taking everybody else down a peg or two.

You know how all children have this creative power. You have all seen things like this: the little girls in our family used to give play after play. They wrote the plays themselves (they were very good plays too, interesting, exciting and funny). They acted in them. They made the costumes themselves, beautiful, effective and historically accurate, contriving them in the most ingenious way out of attic junk and their mothers' best dresses. They constructed the stage and theater by carrying chairs, moving the piano, carpentering. They printed the tickets and sold them. They made their own advertising. They drummed up the audience, throwing out a drag-net for all the hired girls, dogs, babies, mothers, neighbors within a radius of a mile or so. For what reward? A few pins and pennies.

Yet these small ten-year-olds were working with feverish energy and endurance. (A production took about two days.) If they had worked that hard for school it probably would have killed them. They were working for nothing but fun, for that glorious inner excitement. It was the creative power working in them. It was hard, hard work but there was no pleasure or excitement like it and it was something never forgotten.

But this joyful, imaginative, impassioned energy dies out of us very young. Why? Because we do not see that it is great and important. Because we let dry obligation take its place. Because we don't respect it in ourselves and keep it alive by using it. And because we don't keep it alive in others by *listening* to them.

For when you come to think of it, the only way to love a person is not, as the stereotyped Christian notion is, to coddle them and bring them soup when they are sick, but by listening to them and seeing and believing in the god, in the poet, in them. For by doing this, you keep the god and the poet alive and make it flourish.

How does the creative impulse die in us? The English teacher who wrote fiercely on the margin of your theme in blue pencil: "Trite, rewrite," helped to kill it. Critics kill it, your family. Families are great murderers of the creative impulse, particularly husbands. Older brothers sneer at younger brothers and kill it. There is that American pastime known as "kidding,"—with the result that everyone is ashamed and hang-dog about showing the slightest enthusiasm or passion or sincere feeling about anything. But I will tell more about that later.

You have noticed how teachers, critics, parents and other know-it-alls, when they see you have written something, become at once long-nosed and finicking and go through it gingerly sniffing out the flaws. AHA! a misspelled word! as though Shakespeare could spell! As though spelling, grammar and what you learn in a book about rhetoric has anything to do with freedom and the imagination!

A friend of mine spoke of books that are dedicated like this: "To my wife, by whose helpful criticism . . ." and so on. He said the dedication should really read: "To my wife. If it had not been for her continual criticism and persistent nagging doubt as to my ability, this book would have appeared in *Harper's* instead of *The Hardware Age*."

So often I come upon articles written by critics of the very highest brow, and by other prominent writers, deploring the attempts of ordinary people to write. The critics rap us savagely on the head with their thimbles, for our nerve. No one but a virtuoso should be allowed to do it. The prominent writers sell funny articles about all the utterly crazy, fatuous, amateurish people who *think* they can write.

Well, that is all right. But this is one of the results: that all people who try to write (and all people long to, which is natural and right) become anxious, timid, contracted, become perfectionists, so terribly afraid that they may put something down that is not as good as Shakespeare.

And so no wonder you don't write and put it off month after month, decade after decade. For when you write, if it is to be any good at all, you must feel free,—free and not anxious. The only good teachers for you are those friends who love you, who think you are interesting, or very important, or wonderfully funny; whose attitude is:

"Tell me more. Tell me all you can. I want to understand more about everything you feel and know and all the changes inside and out of you. Let more come out."

And if you have no such friend,—and you want to write,—well then you must imagine one.

Yes, I hate orthodox criticism. I don't mean great criticism, like that of Matthew Arnold and others, but the usual small niggling, fussy-mussy criticism, which thinks it can improve people by telling them where they are wrong, and results only in putting them in straitjackets of hesitancy and self-consciousness, and weazening all vision and bravery.

I hate it not so much on my own account, for I have learned at last not to let it balk me. But I hate it because of the potentially shining, gentle, gifted people of all ages, that it snuffs out every year. It is a murderer of talent. And because the most modest and sensitive people are the most talented, having the most imagination and sympathy, these are the very first ones to get killed off. It is the brutal egotists that survive.

Of course, in fairness, I must remind you of this: that we writers are the most lily-livered of all craftsmen. We expect more, for the most peewee efforts, than any other people.

A gifted young woman writes a poem. It is rejected. She does not write another perhaps for two years, perhaps all her life. Think of the patience and love that a tap-dancer or vaudeville acrobat puts into his work. Think of how many times Kreisler has practiced trills. If you will write as many words as Kreisler has practiced trills I prophesy that you will win the Nobel Prize in ten years.

But here is an important thing: you must practice not perfunctorily, but with all your intelligence and love, as Kreisler does. A great musician once told me that one should never play a single note without hearing it, feeling that it is true, thinking it beautiful.

And so now you will begin to work at your writing. Remember these things. Work with all your intelligence and love. Work freely and rollickingly as though they were talking to a friend who loves you. Mentally (at least three or four times a day) thumb your nose at all know-it-alls, jeerers, critics, doubters.

And so that you will work long hours and not neglect it, I will now prove that it is important for *yourself* that you do so.

Bibliography

Beach, R. & Bridwell, L.S. (Eds.). (1984). *New directions in composition research.* New York: Guilford.

Berkenkotter, C., Huckin, T., & Ackerman, J. (1988). Conventions, conversations and the writer: Case study of a student in a rhetoric Ph.D. program. *Research in the Teaching of English, 22,* 9-44.

Berlin, J. (1988). Rhetoric and ideology in the writing class. *College English, 50,* 477-494.

Berthoff, A. E., Daniel, B., Campbell, J., Swearington, C. J., Moffett, J. (1994). Interchanges: Spiritual sites of composing. *College Composition and Communication, 45,* 237-263.

Bizzell, P. (1982). Cognition, convention, and certainty. *Pre/Text, 3,* 213-243.

Braddock, R., Lloyd-Jones, R., & Schoer, L. (1963). *Research in written composition.* Urbana, IL: NCTE.

Brand, A. (1987). The why of cognition: Emotion and the writing process. *College Composition and Communication, 38,* 436-443.

Brand, A. & Graves, R. (Eds.). (1994). *Presence of mind: Writing and the domain beyond the cognitive.* Portsmouth, NH: Boynton/Cook.

Brandt, D. (1990). *Literacy as involvement: The acts of writers, readers and texts.* Carbondale, IL: Southern Illinois UP.

Bridwell, L. (1980). Revising strategies in twelfth grade students' transactional writing. *Research in the Teaching of English, 14,* 197-222.

Brodkey, L. (1987). Modernism and the scene(s) of writing. *College English, 49,* 396-418.

Brodkey, L. (1989). On the subjects of class and gender in "The literacy letters." *College English, 51,* 125-141.

Buxton, E. (1971). Preface. In Emig, J. *The composing processes of twelfth graders.* Urbana, IL: NCTE.

Calkins, L. (1980). Children's rewriting strategies. *Research in the Teaching of English, 14,* 331-341.

Clark, B. & Wiedenhaupt, S. (1992). On blocking and unblocking Sonja: A case study in two voices. *College Composition and Communication, 43,* 55-74.

Cooper, C. & Odell, L. (1978). *Research on composing: Points of departure.* Urbana, IL: NCTE.

Cooper, M. M. (1986). The ecology of writing. *College English, 48,* 364-375.

Cooper, M. M. & Holzman, M. (1983). Talking about protocols. *College Composition and Communication, 34,* 284-293.

Daiute, C. (1985). *Writing and computers*. Reading, MA: Addison.

Dobrin, D. N. (1986). Protocols once more. *College English*, *48*, 713-725.

Doheny-Farina, S. (1986). Writing in an emerging organization: An ethnographic study. *Written Communication*, *2*, 158-85.

Durst, R. K. (1990). The mongoose and the rat in composition research: Insights from the *RTE* annotated bibliography. *College Composition and Communication*, *41*, 393-405.

Dyson, A. H. (1987). Individual differences in beginning composing: An orchestral vision of learning to compose. *Written Communication*, *9*, 411-441.

Dyson, A. H. (1988). Negotiating among multiple worlds: The space-time dimensions of young children's composing. *Research in the Teaching of English*, *22*, 355-390.

Dyson, A. H. (1994). Confronting the split between "The child" and children: Toward new curricular visions of the child writer. *English Education*, 12-28.

Emig, J. (1982). Inquiry paradigms and writing. *College Composition and Communication*, *33*, 64-75.

Faigley, L., Cherry, R., Joliffe, D., & Skinner, A. (1985). *Assessing writers' knowledge and processes of composing*. Norwood, NJ: Ablex.

Faigley, L. & Witte, S. (1981). Analyzing revision. *College Composition and Communication*, *32*, 400-414.

Feldman, P. R. & Norman, B. (1987). *The wordworthy computer: Classroom and research applications in language and literature*. New York: Random House.

Flower, L. (1989). Cognition, context, and theory building. *College Composition and Communication*, *40*, 282-311.

Flower, L. & Hayes, J. R. (1981). A cognitive process theory of writing. *College Composition and Communication*, *32*, 365-387.

Flower, L., Hayes, J. R., Carey, L., Schriver, K., & Stratman, J. (1986). Detection, diagnosis, and the strategies of revision. *College Composition and Communication*, *37*, 16-55.

Flynn, E. (1990). Composing "Composing as a woman": A perspective on research. *College Composition and Communication*, *41*, 83-89.

Greene, S. (1990). *Toward a dialectical theory of composing*. (Occasional paper No. 17). Berkeley, CA: Center for the Study of Writing.

Hairston, M. (1986). Different products, different processes: A theory about writing. *College Composition and Communication*, *37*, 442-452.

Harris, M. (1989). Composing behaviors of one- and multi-draft writers. *College English*, *51*, 174-191.

Herrington, A. (1985). Writing in academic settings: A study of the contexts for writing in two college chemical engineering courses. *Research in the Teaching of English*, *19*, 331-361.

Hillocks, G. (1986). *Research on written composition*. Urbana, IL: NCTE.

Himley, M. (1988). Becoming a writer: A documentary account. *Written Communication, 5*, 82-107.

Hull, G. (1987). The editing process in writing: A performance study of more skilled and less skilled college writers. *Research in the Teaching of English, 21*, 8-29.

Hull, G., Rose, M., Fraser, K. L., & Castellano, M. (1991). Remediation as social construct: Perspectives from an analysis of classroom discourse. *College Composition and Communication, 42*, 299-329.

Jensen, G. H. & DiTiberio, J. K. (1984). Personality and individual writing processes. *College Composition and Communication, 35*, 285-300.

Kirsch, G. (1991). Writing up and down the social ladder: A study of experienced writers composing for contrasting audiences. *Research in the Teaching of English, 25*, 33-53.

Kostelnick, C. (1989). Process paradigms in design and composition: Affinities and directions. *College Composition and Communication, 40*, 267-281.

Kroll, B. (1985). Rewriting a complex story for a young reader: The development of audience-adapted writing skills. *Research in the Teaching of English, 19*, 120-139.

Lamme, L. L. & Childers, N. M. (1983). The composing processes of three young children. *Research in the Teaching of English, 17*, 31-50.

Lay, N. D. (1982). Composing processes of adult ESL learners: A case study. *TESOL Quarterly, 16*, 204-214.

LeFevre, K. B. (1987). *Invention as a social act*. Carbondale, IL: Southern Illinois UP.

Lunsford, A. A. & Ede, L. (1990). Rhetoric in a new key: Women and collaboration. *Rhetoric Review, 8*, 234-241.

Lynn, S. (1987). Reading the writing process: Toward a theory of current pedagogies. *College English, 49*, 902-910.

Matsuhashi, A. (1981). Pausing and planning: The tempo of written discourse production. *Research in the Teaching of English, 15*, 113-134.

Matsuhashi, A. (Ed.). (1987). *Writing in real time: Modelling the production processes*. Norwood, NJ: Ablex.

McCarthy, L. (1987). A stranger in strange lands: A college student writing across the curriculum. *Research in the Teaching of English, 21*, 233-265.

Moffett, J. (1985). Liberating inner speech. *College Composition and Communication, 36*, 304-308.

Murray, D. E. (1991). The composing process for computer conversation. *Written Communication, 8*, 35-55.

Murray, D. M. (1980). Writing as process: How writing finds its own meaning. In T. Donovan & B. McClelland (Eds.), *Eight approaches to teaching composition* (pp. 3-20). Urbana, IL: NCTE.

Murray, D. M. (1991). All writing is autobiography. *College Composition and Communication, 42,* 66-74.

North, S. (1986a). *The making of knowledge in composition: Portrait of an emerging field.* Portsmouth, NH: Boynton/Cook.

North, S. (1986b). Writing in a philosophy class: Three case studies. *Research in the Teaching of English, 20,* 225-262.

Perl, S. & Wilson, N. (1986). *Through teachers' eyes: Portraits of writing teachers at work.* Portsmouth, NH: Heinemann Educational Books.

Pianko, S. (1979). A description of the composing processes of college freshman writers. *Research in the Teaching of English, 13,* 5-22.

Prior, P. (1991). Contextualizing writing and response in a graduate seminar. *Written Communication, 8,* 267-310.

Raimes, A. (1985). What unskilled ESL students do as they write: A classroom study of composing. *TESOL Quarterly, 19,* 229-258.

Root, R. L., Jr. (1991). *Working at writing: Columnists and critics of composing.* Carbondale, IL: Southern Illinois UP.

Rose, M. (Ed.). (1985). *When a writer can't write: Studies in writer's block and other composing process problems.* New York: Guilford.

Runciman, L. (1991). Fun? *College English, 53,* 156-162.

Schwartz, M. (1983). Two journeys through the writing process. *College Composition and Communication, 34,* 188-201.

Selfe, C. (1984). The predrafting processes of four high- and four low-apprehensive writers. *Research in the Teaching of English, 18,* 45-64.

Selzer, J. (1983). The composing processes of an engineer. *College Composition and Communication, 31,* 377-388.

Smargorinsky, P. (1989). The reliability and validity of protocol analysis. *Written Communication, 6,* 463-479.

Sommers, N. (1993). I stand here writing. *College English, 55,* 420-428.

Steinberg, E. R. (1986). Protocols, retrospective accounts, and the stream of consciousness. *College English, 48,* 697-712.

Sternglass, M. (1988). *The presence of thought: Introspective accounts of reading and writing.* Norwood, NJ: Ablex.

Stotsky, S. (1990). On planning and writing plans—Or beware of borrowed theories. *College Composition and Communication, 41,* 37-57.

Strong, W. (1987). Language as teacher. *College Composition and Communication, 38,* 21-31.

Tedesco, J. (1991). Womens' ways of knowing/women's ways of composing. *Rhetoric Review*, *9*, 246-256.

Tobin, L. (1989). Bridging gaps: Analyzing our students' metaphors for composing. *College Composition and Communication*, *40*, 444-458.

Tomlinson, B. (1986). Characters are coauthors: Segmenting the self, integrating the composing process. *Written Communication*, *3*, 421-448.

Walvoord, B. & McCarthy, L. (1991). *Thinking and writing in college: A naturalistic study of students in four disciplines*. Urbana, IL: NCTE.

Witte. S. (1983). Topical structure and revision: An exploratory study. *College Composition and Communication*, *34*, 313-341.

Witte, S. (1987). Pre-text and composing. *College Composition and Communication*, *38*, 397-425.

Zamel, V. (1983). The composing processes of advanced ESL students: Six case studies. *TESOL Quarterly*, *17*, 165-187.

Zawacki, T. M. (1992). Recomposing as a woman—An essay in different voices. *College Composition and Communication*, *43*, 32-38.

Index